W9-DJA-067

WOMEN AND LEADERSHIP IN NINETEENTH-CENTURY ENGLAND

Women and Leadership in Nineteenth-Century England

Lilian Lewis Shiman
Professor of History
Nichols College, Dudley, Massachusetts

St. Martin's Press New York

Scholarly and Reference Division,
St. Martin's Press, Inc., 175 Fifth Avenue,
New York, N.Y. 10010

First published in the United States of America in 1992

Printed in Hong Kong

ISBN 0–312–07912–5

Library of Congress Cataloging-in-Publication Data
Shiman, Lilian Lewis.
Women and leadership in nineteenth-century England / Lilian Lewis Shiman.
p. cm.
Includes bibliographical references and index.
ISBN 0–312–07912–5
1. Women—England—History—19th century. 2. Women social reformers—England—History—19th century. 3. Women—England—Social conditions. I. Title.
HQ1599.E5S54 1992
305.42'0942—dc20 91–43786
CIP

To the women of my family,
in memory of 'Auntie'.
She endured, and she cared.

Contents

Preface

It is the duty, and the joy, of a historian to bring out of obscurity those of the past who have made significant contributions to the development of our civilization. It is a duty to one's own time, furthering its quest for self-understanding. And it is a duty to theirs, helping it to live again in common memory.

In interpreting past to present, the most difficult task is to be faithful to both. The all-too-human tendency, from which historians are by no means exempt, is to mythologize the past, to project present concerns into it. The scholar must constantly be on guard against this, seeking to understand and communicate not only past actions, but also the worldviews that motivated them. Past values must not be confused with present ones; every society has its own priorities.

The history of women in nineteenth-century Britain is only now being understood. Concealed by a mythic mantle of domesticity, for the most part they lived out of the public eye. Even those well known in their own time have been largely ignored by historians; and it is interesting that the women perhaps best known as eminent Victorians – most notably Queen Victoria and Florence Nightingale – were not leaders in the battle for women's rights.

That a group has been historically invisible does not mean that they did not exist, or that they achieved nothing. Trees fall in the forest even if there is no one there to hear them. The historian must raise the question whether there was a lack of achievements by women or merely a failure to publicize and preserve them. We know that some Victorian men quite consciously sought to suppress accounts of female activism as a bad example for their wives and daughters. Considerable effort is needed therefore to learn about women who sought meaningful public lives despite societal pressure against them. While for many their attainments fell far short of their hopes, they helped to open doors through which succeeding generations of women moved to a wider and richer life.

In selecting the women and their activities that are described in this work, my concern has been to emphasize those who, by individual reputation or organizational contribution, had the greatest impact on the women's movement that eventually emerged. There are many women and many activities that have not been included; I hope that this will not be taken as a mark of indifference to their accomplishments. Some of the women have already received considerable attention. The same can be said for certain parts of the women's movement: In particular, the women's education reform movement and the women's suffrage organizations have been well covered in a number of separate volumes. For a different reason the emphasis here has been on English women and organizational initiatives. Distinctively Scottish, Welsh, and Irish developments deserve separate treatment.

This book could not have been written without the help and support of many people both in England and the United States. I must mention first the role of my first Macmillan editor, T. M. Farmiloe, who provided the essential carrot and stick. In the United States many colleagues and friends guided me to crucial source materials. To Frank Baker of Duke University who collected much Methodist material, to Philip Lewis Shiman and his former colleagues of the Manuscript Department of the William R. Perkins Library at Duke University, I owe a hearty thanks for material important in Part One of this book. My thanks also to my long-time friend and fellow researcher in the temperance field, Professor David Fahey, of Miami University, for his help over the years, especially in my work on temperance women.

Much of the research took place in England where I was given time and help in many libraries and organizations. To the ladies of the British Women's Temperance Association who gave me full access to their Minute Books and other records, and to those of the Women's Liberal Federation who likewise kindly allowed me to examine their records from past times I owe a debt of gratitude.

To the National Endowment for the Humanities I am grateful for making possible a very rich summer of study with Professors L. Perry Curtis and Roger B. Henkle and members of their 1989 summer seminar at Brown University. Their comments and criticism of draft excerpts have helped guide me in completing the book.

Without the help of the administration and my colleagues at Nichols College this book might never have been written. They gave me financial support so I could spend my summers in England researching, and also granted me a sabbatical leave which I spent drafting this manuscript. I am particularly grateful to some of my female colleagues: to Professor Louise Nordstrom for moral support; and to Professor Karen Tipper for valuable criticisms of the manuscript. And to Joan Meehan and her cohorts in the Davis Center of Nichols College, I send my hearty thanks: Without their patience in teaching me and then supporting me in the use of the word processor this work would have taken much longer to complete.

Finally, I would like to acknowledge the continuing help and support of my husband Paul. He has read numerous drafts of this manuscript and given me much needed criticism, forcing me to elucidate what I often would have left in obscurity.

LILIAN LEWIS SHIMAN

Introduction: The Walls of Jericho

> 'And the Lord said . . . "See, I have given into thy hand Jericho, and the king thereof, even the mighty men of valour. And ye shall compass the city . . . and when ye hear the sound of the horn, all the people shall shout with a great shout; and the wall of the city shall fall down flat".'
>
> Joshua 6:2–5

> 'The walls of Jericho have fallen before the voices and the confidence in their cause of a handful of women in a manner that is remarkable as any miracle.'
>
> Florence Fenwick Miller
> *Woman's Signal*, 4 January 1894

THE OLD SOCIETY

Medieval and early modern England was a corporate world, a society in which men and women were defined according to their associations. While membership in towns, guilds and other associations was important, the basic social unit was the family.

Extended families provided the physical and psychological support that was essential for individual and group survival, not just in times of need but in everyday life. Families saw to the material welfare of their members, but, perhaps more importantly, kinfolk helped to diffuse tensions that could arise either between individuals within the family, or between kin and members of other families. Conflicts between man and wife or other family members would be mediated by third parties from the family, allowing marriages and other family relationships to endure long after modern nuclear families under similar stresses would have disintegrated. Individual security was achieved through the network of informal support services that kept families and other social institutions vital.

Anyone who could claim a blood relationship, no matter how tenuous, was part of the family, which was, in anthropological language, a clan.

Dominated by the head, usually the one of most senior rank, not necessarily of greatest age, the family took care of its own. Positions, sinecures and other economic advantages were secured for family members as part of the family's responsibility, and through the family the individual could achieve a position in society which might enhance the situation of the rest of the clan. Marriage was one important means by which the power of the family could be expanded. What was said about the Hapsburgs could be said about any major European family: They became powerful through the formation of alliances through marriages. Both men and women married where it was of advantage to the family and usually accepted this as the price of their kinship.

The individual was of lesser importance than the greater whole; private desires had to give way to the needs of the larger society. Marriages were not private affairs: They affected the whole community and so were matters of public concern. Men and women of the same families believed themselves to have a common interest. They perceived divergences of interest between classes, religions or families but not between the sexes within a family.

In the eighteenth century this collective worldview was undermined, particularly by economic forces but by others as well. Evangelical religion for instance contributed to a new focus on the individual by affirming the personal character of Christian salvation. Church attendance was no longer to be a family and community activity performed out of habit according to tradition, but rather an expression of personal commitment. By the mid nineteenth century individualism had largely triumphed; the highest value was now placed on the individual as a producer, citizen or public figure. Unsurprisingly, autobiography and biography became the most favored literary genres, presenting successful individuals to the public for admiration and emulation.

One small segment of the English population, important beyond its numbers, managed to hold on to its traditional lifestyle much longer than the other classes. The aristocratic families of England were not at first greatly affected by the industrial changes because their connection with the land continued to give them their primacy in English society. Their wealth might now come from canals, coal or other sources, but their prestige still derived from their estates. Regardless of monetary worth, true value in traditional English society came from the land – *real* property. The family estate was the physical and symbolic center of the aristocratic family.

But the prerogatives associated with landholding began to decline when commerce and industry emerged as dominant forces in the economic life of the country. As the land itself played a declining role in England's wealth, money became increasingly more valuable than land. Individuals accumulated large amounts of it as a means of gaining status and independence in English society. By the last quarter of the nineteenth century, when England had become an industrial country, it was in industrial development that fortunes were made. Landowners slowly lost their influence in English politics and society as the country turned to imports to feed its population – imports paid for by earnings from industrial exports. Lady Nevill, in 1910, looking back over the changes in English society since her girlhood, was impressed by the increased importance and availability of money. To be a leader in the early nineteenth century required little money, she wrote, while later great sums were needed in order to maintain one's position.[1]

THE NEW SOCIETY

The change from land to money as the basis for power and status most benefited a new class. There had always been bankers, industrialists, managers, professionals and investors in the traditional landed society, but in industrial England they increased both in numbers and in power. Members neither of the landed aristocracy nor of the propertyless working class, they became the new middle class, inhabiting the more prosperous areas of the major urban centers. Their growing impact on British political life was signalized by the 1832 Reform Bill, after which they began to take control of the government from the declining landowners. The Liberal Party came to represent their interests, promoting a society which encouraged and rewarded entrepreneurialism. Their political motto was *laissez faire* – unless, of course, government action was to the interest of the merchants and masters. Thus they objected to government regulation of domestic working conditions but not to governmental protection of overseas trade. By the second half of the nineteenth century the middle class was politically dominant.

Lower down the social and economic scale in this new English society a large working class was emerging. As workers moved to the city to find employment in the workshops and factories, they found they had to adjust to a completely new life, working long hours in poor conditions. No longer part of a viable community, they became 'hands' in a factory, numbers on a factory roster. Each factory hand simply represented a unit of labor to the employer, just as the horse or ox did in the fields. Gone was the community of the workplace, the old easy association between master and workers, replaced by an impersonal hierarchy where levels of authority isolated the employers from their now faceless workers. As the industrial organizations grew larger so did the sense of isolation and alienation of the workers.

Conditions in their domestic environment were no better. To men who had grown up in towns and villages where generations of their families had lived and worked, the new cities were cold and uncaring places. In their new homes the successful and prosperous were segregated from the less successful through a series of graded suburbs: The district in which a man lived indicated his place on the social ladder. Local government of the towns came to represent their middle-class residents, who were not interested in paying higher taxes to improve conditions for the poorer citizens. Public facilities were therefore poor and social services minimal: The workhouse was a constant threat. Needing to negotiate both working and living conditions with powerful opponents, the working classes looked to the government for help; but to obtain it they needed the franchise. The most active working class agitations in nineteenth-century England were over the franchise.

Changes in government role in nineteenth-century England were prompted not only by economic developments but also by the social and political message of the French Revolution. Out of its turmoil a new concept of citizenship emerged, attaching its rights and duties to persons within the boundaries of a state, regardless of social and economic position. With other radical ideas this travelled across the Channel and eventually had a strong impact on English politics. The Parliamentary franchise was increasingly seen as a fundamental right of citizenship, and the primary key to responsive government.

But in the first Reform Bill of 1832, property rather than citizenship was made the uniform basis for the franchise. Furthermore, only male property owners were enfranchised, in a vestige of the old collective thinking that society is composed of families, politically and legally represented by the father. As the century progressed the property basis of the franchise became increasingly unacceptable to the propertyless working classes who needed the protection of the government against their employers. Parliament was forced to open up the franchise to the lower classes by allowing lodgers to have the vote. Women, however, were still barred from the parliamentary franchise, in theory protected within the domestic sphere from the rigors of male public life.

With successive enlargements of the electorate came reorganization of the political establishment to provide linkage between the new voters and the government. Modern political parties were born. These parties became the agencies for communicating the desires of the electorate to the politicians and the policies of the politicians to the electorate. Especially for the latter purpose an essential means was the new institution of the 'public platform'.[2] Although individual reformers had spoken at public meetings in the eighteenth and early nineteenth centuries, such gatherings were special events. According to Herbert Asquith, 'the organized use of the platform as an instrument of propaganda' dates from the early 1840s.[3] Throughout the nineteenth century serious journals reached only a small segment of the population; and mass popular journalism did not develop until the beginning of the next century. Until then the public platform was the only way to reach large numbers of English men and women.

WOMEN IN THE NEW SOCIETY

The majority of English women long accepted the view that their well-being was bound to that of their families as represented by their husbands and fathers. But as they found themselves excluded from the benefits many of their menfolk enjoyed in the new nineteenth century economic and political order they began to question their situation. Men were liberating themselves from the old community bonds; but women remained tightly controlled by economic, social and legal constraints. They were expected to accept second-class citizenship in a separate domestic sphere under the protection of husbands. Many 'surplus' women were in fact deprived even of this status. Women depended on the goodwill of men for a decent life and this was not always forthcoming. Slowly the women came to understand that their interests did not always coincide with those of the men. Out of this realization of diverging interests the women's movement was born in the last half of the nineteenth century.

Although there were upper class women in leadership positions and working-class women in the ranks, the movement was primarily composed of middle-class women. This was the segment of the female population most affected by the restrictions of the new economic order, the exclusion from businesses, trades and professions and public life generally. Working-class women did not experience such a great alteration in their lives: They continued to work as before, and still found support in kinship networks.[4] Upper-class women who lived closest to the old preindustrial ways were the last to perceive a special interest for their sex. For most of the nineteenth century they gave primary allegiance to family and class rather than gender.

This book tells the story of the painful emergence of exceptional women from the corporate community of traditional English society into positions of significance in the new public life. Part One, *The Voice of the Lord*, is concerned with leadership roles of women in early industrial society, particularly in the new evangelical movements. Women took to the evangelical sects with great enthusiasm; and women preachers, many very popular and with wide reputation, had a strong impact in the early years. But as the sects became institutionalized as churches the women found themselves once more excluded from the pulpit, expected to serve as handmaidens to an exclusively male authority. A similar pattern is found in political and social movements of the early nineteenth century such as anti-slavery and corn law reform: Whatever their initial roles, women ended up either in subordinate roles or in segregated ladies' associations.

The second part of the book, *The Sound of the Horn*, carries the story into the mid nineteenth century. In this period public activity among middle-class women especially reached a low point. However, there arose some strong individuals who inspired others to leave their domestic world and enter public life. These pathfinding women, like those of a previous period, believed they were called by their Lord to do this work. As John Wesley had put it, they answered to an 'extraordinary call',[5] some to preach and others to work at the various reforming missions and religious orders that proliferated at this time. Writing and speaking about their own experiences, they raised the consciousness of many women by challenging them to ask 'What can I do?' The cause of temperance, a major reform in the second half of the nineteenth century, was especially effective in attracting many women out of their domestic world and into socially acceptable public work: It was a domestic concern that was acknowledged to require public attention.

By the last quarter of the nineteenth century 'The Woman Question' had emerged into public consciousness at all levels of society, alongside 'the Irish Question', 'the Drink Question' and others. Part Three, *The Great Shout*, shows how women of this period, realizing the need to influence the public as well as the government if they wanted to improve their position, learned to 'organise, educate and agitate'[6] in support of women's issues. Josephine Butler's Ladies National Association provided the inspirational prototype; the British Women's Temperance Association followed as the working model; and finally the political organizations – the Primrose Dames, the Women's Liberal Federation, the Women's Liberal Unionist Association and the various women's suffrage societies – applied the lessons learned in sophisticated large scale politicking. These organizations became full-fledged women's political lobbies counting some of the country's most effective orators among their leaders. The walls of exclusion from public life were falling.

The connection between the great eighteenth century Methodist preacher

Sarah Crosby, and Lady Carlisle, the aristocratic Liberal leader of the late nineteenth century, is a direct one. Their public roles were, of course, very different, because they lived in societies that were very different. English public life in the time of Sarah Crosby was largely framed by religion and couched in its language. By the late nineteenth century, England had become a predominantly secular society in which the public platform was replacing the pulpit as the vehicle for public address and betterment. As Crosby preached that the great day was dawning when all Christians would share equally in final salvation, so did Lady Carlisle proclaim the coming of the day when all citizens would get their just due. The rhetoric and the worldview had changed but it may nevertheless be said that Sarah Crosby and Lady Carlisle shared with many other exceptional women an extraordinary call to leadership in the struggle for equal rights for women.

Part One

1750–1850: The Voice of the Lord

Part One
1750–1850: The Voice of the Lord

> 'As in all the churches of the saints, the women should keep silence in the churches. For they are not permitted to speak, but should be subordinate, as even the law says. If there is anything they desire to know, let them ask their husbands at home. For it is shameful for a women to speak in church.'
>
> Paul, I Corinthians, 15

> 'We entered the house of Philip the evangelist . . . and he had four unmarried daughters who prophesied.'
>
> Acts 21

THE DAUGHTERS OF EVE

The twentieth century women's movement has aroused discussion in many areas, but especially in the field of religion has the position of women been ardently debated. The strong passions generated by these theological and organizational debates indicate the continuing importance of religion in our society. Or perhaps they should be viewed as a lingering consequence of past ages when church writings and traditions were an instrument to keep women subordinate even within secular society. Throughout the centuries the major Christian churches, with few exceptions, have been antagonistic toward assertion of women's rights. But Christanity has also been, paradoxically, an important avenue for the expression of those rights.

The patriarchal values of the Hebrew society were evident in its male-dominated institutions, laws, moral values and traditions. However, the Old Testament did not relegate all women to a silent and passive role. There were heroic women who at various times played a critical role in the survival of the Hebrews. Thus Miriam rescued Moses from a watery death, Queen Esther was active in saving her people from their enemies, and Deborah, 'a Mother in Israel', was prophetess and judge.[1] A number of women were recorded as speaking out publicly in the old Hebrew society and taking action, sometimes violently as a man would, if their people were in peril. No doubt the majority of women were completely involved with families, but this could also be said of men.

In the New Testament, in its traditional interpretation, a quite different view of women comes to prominence. Women are now identified with the Eve who tempted Adam.[2] Furthermore, the subordination of women appears to be quite clearly asserted in instructions from the Apostle Paul.

The Bible, however, is a collection of ambiguous writings that can be made to support a plethora of interpretations. If in the oft-quoted passage Paul said women should be silent, Paul is also the one who said 'in Christ there is no male and female'.[3] If Timothy states that women should not teach religion to men,[4] in another part of the New Testament we find the four daughters of Philip the evangelist prophesying and openly preaching.[5] Other women such as Mary Magdelene also preached and played an active role in the time of Jesus. And the teachings of Jesus himself did not discriminate by gender.

The question is not whether the Bible says these things, but rather why certain biblical writings become established as authoritative, while other apparently conflicting parts are ignored. Perhaps each generation interprets the teachings of the Bible in its own way so as to reinforce contemporary values. Almost every political and social position can find support somewhere within the Bible, and just as current popular values achieve biblical confirmation, so do parts supporting unpopular ideas become 'forgotten'. Such is the case for the role of women in Christian life. Even in the churches, where they made up the greatest number of regular supporters, women had no authority. They were the daughters of Eve and the temptresses of all the Adams. Only when they had an 'extraordinary call' from the Lord were they allowed to speak out, and even that permission was grudgingly given.

1 They Sat Not Still

If Christians were 'all one in Christ', there could be no gender discrimination in Christianity. But when the Christian Church was organized in Roman times, there was a customary division between men and women, and biblical texts were searched to find justification for continuing this separation.[1] We find rules and structures being developed to 'protect' the church and the class in power. By the time of the Reformation the status of women in the Roman Church had been clearly defined. No matter how intelligent or gifted a woman might be, she still had the fatal flaw of Eve. The most that she could hope for was control in her own sphere, albeit always subordinate to male authority.[2]

Not all early Christians accepted this separation by gender. In Anglo-Saxon England the Celtic Church had religious houses where both men and women were equal members, some with women leaders exercising power over men.[3] But this did not last long. When the Roman Church took control of the English church, segregation by gender became the rule: monasteries for males and separate convents for females.

Historians have claimed that many women found a great deal of freedom from male authority within the medieval convents, that the head of the convent, the Mother Superior, was able to make decisions, and that her power and authority exceeded that of most females in the secular world.[4] To a limited extent this was true, but the ultimate Christian authority, the priest, was always male and without him there could be no giving of the sacraments – a crucial part of the religion. Furthermore, it was a rare convent that was free from the authority of the local hierarchy of the Church, which was also always male.

THE PROTESTANT REFORMATION

The Reformation broke up more than a religious institution; it introduced new ideas and beliefs into the Christian world that led to a new theology as well as new churches and new institutional structures. In England the actual break with Rome came not from religious motivation but from a monarch who wanted to make decisions without papal interference. But the reforming ideas that fomented doctrinal questioning and change in

Continental Europe came eventually to England and were to undermine the traditional rules that had controlled the religious establishment, including those pertaining to the position of women. The Bible, especially the Old Testament, was given primary importance in the Reformed religion, leading to a new appreciation of the Hebraic attitude towards women and their role in society.

Women were active in the many nonconformist groups that rose in opposition to the traditionalist established church. How active we do not know because the role of women in religious life was often discounted, if even mentioned, by male chroniclers. Residual prejudice against female leadership was hard, if not impossible, to overcome. Evidence does exist, however, that women played an effective part in the printing and dissemination of 'subversive' religious ideas, sometimes working alone and sometimes in unison with husbands, fathers or other male family members.[5]

However, in the sixteenth century deep religious questioning was muted in England in reaction to the emerging Counter-Reformation. All discord, both political and religious, was seen as treasonous as the English united against the Roman Church and the power of Spain. By the beginning of the seventeenth century when this threat was overcome, religious agitation was too strong to be suppressed any longer; coupled with growing political discontent, it led to civil war, one that unleashed a great new surge of religious feeling.

With the collapse of civil government and its power to enforce religious conformity, men and women were free openly to embrace new religious ideas and groups. And so the 1640s and 1650s were decades of religious enthusiasm that drew in English men and women of all classes intent on finding their own salvation. A strong millenarianism accentuated the urgency of seeking the 'will of the Lord'. Government, church and even family authority were rejected by those convinced that true authority was exercised through those whom the Lord had chosen to reveal his word.

The two main established churches rejected these new ideas and remained loyal to their own traditions. The Church of England which had retained the institutional hierarchy from Rome, except of course the authority of the Pope, had also kept most of the doctrines inherited from the old Roman church. The position of women changed little except that the convent was no longer an alternative to secular life. The Presbyterian church, established in Scotland and elsewhere, likewise retained its traditional male authority; in both churches women continued in a subordinate position.

WOMEN AND THE SECTS

It is in the sects that we find the enthusiasm and the religious radicalism that was to lead to changes. Many religious communities were being formed by individuals who were converts to some particular set of beliefs. Women were leaders as well as followers at this time – moving around, like the men, among the various bodies, searching for a religious home.[6] Some of these communities developed into sects and a few survived to become nonconforming churches of the post-Restoration period. Prominent among these enduring sects were the Baptists, Congregationalists, and Society of Friends, where women made up a large part of the membership and sometimes a part of the leadership during the 1640s and 1650s. It is illuminating to look at women's roles in their subsequent development.

The Congregationalists and the Baptists had a common origin. Both trace their history back to the beginning of the seventeenth century when a sect of radical Puritans separated from the Church of England and went to Holland. Both men and women went, in families and singly, with some individual women leaving their husbands behind in England.[7] Most of these 'separatists', as they were called, soon returned to England and, though some went on to Plymouth Colony, others stayed in England to work in the religious underground. Puritan women were particularly active in writing and printing proscribed pamphlets.[8] If caught these women suffered the same punishment as men: imprisonment, torture and, in some cases, death. In these early years women as well as men were appointed deacons of the church and, though not officially allowed to preach, women thought to be 'spiritually endowed' did so.[9]

In these first decades of the seventeenth century the contribution of women was especially important for the Puritan faith because, being illegal, it had no churches or other official centers in which to meet or pray. Acting in their capacities as housewives and mothers, women organized their homes as religious centers and saw to it that all members of the household were taught Puritan principles. Without the action of these women within their traditional roles, the Puritan sect would not have flourished.[10]

But it was in the religious turmoil of the 1640s, when a great many new members joined the Puritans and then split off to form other sects, that the role of women itself changed. Many of these new members brought with them new beliefs and new values that were to free many Puritan women from their traditional restraints and enable them to take new leadership responsibilities. We have no evidence that any women at this time were officially ordained,[11] yet many preached in public and, perhaps more importantly, some established and maintained new churches.[12] At this time too we find women and men as 'ordained Deacons' of the Baptist sect, female deacons having the same status as their male colleagues. They were paid by the church, but their work was mostly with the sick.[13]

SOCIETY OF FRIENDS AND OTHER NONCONFORMISTS

For a more drastic and permanent change in the female role in religion we have to look to the Society of Friends or Quakers. So numerous were the women in this sect and so public their activities, that in some places it was believed only women could be members of the Society, that it was a special women's religion.[14] Based on a different attitude towards the Bible the Quakers believed they were living in a post-biblical era – when the world of the 'Spirit' had succeeded that of the 'Word', and all people, men and women, possessed part of this spirit, or 'inner light', without gender discrimination.

The Bible, however, was not ignored; it still had an important place in this new religion. Like their Puritan predecessors, the Society of Friends quoted it to support new positions, but the passages they quoted were those that had been previously been little valued, or ignored altogether. New importance was given to the chapters that emphasized the work of women, both in the Old and the New Testaments. George Fox, the early leader of this sect, was personally committed to gender equality, and believed that 'in Christ there is no male and no female, that all are one'.[15]

At his insistence, and against great opposition, Fox organized special Women's Meetings that were to meet regularly as part of the organizational work of the Society.[16] Here women were free to speak without pressure, overt or subtle, from male members. Though primarily a gathering for worship, these meetings also dealt with wider topics than the immediate affairs of the group: Serious decisions were made on matters that Fox considered women could manage better than men. Working with other women and with children took up much of their time, but they were also responsible for investigating and dealing with the problems of the poor. They handled considerable sums of money from two funds: the collections from their weekly meetings, and their trust fund that came from many sources – their businesses, legacies and donations. This money was used for various purposes: ministers' expenses, apprenticing children, loans to fellow Quakers for their businesses, and so on. The women took their responsibilities seriously and expended much time and energy in carrying out their duties. They also learned to buy property and to deal with business matters, valuable training that few women (or even men) then received.[17]

Describing some of the women's work, one male contemporary chronicler wrote:

> These women did also enquire into and inspect the wants and necessities of the poor, who were convinced of the Truth; and they sat not still, until the cry of the poor came to their houses, but when they did suppose or discover a want of help, their charity led them to enquire into their conditions, and to minister to their necessities.[18]

Women's Meetings as well as Men's Meetings had to approve of all marriages, an authority that later upset many men because it was seen as infringing on the masculine right to make such family decisions.[19]

Women of the Society of Friends were encouraged to get up and 'testify' in public, to speak to others. There were no privileged groups, no titles, in these first years of the Society: All Friends, both men and women, were 'spiritually endowed' and any could preach as the Spirit moved them. This religious equality affected the position of women in the Quaker families, both at home and at meetings. Women's opinions were considered important, and not just those of a few female luminaries.

Such a radical attitude was bound to have a strong effect on the economic position of women within the Quaker community. Most members were farmers or artisans; they worked for a living, with the family as the primary economic unit. Their businesses and farms were family enterprises in which women and men worked alongside one another as co-workers. As was true for English working society as a whole, there were no 'separate spheres' at this time, and women worked in the fields doing heavy manual labor, without worries about 'the weaker sex' or 'delicate females'.[20]

It was a Quaker custom that when the husband died, the family business was inherited by the wife who would run it as her enterprise.[21] If there was no family business, independent work was found for Quaker women, single or married, just as was done for the male Friends.[22]

With the restoration of the Established Church in 1660, the Quakers were proscribed and suffered great hardship along with all the other sects. But the women as well as the men persisted, working both at home and abroad to spread their beliefs around the world.[23] In 1671 the London Women's Meeting attempted unsuccessfully to organize all the women's meetings into a federation for Quakers at home and abroad.[24]

It is easy to exaggerate the changes in the lives of Quaker women. Centuries-old traditions and social attitudes do not change overnight. Quaker males could agree in theory that all are created spiritually equal, men and women, that each possesses the same religious light, but it was harder to accept this equality in everyday life. Men used to controlling the family and making its decisions must have found it difficult to accept sharing family power. And so it is not surprising to find that there was much opposition among the ordinary members of the sect to the new status of women, especially after the first generation of Quakers had passed away. There was a whittling away of the rights of women, so that, by the beginning of the eighteenth century, they were less than equal to men, both in spiritual and in secular matters.[25]

WOMEN AND THE SECTS IN THE EIGHTEENTH CENTURY

The real test came with the formal organization of the Quaker Church. With the Toleration Act of 1689, all the sects were allowed legal existence. Though they still had to suffer severe disabilities, the passage of this act invigorated for a time the Quaker efforts at proselytizing and women again became active in preaching and missionary work. But at this time the Society started to place the names of recognized preachers in a special book, leading to an official separation between professional and lay preachers. There then developed debates over the appointment of lay preachers: whether those who were self-appointed should be recognized by having their names placed in the book and, furthermore, whether women's names should be placed in the book on the same basis as men's. The Society was changing from a sect to a church.

In the development of the other sects we find a similar pattern. Although women did not play the same important part in the Baptist and Congregational sects, they had been active preachers during the Civil War. Then, with peace and the organization of the churches, women lost the advantages they had gained in the founding years and found themselves back in a subordinate position. As both sects built chapels and organized a professional clergy, women were excluded from any major institutional role. In the Baptist church throughout the eighteenth century, there was a decline in the position of women.[26] Women continued to be appointed deaconesses, but they were no longer ordained and did not have equality with the male deacons.[27] Although the Congregational Church was considered by some in the late nineteenth century to be 'one of the few Churches not hostile to women',[28] it never ordained women or gave them authority within church structure.

The acquisition of permanent meeting places by these new churches was often a turning point. It was logical for each church to have its own buildings and thus be less dependent on its members or sympathetic property owners for a place to hold services and other church activities; however, such ownership required a more structured organization. Owning property tends to make people very conservative, and the eighteenth-century nonconformists were no exceptions. In setting up their establishments, the new churches looked to the older denominations for models and copied them. Because the older ones had been based on the traditional patriarchal society, this became the pattern adopted by later religious foundations.

The Society of Friends, too, became involved in building programs. New gender-related problems arose with these changes. For example, it was discussed whether in the new meeting halls women and men should sit together or if the two sexes would be more comfortable apart. This issue was given greater consideration when it was discovered that young men tended to 'crowd' the women in the new halls, which made the women unhappy. The decision was made to seat the sexes separately.[29]

In the eighteenth century the Society of Friends went through a time of 'quietism'. Both men and women withdrew from most of their traditional proselytizing and missionary work to devote themselves to their own Quaker circles. Women continued to play an active part in their local meetings and in other charitable work. Compared to their contemporaries in other churches, they had a great deal of freedom and non-domestic responsibilities; but when compared to their Quaker predecessors of the mid seventeenth century, they were fading into the old female subservience. The economic position of the members of the Society was improving and many were becoming prosperous. As a consequence of this change and the subsequent greater involvement with the non-Quaker world, the Friends moved into greater conformity with the practises of the rest of English society. Nevertheless, the Quaker women did manage to retain some of their improved status at meetings and in the Society generally; and, as we shall see, in a propitious time they were to emerge again as leaders in many social causes, disproportionate to their numbers in the population as a whole. Mr. Crouch was right about Quaker women when he wrote: 'They sat not still'.

2 The Call to Preach

THE METHODIST REVIVAL

During the first half of the eighteenth century English religious life generally appears to have stagnated, as though exhausted by the clamour and demands of the reformers of the previous century. With the Act of Toleration of 1689 overt persecution ended and the nonconforming groups could establish themselves within certain parameters. Most English men and women chose to remain within the Anglican fold, though nominally in many cases. It was not an era of religious agitation, but rather a time of digesting the previous changes.

This state of general inertia was broken with the emergence of a new evangelical movement within the Church of England led by John and Charles Wesley and George Whitefield. They and their cohorts encouraged and guided a great revival of religious enthusiasm that created a new spirit, new sects and eventually new churches. The roots of this new 'revivalism' went back to the late 1720s when the Wesley brothers and George Whitefield formed the Holy Club at Oxford. The Wesley brothers came from a religious family. Their father was an Anglican clergyman and their mother the daughter of a nonconforming minister. A deeply religious woman, she had converted to Anglicanism after a period of self-examination and study.

When the Reverend Wesley was away from home Susanna Wesley, the mother, led the family prayers and often preached to these gatherings. Sometimes outsiders were invited to attend, but even the presence of strangers did not modify her role on account of her sex; she conducted these services as her husband would had he been at home.[1] Through her domestic religious activities, Susanna Wesley played an important role in laying the foundation of her sons' acceptance of a strong female position in the Methodist revival.[2]

The founding of the Methodist Society in 1742 had a profound effect on the religious life of England. Whereas the population of England increased greatly in the eighteenth century, the Church of England did not expand its church places. After a hundred years of Anglican domination and, in many instances, neglect, and with the dissenting (nonconformist) churches withdrawing into themselves, a large number of Englishmen had little connection with any religion. The country was ripe for a religious awakening. Women found in this new evangelicalism an opportunity to participate more fully in religious activity; and it is not surprising to find them, as in the Civil War days, among the ardent proselytizers for the new faith. Their role was only possible because in its beginning the sect was not officially authorized by the Church of England; according to the Established Church tradition, neither laymen nor laywomen were empowered to preach publicly in the Anglican church.[3]

The original Methodists started as a Society within the Church of England in the 1740s. All members had to be communicants in the established church and were expected to attend the regular Anglican services. However, they differed from the regular church members in seeking a more personal commitment to their faith than was offered by the eighteenth-century Anglican church. As their numbers grew and the local methodist societies became increasingly impersonal, smaller groups were organized. All-male and all-female bands were set up as study groups to help the members spiritually. It was a purely voluntary attachment with no coercion. Meetings were, for the most part, in the homes of members. The separation of the sexes was important for the women, particularly in the early days, because it allowed them to develop leadership, public speaking, and teaching skills that would not have been allowed to emerge in most mixed groups. The majority of female preachers began their careers in these female bands and later expanded their activities to the public in general.[4]

In its early days the Methodist Society also organized groups which it called classes. Unlike the bands, enrollment in a class was required of all members of the Society, who put themselves under its discipline. Men and women usually met together in the homes of members with twelve members making up a class, one of them appointed leader. The function of the class was to integrate and teach the new recruits as well as give support and ongoing instruction to established associates through bible study, prayers and discourses. The job of the leader was to visit the homes of the class members to see that they all remained faithful and adhered to the rules of the Society.[5]

Most of this leadership work was carried out by laypeople, members of the community who had, in many cases, a natural talent for the task. It was within these classes that women came to the fore – even within mixed groups many of the class leaders were women. Often talented and charismatic personalities, the best of these women attracted so many new members that they eventually had to leave the small classes and go into larger public arenas where they could preach to hundreds.[6] The reputations of some women was so great that they were instrumental in bringing into the Methodist fold large numbers of formerly uncommitted men and women. No doubt, some came initially to hear a woman speak, a novelty that pulled into the Methodist orbit 'many persons who without it would not come'.[7]

At first John Wesley was unhappy with women preaching at Methodist meetings. He was an ordained minister in the Church of England and despite his radical actions in setting up and organizing the Methodist Society, he was basically a conservative who saw his Society as an auxiliary of the Church of England and insisted, in the beginning at least, on its members adhering to Church of England rules. Accepting the traditional view of women's role in the church, Wesley initially forbade women preaching; in 1761 he wrote a letter to Sarah Crosby, a leader among these well-known women preachers, to tell her that 'the Methodists do not allow of women preachers'. However, he realized that women like Crosby were playing a very important role in the Methodist revival and, unwilling to lose their talents, suggested that she 'read to the people the Notes on any chapter before you speak a few words . . . '.[8]

Sarah Crosby found this restriction unacceptable and in a letter dated July 7, 1765 wrote, 'I do not think it wrong for women to speak in public provided they speak by the spirit of God.'[9] It was an important issue, one that could not be ignored as increasing numbers of women were taking prominent public roles and gaining great reputations as evangelists. In 1769, four years later, John Wesley wrote to Miss Crosby telling her that she could now make 'short exhortations' at Methodist meetings.[10]

OPPOSITION TO WOMEN PREACHERS

The matter of female preaching and teaching continued to be agitated within the Methodist Society, for many of whose members the established Pauline prohibitions were Christian law. In 1771 Mary Bosanquet wrote a letter to John Wesley listing the criticisms many women had to face when preaching in public. Her reason for writing was the opposition she experienced when travelling in a Methodist missionary group of one man and two women in Yorkshire. Because many of their flock had 'a dislike of preaching houses', such evangelists preferred not to use regular churches, although they sometimes had no choice: Churches were often the only buildings large enough to accommodate the numbers that came to their gatherings. At one of these meetings held in a local church a Methodist preacher told Mary Bosanquet that he 'thought it quite unscriptural for women to speak in the Church, and his Conscience constrained him to prevent it.'[11] When others attending the meeting voiced similar objections she determined to stop her work, as the easiest course to take.[12] However, on reconsideration she changed her mind, convinced that she was called to do 'all I can for God', and that if she refused to preach to the 'hundreds of unawakened persons' who came to their meeting then God would say 'their blood will I require of you'.[13]

According to her letter to Wesley she then continued her work in a modified way, not openly preaching but 'talking' to the people. Again there were objections both from within and without the Methodist circle. The biblical injunction that 'a woman ought not to teach nor take authority over the man' was cited by those who opposed her. In responding, Mary Bosanquet suggested that the Pauline proscription was relative to the circumstances that gave rise to it:

> But the Apostle says, I suffer not a woman to speak in the Church but learn at home. I answer, was not that spoke in reference to a time of dispute and contention, when many were striving to be heads and leaders, so that his saying, she is not to speak, here seems to me to imply no more than the other, she is not to meddle with Church Government.[14]

In response to the objection that 'improper women' might preach, she asked what happens when 'improper men' preach, and answered, the Church 'has power to stop his mouth'. Why then cannot the same action be taken in the case of females? That there may be improper men preaching does not lead to a prohibition of all men preaching; the same should be true for women.

In her letter Mary Bosanquet then turned to the argument against women preachers based on the weakness of women: that women are more easily deceived than men and have 'passions more tender'. Accepting the premise, she argued that the problem it creates can be solved by making sure that a woman evangelist 'acts according to the Oracles of GOD, and while she speaks according to the Truth she cannot lead the people into an Error'.

Considering finally the conflict that could arise with the old traditional virtues of 'modesty, purity and humility' believed essential to a good Christian woman, Mary Bosanquet pointed to the virtuous women in the Scriptures who played an active public role. Mary, she wrote, could not be 'accused of immodesty when she carried the joyful news of her Lord's Resurrection, and in that sense taught the Teachers of Mankind'. The woman of Samaria when she 'invited the whole City to come to Christ' could not be accused of immodesty. The wise woman of Abel, spokesperson for a whole city,[15] and Deborah, the prophetess, are evidence that the Scriptures approved of women who would take the initiative when it was necessary. Mary Bosanquet thus laid out her problems of female authority before John Wesley and asked for his guidance.

From the beginning the Methodist Society had stressed the importance of a personal commitment to God. An individual relationship between the Lord and the believer with no important intermediaries lay at the heart of this revival; the individual believer, not the organization, was the main focus of the Society. Under these circumstances, it was difficult to forbid women to preach or teach when they appeared to have a special mandate to do so from God. Who was to declare that God did not speak to women when their preaching showed otherwise? If the Lord 'calls' a woman to preach his Gospel, who is to deny it? That was John Wesley's final position when asked for his ruling on women preaching. He put it unequivocally, so that no misinterpretation could be made by those who might disagree with it. Writing on June 13, 1771 to Sarah Crosby, he said:

> I think the strength of our Case rests there in your Having an *Extra-ordinary* Call. So I am persuaded has every one of our Lay-preachers; otherwise I could not countenance his preaching at all. It is plain to me, yet: the work of God termed methodism is an Extraordinary dispensation of HIS providence.
>
> Therefore I do not wonder, if several things occur therein which do not fall under ordinary Rules of Discipline; St. Paul's ordinary rule was 'I permit not a woman to speak in the Congregation': yet in Extraordinary Cases, he made a few exceptions: at Corinth in particular.[16]

Unfortunately for the Methodist female preachers opposition to their work persisted, and they were ultimately forced to repeat the pattern of their Quaker sisters. Just as a large proportion of the first Quaker preachers who were women were later silenced by sheer weight of opinion from their Society as a whole, now, over a hundred years later, the Methodist women (in such large numbers at the beginning that the Methodist Society was accused of being a Quaker sect),[17] found themselves under pressure to be silent also. To the accusation of Quakerism, John Wesley replied that his Society had a totally different attitude towards the biblical prohibition of women preaching than did the Quakers. 'They (the Quakers) flatly deny the rule itself excluding women from preaching . . . . We allow the rule; only we believe it admits of some exceptions.'[18] The basic conservatism of the Methodists on the role of women comes through here. Whereas the Quakers had supported the right of women to preach on the same basis as men – all members, men or women, could preach – for the Methodists, while all men and women *who were called* could preach, the Pauline rule still held and ordinarily women were to be silent in the churches.

Using the Bible as their guide, the early Methodists did not introduce radical interpretations of the Scriptures but wanted to spread the message of established Christian doctrines to a wider audience. Since they were not endeavouring to change the social arrangements, there was little attempt to foster gender equality. Many female Methodists like Mary Bosanquet accepted the traditional views, Church and secular, of their sex: Females suffered under emotional instability, weakness of female intellect, and other gender handicaps. But the preaching women thought of themselves as distinctly different from the ordinary females – divinely appointed to be dissimilar. Like so many earlier and later women leaders, they unintentionally enlarged the scope of women despite their own beliefs in female inferiority. Their public work and actions denied female inadequacies that traditional Christianity had stressed.

Female activity in Methodism during the second half of the eighteenth century was notable for the diversity of its social backgrounds. The evangelical call crossed social lines and drew into the Methodist revival women from all classes. Mary Bosanquet was a well-to-do woman from an Anglican family who became converted to Methodism and used her personal fortune to set up an organized community of Methodist women. Sarah Crosby came from a humble family and at times suffered great hardship because of her impecunity. The majority of the women preachers appear to have fallen somewhere between these two extremes. There was no 'typical' woman preacher. Some women remained single while others were married – often to other preachers; and some came from a religious background while others grew up in a nonreligious environment. They all felt personally called by God to do His work and so were confident of the rightness of their activities.

But even if the women were sure of their mission, their position in the organization was always tenuous despite the approval of their leader. With the formation of the Methodist Connexion after the death of John Wesley, new forces took control of the Methodist Society and worked to create an independent nonconforming church acceptable to the rising middle classes. By this time the Wesleyan Methodists had changed their goals and adopted new values that were more in keeping with their improving economic and social position. The Wesleyans became intent on creating a respectable church with a professional clergy. This meant, among other things, an end to women teaching men and speaking in public, even with an 'extraordinary call' from God.[19]

THE WESLEYAN CONNEXION AND OTHER METHODIST SECTS

In 1794 when the Methodists decided to split from the Church of England and set up their own church, they also sought to create a more professional environment for their work. A chapel building program was inaugurated and new controls imposed on the preachers. Into the old Methodist world of classes, outdoor meetings and lay preachers now appeared rigid institutional divisions between member and nonmember, layman and preacher, and preacher and superintendent. Also created was a new hierarchy with various officials, both at the center as well as at the local level, to run the church.[20] To be recognized all preachers had to have their names on official lists, and only those acceptable to the newly formed hierarchy would be admitted to the roster.

In this new church women were given no place in the professional ranks. Despite the official acceptance of female preachers at the conference of 1787,[21] there had always been much hostility towards their work. But the elimination of female preachers did not occur immediately. For ten years after John Wesley's death there was a great revival in evangelical religion throughout the country, and women preachers remained very popular among the people, especially in the north where Methodism had a firm hold. By the beginning of the nineteenth century Lancashire and Yorkshire had the largest percentage of Methodists,[22] and it was in these northern industrial areas that women were the most active.[23]

Women preachers, therefore, could not be eliminated immediately in a frontal attack by the conservatives. Instead the women found themselves being slowly nudged to the periphery of Wesleyan activity. Some were harassed by accusations of wrongdoing. If their enemies could find nothing true to use against them, innuendos or downright lies were circulated.[24]

The first direct prohibition of female preaching for Methodists took place at the Dublin Conference of 1802, but this was not effective in England. The following year, in Manchester, the Conference of Methodist Preachers moved to reduced their role, claiming a large majority of Methodists were against women preaching. The conference decreed that only where there were not enough men preachers to do the work could women do it. If a woman had 'an extraordinary call', she should be allowed to preach but even then her work should be limited to women's groups. [25] Furthermore, the conference ruled, no female preacher was to preach without the permission of the local superintendent. Thus women once again found themselves placed in the traditional female supportive position: Sunday School teaching instead of public preaching, welfare work instead of evangelizing. By the 1820s few official women preachers remained in the Wesleyan Connexion, though they were not formally banished until 1835. Even the important contributions of the early women preachers were diminished in official journal accounts in order to prevent their use as exemplars for young Methodist women.[26]

Increasingly conservative and authoritarian, the Wesleyan Methodists soon rejected all lay preaching, thereby effectively excluding all females from this work. Men and women who claimed to have an extraordinary call to preach, came to be seen by the new Methodist leaders as undesirable 'fanatics'.[27] Camp meetings were replaced by services in the new chapels, the center of Methodist activities, and a strong new discipline was imposed on all members. Women once again disappeared from the public platform, at least the religious one.

As the Wesleyans pursued their goal of middle-class respectability, abandoning their open air and camp meetings along with their reliance on lay preachers, not all of those connected to the Methodist evangelical movement were happy with the changes. Many English men and women did not want to belong to this new connexion now apparently just as rigid and dogmatic as the established churches. Also, some of the religious needs that John Wesley and his followers had sought to fulfill were not being met by the new body. Consequently, a number of breakaway groups formed in the years 1796–1815 to retain the original methods and purposes of Methodism: The Independent Methodists, the New Methodist Connexion, the Primitive Methodists, and the Bible Christians.

Even before official banishment women preachers had already felt the cold winds of disapproval emanating from some of the male leaders, and by the end of the eighteenth century many had already left the Connexion: some to remain independent of any church, some to link up with local groups still evangelizing among the unattached, and still others to join the more hospitable breakaway sects. A small minority left Methodism altogether and joined the Quakers,[28] but the great majority joined either the Independent or Quaker Methodists, the Primitive Methodists or the Bible Christians. Female preaching was never fully accepted by all members of the sects, but the leaders of both the Bible Christians and the Primitive Methodists rejected any claim that there was a Biblical prohibition to women preaching.[29] William O'Bryan, the founder of the Bible Christians, was married to a popular preacher and he strongly supported her work. Of all the connexions the Bible Christians was the only one at this time to give 'full authorization of women itinerant preachers'.[30] Between 1819 and 1861 the Bible Christians had more than 71 female itinerant preachers; the peak years for women preachers in this sect were the 1820s, mostly in the South of England.[31]

Men preachers in this connexion were encouraged to marry their female counterparts.[32]

In the ranks of Primitive Methodism were to be found some of the most popular women preachers of the early nineteenth century, especially in the north where this connexion had its greatest support. Hugh Bourne, the Primitive Methodist leader, encouraged women preachers, realizing their value in evangelizing among the unchurched. He saw to it that these women like the men were paid a salary, even if their remuneration was only half the amount men received and some of them, like their male counterparts, had to raise the money themselves.[33] In 1818 one out of five Primitive Methodist preachers was female.[34] Women were also officially ordained as ministers in the Primitive Methodist sect.[35] Some of these women preachers worked at home and ran local societies. This allowed them to maintain their homes and raise families while continuing their evangelizing.[36] These women while being useful to their sect were also examples of domestic piety.[37] However, they were not given real authority and publicity within the connexion. In 1824 the connexion banned female superintendents and did not allow women to vote on quarter day boards.[38]

The women who managed to combine their home life and their religious responsibilities successfully were not numerous, because the work was not easy and the hours long. But the hardest situations for both men and women were those of the itinerant preachers. They were expected to travel to isolated villages and farms and then preach, often twice a day, outside if necessary, no matter what the weather. Home life must have suffered when the husband or the wife, particularly the latter, was away. Nevertheless, women continued to work as itinerant preachers in these sects.

Some women rejected affiliation with any of the established connexions and preferred to set up their own independent chapels. One very successful sect was that of the Countess of Huntingdon. Coming from a wealthy aristocratic family, the Countess was able to organize and support her own chapels, both economically and socially. A pious woman, she was introduced to Methodism by her sister-in-law, who had been converted by a Wesleyan minister in the 1740s.[39] It was during an illness that the Countess decided to take an active role in promoting the gospel. At first, like John Wesley, she tried to work within the Church of England, supporting Anglican doctrines and ceremonies, but she came into conflict with the hierarchy of the established church, and, like the Wesleyans, eventually set up her own organization.

The husband of the Countess was not a convert to her new evangelicalism but was sympathetic, allowing their home, Ledstone Hall, to be a center for travelling preachers and his fortune to be used for their work.

After his death his widow made Ledstone Hall a center for her religious work. George Whitefield, the associate of John Wesley, was appointed her chaplain and many missionary groups were organized, including all-women groups.[40] The Countess did not herself preach but hired others to do so. She gave both financial and social support to many evangelical groups and individuals and eventually organized a chapel. This led to a connexion that ultimately included a college for the training of ministers and a number of chapels. So firmly established was her sect that it continued to expand long after her death. In her lifetime it had seven chapels, but by 1891, one hundred years after her death, there were thirty-three. More than one hundred other chapels were also associated with her connexion.[41]

The Countess was not a feminist and did not deliberately work to enlarge the opportunities for women in the society;[42] but, like her nineteenth-century counterparts, she encouraged all women to be active in the work, including upper-class women who were persuaded to hold 'Drawing-Room' meetings for the evangelical reform.[43] Her fortune along with her social status allowed her an independence of action that few individuals, men or women, enjoyed. She had an impact on all classes and the example of her leadership was of great importance for later women evangelists and activists.[44] However, because she was a woman her work had to contend with traditional views that diminished any female contribution to religious development. The role of the Countess of Huntingdon in eighteenth-century English history remains in need of better evaluation by scholarship free from gender bias.[45]

INDEPENDENT WOMEN PREACHERS

The majority of female evangelists in the late eighteenth and early nineteenth century preached independently of any church. Some of the women created their own circuits, travelling around the country to preach and drawing in listeners through their own reputations. Some set up chapels as centers for their work. If the preacher had access to funds for such a building, as some did, there was no great problem. If the missionary had none, there were usually some sympathetic supporters willing to give or lend money for such a cause.

A good example of an independent mission was the chapel organized by Ann Carr and a group of female revivalists in Leeds in 1825. These women were popular preachers among the Primitive Methodists but eventually severed their connection with this sect when it tried to exercise control over them. Fortunate to have some financial support, they bought land in the middle of a Leeds slum where they built Leylands Chapel as well as cottages and workshops. This mission became a center for help to the poor of the area, attracting support from many diverse groups and individuals. William Taite, a Quaker from a well-known Leeds family, supplied the initial mortgage money, while continuing religious support was given by various area ministers, some of whom would lead the services. More than just a religious organization, the Leylands Chapel mission supported a Sunday School, a Sick Society and a temperance society. Subsequently, a second chapel and a third were opened.[46]

Such local relief work was carried out by many religiously inspired women throughout the nineteenth century. Some of these chapels became local landmarks, but they were basically one or two-person operations, frequently supported by family funds, and rarely outlasting their founders. It was not unusual for these missions to employ, full- or part-time, men and women to work with the poor. If expenses were greater than the evangelists could bear, funds could be raised from local philanthropists, especially Quaker merchants. Eventually the few that survived were joined to a regular denomination, as was Ann Carr's Leylands chapel after her death. Although most had only a fleeting existence, whether they had a long or short life span they did very important and useful work in their local districts. The evangelists lived within the community, among the poor and unhealthy, working to ameliorate the worst of the slum conditions. Widely known and usually appreciated in their own neighborhoods, they rarely received recognition beyond it. Most of them did not limit their mission to narrow religious teachings. Along with their evangelizing they supported various social reforms, especially temperance in the second half of the nineteenth century. They recognized that their religious message would be ineffective among those too cold, too hungry and too intoxicated to understand it.

DOMESTIC RELIGION

There was nothing new in England in making the home the center of religious activity. Since the days of the Lollards and the rise of the later Protestant sects, private houses had been the scene of much evangelizing. When the break with Rome came in the fifteenth century, many sects joined the Church of England, but a few did not and preferred to remain domestic religions. This was partly because some Englishmen, especially in the lower orders, distrusted all institutionalized religion, where they rarely had any voice.[47]

Methodism and domestic religion had much in common and were often intermingled, especially in the rural areas of the north of England where they reinforced one another. The early Methodist system of classes and other religious gatherings, led by lay men and women in informal settings, was attractive to those suspicious of institutional religion. Particularly in the late eighteenth century, a time of active Methodist evangelizing, homes were utilized for such religious meetings. Later, however, when the Methodist religion became more formally established their chapel was as much distrusted by some villagers as was the local parish church. For many living in isolated villages and farms there were no viable religious organizations, and home-based religion was the only one available.

Out of this amalgam of Methodism and domestic religion a new cottage religion developed. Family kitchens and parlours became the centers of this nonconformist religion born in working-class villages with few resources. Into the small parochial world came visiting evangelists, women as well as men, bringing not only new faces but also new teachings, thus connecting home groups to the larger religious world. Eventually cottage meetings were to develop into a loosely connected network that had a strong impact on local life in the late eighteenth and early nineteenth centuries.[48]

Women, because they were usually in charge of the home, were given a prominent role in this domestic religion. They made their homes available to the classes and other groups and gave hospitality to itinerant preachers, dependent on their generosity for daily bread and a bed at night. A warm kitchen was a good meeting place for neighbors, and a simple meal would suffice. If there were no bed the floor would do.[49] Many of these wandering evangelists came from modest homes and knew how to make do on little, and so long as they felt they were doing the Lord's work they were content.[50] Such hospitality meant that almost anyone could be active in evangelical work; they needed no organization or financial support to carry out their mission. The day-to-day work of the local religious effort was carried on by individuals of the community who had some natural organizing ability. Without much fuss or ceremony they would speak, discuss, and learn together.

As in revivalist meetings, participants at these home meetings discussed publicly their religious experiences, and women as well as men were encouraged to speak out. Because there was no hierarchy involved and no outside discipline to be adhered to, the gatherings were democratic in both their spiritual functions and their secular arrangements. In the preindustrial community, where work and home were intermixed, there was not the separation that was to appear in the later industrial society. There was, similarly, little separation between religion and daily life: Prayers in the kitchen were part of normal living. There was rarely the institutional ritual commonly associated with churches and even chapels.

Providing a supportive fellowship and framework to many individuals and families, these small religious groups were as much social as religious. Thus, when the family or the individual migrated to the city, as many did in the early nineteenth century, they took their religion with them. In the strangeness of their new environment these immigrants tried to recreate the communities left behind and many kept their cottage religion, with all its associations, until they became more acclimated to their new surroundings. Therefore, in this transference of village life to city, women played an important part.[51]

Once firmly established in their new homes, the immigrants sought a wider community. They joined the sects, particularly the various independent bodies of Methodists which had not merged with the Wesleyans. Most sects had retained much of the old evangelical simplicity, including lay preaching. In the 1830s and 1840s immigrants to the towns who did not join any religious organization sought fellowship in other groups, political or reform, such as Chartist clubs or temperance societies. Women played no leading role in these organizations, though they were sometimes involved in their activities. However, involvement of women in evangelical work continued throughout the nineteenth century, some of them we shall find having a powerful impact on the religious lives of many Britons.[52]

3 Class and Politics

TRADITIONAL UPPER-CLASS POLITICAL LEADERSHIP

In preindustrial Britain, Parliament was mainly concerned with foreign affairs and keeping the domestic peace, and its work did not affect the majority of Englishmen. More important to the common people was the role of local government, where landowners ruled and tenants obeyed. Both in town and countryside, authority was in the hands of local elites, whether the squire, vicar, or urban guilds.

Parliament had the right to make the laws dealing with the general welfare, regulating the economic as well as the social life of the people. But in normal times the national government preferred to leave most of the local exercise of power in the hands of the county and other local authorities, who were given great freedom in interpreting and enforcing the law. If the central government prescribed no solution to local problems, local authorities devised their own. There were no effective political parties in preindustrial England, only personal affiliations. Social and economic problems, as a rule, were not aired during elections:[1] An election campaign was a contest between personalities not programs.

The great political families of the eighteenth century are well known to students of political history; a relatively small number of them controlled the national government. Only men could be elected to Parliament, but they were representatives of their families, and the process of getting them elected was a family affair. A man or woman was still identified according to his or her connections, and the achievements of one member could benefit all. Elections in the eighteenth century were not the critical events for politics that they became in the nineteenth, nor were they contests with huge numbers of voters to influence. Often there was no campaign: The Member of Parliament was simply the appointee – often a member – of a family that controlled the seat. In 1793 it was estimated that 1,500 voters sent 100 representatives to Westminster.[2] As late as 1832, in one of the last by-elections of the unreformed Parliament, Benjamin Disraeli fought his first contest trying to win the votes of thirty-two electors. He lost twelve votes to twenty.[3]

The House of Lords, controlled by the aristocracy, was still the most powerful body in the eighteenth century, with the House of Commons dominated by landlords, often younger sons of the political families of the upper chamber.[4] Social and political life was carried on in the homes of the politically active aristocratic families, who relied on the talents of their women to further their political ambitions. Holland House, for example, was a center of political activity with Lady Holland and her hospitality famous among the leading politicians.[5] Such a celebrated hostess could bring to her table the great men and women whose influence could be essential in developing a career. Some of these hostesses were nationally and even internationally famous.[6]

Women in upper class political families continued to be active in supporting their families' political ambitions in the nineteenth century. Wives and daughters were important workers in seeking political support for their family men and expected to canvass the district if necessary. Many wives and daughters identified with the political affiliations of the family. Lady Stanley of Alderley, for example, active in Whig politics throughout her life, was the daughter of Viscount Dillon, an ardent Whig and a friend of Charles James Fox. As a girl in Italy, she would not dance with officers of the Austrian Army because it offended 'her Whig principles' (fairness required her to acknowledge that Austrian officers were the best dancers). Later she married the second Baron Stanley of Alderley, an active Whig, and helped his political career. She became so identified with the Whig cause that Lord Palmerston introduced her to a foreigner as 'our Chief of General Staff'.[7] On the Tory side, according to Walpole, there was one unnamed 'great lady' who during an election campaign at Westminster, 'harangued the mob' at the hustings from the window of her hotel. She was credited with helping the Tory candidate to victory.[8]

After her husband died Lady Stanley continued her public role, becoming a founder of the Women's Liberal Unionist Association. Also interested in science, she was instrumental in the establishment of Girton College, Cambridge. Two of her daughters became well known in public life: Maude remained unmarried and worked for various philanthropies, including setting up girls' clubs,[9] and the youngest daughter Rosalind, Countess of Carlisle, became the first woman president of a national temperance organization in the 1880s and in the 1890s president of the Women's Liberal Federation, a rival of the association her mother had helped inaugurate. Commenting on the family's influence on the politics of daughter Rosalind, the Countess' biographer wrote: 'she [Rosalind] had ceased to be a Whig . . . but she carried on during all her life much that she inherited from her Whig forbears'. Although mother and daughter disagreed in politics, they maintained a close affectionate relationship.[10]

THE MIDDLE-CLASS TAKEOVER

The leadership of such families was challenged in the late eighteenth and nineteenth centuries by the emergence of a new middle level in society between the lower orders – the basically nonpropertied workers and laborers – and the landowning upper orders. This new middle class owned property but also worked in trade, industry and the professions – activities often scorned by the upper classes. Although there had always been merchants, lawyers, and doctors in the towns of preindustrial England, their numbers were not large. With the development of industry and the resultant expansion of the cities, this class not only grew in numbers but also in importance. The upper part of the middle class became the leaders in English society, while the lower middle class, the *petite bourgeoisie* of Marxian writings, were ardent followers. Aided by a Queen who was in her values more middle class than upper class, the industrialists, merchants, bankers, and professionals from the middle of the nineteenth century set the standards to which most Englishmen and women sought to adhere.

A new urban life style emerged centered on a nuclear family structure. Once a public concern, families now became a private matter and the traditional community life made up of interconnecting families was now weakened if not destroyed. Each family in the nineteenth century aimed to live in its own isolated world, connected to the larger community only through the formal ties of church, club, and school. Men, women and children had their own sphere. While the wives took care of domestic matters and the children were at school, the men were free to concentrate on business and take part in public affairs. Away all day, many of these men came home in the evening, but not a few lived apart from their families and only returned to their homes at infrequent intervals.[11] Public and private life thus became separated and the home where the wife saw to the welfare and comfort of the rest of the family was the private world of which nineteenth-century Englishmen were so proud.[12]

We see some of these changes clearly in the new roles of women in English society. Middle-class women were under pressure to conform to new requirements, to act as supports of their husbands. Standards of respectability were introduced to separate those who conformed to these expectations from those who did not. There were always a few dissidents who refused compliance, but it was a brave woman indeed who was willing to risk the disapprobation of neighbors in order to follow her own star. The majority of citizens, as in all times and cases, followed the accepted modes.

In late eighteenth-century England the middle classes emerged as a growing force in the political life of the country. These newcomers to the political scene consolidated their power in local matters first, and then, after the first parliamentary reform act of 1832 gave all middle-class male householders the franchise, in national affairs as well.[13] With the vote they obtained also the right to stand for Parliament.[14] By the middle of the nineteenth century they had become a partner – albeit still a junior one – to the landowning aristocrats in the government of England.[15]

While hospitality at home was the general practise among the affluent who had large homes to accommodate the guests and a domestic staff to care for their needs, this was impossible for many of the new politically empowered middle classes with neither facilities nor traditions for private gatherings. In an environment where public affairs were becoming more truly public and not just the concern of a few private families, the substitute for the private dinner was the public dinner. Instead of a private invitation, there were tickets to be bought by those who wished to attend. These public dinners, organized for political purposes, were all-male; women played little or no role.[16]

Accompanying the rise of the middle classes was a new importance of Parliament and central government. Previously most Englishmen had looked no further than to local issues and local authorities. In the economic transformation of England from an agrarian to an industrial nation, however, Parliament was the agency to make national laws controlling working conditions as well as wages, and it became increasingly the focus of middle-class political agitation. Workingmen in the new industries, too, saw it as the only institution with power enough to protect the interests of the lower ranks of society against the new industrial establishments. If the working groups gained influence in the halls of Westminster then they could find the protection that employers, whether rural or urban, declined to give because it often went against their self-interest.

Another development focused political attention on Parliament: the French Revolution of 1789. Throughout Britain and the western world word spread of the coming of a new political era. The rhetoric of this new revolutionary spirit loosed a fanaticism that heretofore had been reserved for religious causes. It spread so far and deep among the lower orders in England that the English elites, originally willing to agree that their French neighbors' government was archaic and needed reform, became apprehensive over potential English rebellion. After the King of France was executed and France experienced a 'reign of terror', the English establishment panicked and proscribed all domestic dissent: Any call for change was now viewed as a precursor of violent upheavals. Doubting the ability of local governments to take care of their own agitators,

Parliament became the vehicle of repression against all reform efforts. 'Conspiracy' was the accusation even for the most harmless of meetings, and laws were passed to make all workingmen's gatherings illegal. But the new political ideas that emphasized citizenship, rights, and reason rather than subjects, duties, and traditions, nevertheless permeated every level of society, politicizing unenfranchised segments of the population. A new attitude towards government and authority spread throughout England. Politics came to replace religion as the issue of greatest concern among Englishmen of all classes,[17] and the problem that dominated early and mid nineteenth century politics concerned the franchise and who should have it.

WORKING-CLASS WOMEN AND REFORM

Very few people in England had a vote in the old unreformed Parliament. Those who did had obtained their votes in a variety of ways allowed over the centuries. A tremendous variety of franchises existed. In some towns all householders had the franchise: In Preston, for example, a 'scot and lot' franchise gave all owners of a hearth the vote – even women. In other towns there were no franchises at all. For the borough franchise it all depended on the individual borough charter.[18] New settlements were not enfranchised automatically when they reached a certain limit, as is done today, and consequently many densely inhabited areas were completely unrepresented. It was not seen as a great problem because Members of Parliament were supposed to represent all of England, not just their electors – at least that was the theory. Needless to say, the upper orders mainly controlled the votes and ran Parliament according to their own needs and desires.

Thus the vast majority of English men and women had no input into their government's decisions in the years before the first Reform Bill of 1832. This caused great unhappiness, particularly among the upper levels of the working classes. The only way to express negative feelings about public matters was by peaceful demonstrations and rioting, the former often deteriorating into the latter. The eighteenth century was a time of much unrest: More than one mob 'came to fight for their liberties.'[19] Daniel Defoe worried about disgruntled workers thrust together in the workshops: '. . . will they not have it more in their power . . . . to break out into mobs and riots upon every little occasion?'[20] If the price of bread rose there were bread riots, and if there were changes in religion there were church riots. Because riots were so common and accepted as a general practise, only the most widespread or unusual civil disturbances were noted by chroniclers or historians, but there were many, especially in towns where groups could easily congregate. Such unauthorized disturbances had a positive as well as a negative side. They allowed the populace to feel they were making their wishes known to authorities, while at the same time providing an opportunity to let off steam in a traditional and somewhat controlled manner. When a riot sometimes got out of hand and became more than just a demonstration of dissent, the immediate issues were not the true reason. Such were the Gordon Riots which occurred in London in 1780, ostensibly over Roman Catholic influence; historians have ascribed other, economic and political, causes for the violence.[21]

It was not uncommon for women to initiate demonstrations, particularly over rising prices, as in Taunton in 1753.[22] Many of these incidents went unnoted, as they were considered part of normal behaviour. Women were also found in the midst of the industrial unrest plaguing England in the early nineteenth century. In the anti-machine Luddite violence of 1811–12, the women Luddites did not restrict their demonstrations to protesting the introduction of machines. 'Lady Ludd', the female equivalent of the mythical male leader, 'General Ludd', appeared in Nottingham to lead a demonstration against bakery price rises.[23]

One advantage enjoyed especially by married women and denied their menfolk was the reluctance of authorities to arrest women. Even when caught in violent acts, women were rarely taken into custody, partly because of the *femme couvert* tradition that made the wife the responsibility of her husband and not individually responsible for her own activities. Like the children in the family, a married woman was legally accountable to its head, her husband, who was to answer for her misdeeds. But the reluctance to arrest women was also due to the practical problems that would ensue if a wife and mother were unable to carry out her normal domestic duties. Thus most women could demonstrate and throw stones with impunity knowing that they would likely be ignored by the authorities.[24]

Few women had the vote at this time, but franchise restrictions were not couched in gender terms. If it happened that a woman could qualify for the vote then she was allowed to exercise this right.[25] A number of the vast majority who did not so qualify were active in the agitations for Parliamentary reform in the pre-1832 era.

The famous gathering at St. Peter's Fields in Manchester in August, 1819, held to promote political reform, was attended by a number of women; in fact, a group of married women headed the procession.[26] Samuel Bamford in his autobiography tells of his wife's determination to go even if her husband disapproved. She went, not with her husband but with a group of women, all 'decent married females'.[27] Later she wrote her account of the proceedings, which was included with that of her husband. We can discern from her observations some of the problems females experienced in such meetings. Public behavior was then not so controlled as perhaps we expect today and, when the women stood together 'surrounded by strange men', they were pushed and pulled.[28] When violence broke out at St. Peter's Fields women were caught up in it. Out of the eleven demonstrators killed at this 'battle of Peterloo' (as it was derisively named by the public because mounted armed soldiers charged an unarmed crowd), two were women. The authorities who had panicked at the assembly of such numbers tried to cover up their own culpability by putting on trial the organizers of the meeting; among the radicals thus charged was one women, Elizabeth Gaunt.[29]

Working-class women in the early nineteenth century also played an important role in political organization by giving home hospitality to visiting radical leaders. As women had welcomed and provided a meeting place for the itinerant religious preachers in previous times, now they did so for political leaders. At a time when there were few if any facilities for public meetings, individual homes became important centers for the spread of political ideology. William E. Adams, for example, growing up a Chartist and radical, was raised by his radical grandmother, who idolized the working-class leader William Cobbett and made her home a center for radical discussions. This was the political nursery for her grandson.[30] Many other working-class and radical leaders must also have had similar experiences. The home was the best place to avoid government spies, especially in troubled times when taverns and other public meeting places were under hostile scrutiny.

Women also created their own reform organizations, particularly in the north of England during the period after Peterloo when there was a great surge of radical activity among all the working classes. A large proportion of these working women were used to making their own decisions as well as their own way. The Manchester Female Reform Society was started during the great excitement over reform in 1819 and quickly recruited more than a thousand members. Similar groups appeared in other northern towns, particularly in Manchester, which had a tradition of political activism.[31] The hostility of authorities was double-barrelled for these women, aimed first at their reform politics and then at their gender – 'petticoat reformers' they were called, and treated as a joke. Their independence was also disapproved by middle-class women who wanted to hire docile female labor.

A play called 'Female Government', performed in 1834, is described in the journal of William Lechmere, a London lawyer and curate, and typifies attitudes of the day toward women in politics. It was a farce about an island governed by women. The men in this play 'were considered as the weaker part of creation'. Then one day part of a ship's company accidentally lands on the island and the men become the lovers of the women rulers. In the end the 'petticoat government' resigns and the women put their power 'into the hands of their lovers'.[32] The piece was judged by Lechmere as 'a laughable and rather ridiculous affair', a common view of women in politics. This play was performed soon after the Reform Act of 1832 had introduced the first specific gender restriction on the franchise.

Ridiculing a group that was demanding power denied them was an old but effective English tactic to keep outsiders ineffectual. It undermined their self-confidence at the same time that it dissuaded potential supporters from coming to their aid. Working-class males were also ridiculed by their 'betters' who thought them 'intellectually' unsuited for leadership – not just because of lack of training but because of natural inferiority: God had placed them in the ranks to which they belonged. This was always the ultimate answer for the early Victorians – the world as ordered by God. Later science was given its due in authoritative statements that women, or other inferior beings were proven to have smaller brains or some such deficiency. Those in power used the current value system to validate their own control and deny it to the dispossessed.

But despite the ridicule, throughout the 1830s working-class women like the men were active in all areas of political agitation and, as at Peterloo, they were leaders as well as followers. Women were to be found on the platforms as well as in the audiences, at the front of the processions as well as in the rear, fighting for their rights and those of their menfolk. Some became Owenite socialists and supported the new world that such political precepts promised. During the 1820s, 1830s and 1840s women were found in the ranks of many movements of protest. They were active for instance in the anti-poor law movement which swept the land after the 'reformed' Parliament tried to solve the old problem of local poverty by imposing national standards for relief which created new hardships on families unable to earn enough to live on.[33]

With the restriction of the vote to middle and upper-class males in the 1832 Reform Act, working-class males and all females were excluded from the franchise. The dissatisfied men and women of the working classes joined together in a revival of political agitation through the Chartist movement. Recently there has been much interest among historians in the role of women in the Chartist movement. Originally women were seen as outside the movement, and hence were ignored altogether.[34] But in a number of works this earlier impression is being corrected. One of the main problems, of course, is the lack of solid information about the contributions of working-class females. There was a growing prejudice, shared by working-class males and middle-class chroniclers of the times, against women in public life. Public speaking and demonstrations by females of any class were viewed as socially undesirable, not to be publicized lest they influence other younger, impressionable girls to follow the same path. Only in extraordinary cases were such activities by women written about. Even women writers often disapproved of the so-called 'immodest behavior' of many of these outspoken women.[35] Therefore, it is difficult to discover the full extent of women's participation in public activities in the 1830s and 1840s even with solid evidence that women were working in the Chartist cause, organized a number of female Chartist groups, and attended Chartist rallies. The five-point charter that these reformers supported in its first draft called for the enfranchisement of women.[36] Without women's support the men Chartists would not have had the same impact on the country, and though these reformers were unsuccessful, they did apply great pressure for changes on the government.

It has been claimed by at least one historian that the women who had been so active in many reforming causes left the field of political agitation in the post-1848 years and that working-class women withdrew permanently from the political field and simply retired to their domestic concerns.[37] Other historians have disagreed with this conclusion, believing that some working-class women continued to be involved until at least the late 1850s[38] when the Chartist movement declined. Its place in radical working-class politics was taken by new burgeoning reforming organizations, such as the Manhood Suffrage Association and the Reform League, which neither had nor wanted female support. Later, in the 1860s and 1870s, few working-class women were active politically – just at a time when their middle-class sisters were beginning their agitations.

Perhaps this is only part of a greater change in English society. Many men and women who were working-class in the early part of the nineteenth century became successful enough to count themselves as middle-class in the middle and later part of the century. Upwardly mobile men and women who achieved a middle-class lifestyle became, in their own eyes and in those of their associates, members of the respectable classes. In seeking to emulate the values and behavior patterns of those above them on the social scale such men would stop going to the taverns, and their women would stay at home in complete domesticity (for anything less would surely cause them to be seen as not having quite made the transition), and both would be active in the local chapel world. If the women continued to work for political reform it was with different concerns and methods. For instance, demonstrations and public speeches to a mixed audience were deemed improper for women of families belonging to the genteel classes: The rules of behavior for this group were more circumscribed than those for working-class women. Now they went from house to house publicizing their causes and collecting signatures on petitions to local and national government. Middle-class women became particularly effective in canvassing residential areas and circulating petitions, because they had time and, more importantly, they had domestic connections that allowed their admittance into many homes.

If we examine the lower middle-class families of the 1860s and 1870s, we will find the majority had their origins in the lower classes. Typically these successful families believed they owed their rise in the world to various personal factors such as self-help activities. Whatever the cause, and many were offered, these families had tended to activism in the first part of the century, and from their ranks early working-class leaders, both men and women, had arisen. They were the 'talented tenth' that rose through the ranks as opposed to the 'sunken tenth' that dropped. Naturally in their new environment they did not stand out as much. They were competing on a higher level with different rules.

4 The Call to Social and Political Action

THE CHURCH OF ENGLAND EVANGELICAL MOVEMENT

The national mood of hostility towards change was strong in England after the French Revolution. There were fears that any deviations from the norms were precursors of further destructive revolutionary action. If changes were needed it was not the institutions that should be altered but the individuals and the society made up of those individuals. Furthermore, all social reforms should be carefully controlled. The best way of doing this, believed contemporary Britons, was to establish associations that conformed to strict patterns of organization, with modes of behavior and leadership directed by so-called responsible members of society – such as bishops and government officials – who could be trusted not to stray too far from established norms.

The Church of England, the most conservative institution of the establishment, committed to the maintenance of social order and the *status quo*, was the perfect body to direct such reforms. They were in keeping with its mission of 'putting conscience into public life', emphasized by evangelicals of the late eighteenth and early nineteenth century.[1] But there was the problem of a hierarchy uninterested in change or reform if it could be avoided. There were many 'Neros' in the Church who preferred 'to fiddle while Rome burned' rather than call the fire brigade. There was also a lack of funds with which to expand the work of the Church. Parliament was unwilling or unable to increase its financing of the established church, especially at a time when the Napoleonic Wars and their aftermath were causing economic depression and other serious national problems.

Just as John Wesley and his fellow evangelists in the mid eighteenth century set up a private Methodist Society to improve the religious teachings of the established church, so now did the Evangelical Party within the Church of England make use of private individuals and organizations to improve the secular work of the Church. The late eighteenth and early nineteenth century saw the appearance of a number of voluntary associations to deal with specific problems. This type of organization was not new. Many had been set up for various purposes in previous times but for the most part did not survive long. The Proclamation Society started by William Wilberforce in 1787 is seen by historians as the start of the evangelical movement in the Church of England.[2] Through this society an attempt was made to reform the manners and customs of English society by means of an active Christianity that was to reach out to all Englishmen, encouraging adherence to a better Christian life.

Other societies soon followed, organized to take care of various ills within British society. Because there was little Church money for such work and also little support from the upper echelons of the Anglican hierarchy, the organizers of these efforts turned to lay men and women for support. Some of them even joined forces with members of nonconformist religions whom they believed had a mutual interest in the work. As can be expected, such cooperation was not always applauded by the most rigid churchmen who feared that the dissenters would increase their influence at the expense of the established church. The Religious Tract Society founded in 1799 was such an interdenominational organization.

The antecedents of many of these new societies can be found in the individual efforts that had sprung up locally to take care of a specific problem. The first Sunday School is believed to have been set up in 1781 in Gloucester, although there is disagreement as to the founder of the first school – Robert Raikes or the Rev. Thomas Stock, a clergyman in Raike's town.[3] Other Sunday Schools quickly followed in many towns, but not until 1803 was the national Sunday School Union formed. The Ragged School Union, formed in 1844, had a similar development with individual schools for very poor children organized and paid for by local philanthropists; later a national network was created to bring them together.[4] However, only after the national Union was formed and the work was given wider publicity do we find many adult men and women being enrolled. Regardless of the cause, the pattern of organization was the same: Men were appointed to the organizing bodies and served as executives, while women provided most of the labour. In the Sunday Schools women taught the classes but did not run the schools.

Another such society founded a year later was also one of the most successful: the British and Foreign Bible Society. Originally established to distribute Bibles to poor families, it extended its work to the publication of tracts. Later members visited homes to read and talk about the Bible and religious topics to families who were mostly unaffiliated with a church or chapel. The Society needed to attract money and support from the wealthier citizens of all religions, and hence required tracts and other writings to publicize its needs. Women who were hired to do the writing produced all kinds of publicity for the Society, including tracts, stories and other material. Hannah More, one of the best known evangelical women, wrote for the Bible Society.[5] It also found women to be the best agents for distributing Bibles to lower-class families.

Large numbers of women were enrolled by the Bible Society, most of them as members of what were called ladies' 'associations'. So successful was the Society in its recruitment that by 1824 there were 500 such ladies' Bible associations. In these separate and unequal women's auxiliaries, the females had some control but were never allowed to make ultimate decisions, which were always reserved for the men. The evangelicals in the Anglican church were great proponents of distinct roles for men and women. Motivated by the teachings of the established church, they saw such a division as ordained by God: Women, because of their sex and physical differences, were not meant to compete with men but had their own domain. The exclusion of women from governing bodies was to be found in many of the reforming movements throughout the nineteenth century.

In one area of endeavour, women were allowed to show their talents in public. Whether in producing religious tracts, temperance tales or children's stories, women writers, particularly from evangelical families, were very active.[6] The publicity women received for this kind of work was acceptable to nineteenth-century society, perhaps because it was done at home and thus did not take the writer away from her protected domestic scene. To keep to the domestic sphere yet be useful was the aim. It was also true that any publicity that she might get could be downplayed – her scribblings discounted by being trivialized.[7] Furthermore, if the women kept to certain topics – to hymn writing, domestic stories, and so on – then they would not be seen as serious writers, because the values assigned to the women's activities were ones imposed by a male hierarchy; anything it did not acknowledge as important was regarded as marginal. Novel writing, for instance, was serious, while hymn writing was not.

A very few women writers succeeded as 'serious' writers. Among the best known of this group were George Eliot who emerged from an evangelical background, and the Bronte sisters, daughters of an evangelical Anglican minister who helped organize local improving groups.[8]

Although in the third and fourth decades of the nineteenth century women appeared to be disappearing from leadership positions in religious evangelizing, after a brief period of high visibility during the early Methodist period, the ground was being prepared for a new upsurge of female activity that was to carry the public work of women into new areas. Despite its conservatism the Church of England had an unintended impact on the changing role of women in nineteenth-century England through the many volunteer and paid lay positions it created. Later when it utilized zealous women as a pool of inexpensive workers, no one foresaw that those women would not be content to keep a subordinate role. When in the middle of the nineteenth century the church faced a growing call for new roles for women within the established church, many of the activists would be drawn from the ranks of these church workers. And what began as marginal auxiliaries for women were to become an important component for all reforming organizations, even if public recognition was withheld.

THE ANTI-SLAVE MOVEMENT

The official national anti-slave societies in England like all the other evangelical organizations were controlled by males. But in them women had a far greater influence than in any other reform movement of this time, largely because this cause was predominantly the concern of the Friends before the evangelicals adopted it, and many Quaker women had traditionally been actively involved. Quaker girls were taken to public anti-slave meetings by their fathers; and Quaker children playing at being adults included 'going to anti-slave meetings' among the adult activities viewed as a natural part of both a father's and a mother's world.[9]

The male leadership of the anti-slave movement retained a firm hold on the mixed-gender organizations. However, important for the movement was the Society of Friends' continuing tradition of Women's Meetings, meaningful organizations controlled by women whose members were expected to make contributions to community improvement. They were not *auxiliaries* to the main (men's) effort, but genuine contributing *associates* of other groups. There were female anti-slave societies with a large number of Quaker women taking an active and innovative role in forwarding the work. As early as 1788 women were giving significant support to the anti-slavery reform in England,[10] They went door-to-door to get signatures on petitions to Parliament against slavery; and they printed and distributed publicity aimed at arousing public sympathy for the movement.

The zeal of Quaker women eventually brought many of them into conflict with their male associates: They did not believe that the men were taking strong enough action to end slavery. The policy of 'gradual emancipation' of slaves, which Parliament and the male-dominated movement adopted, was unacceptable to many Quaker women who felt very strongly about the evils of slavery. Elizabeth Heyrick, a Quaker from Leicestershire, wrote a tract *Immediate Not Gradual Abolition* which became so popular that it went through three editions in 1824. In it she called for an immediate end to all slavery in British possessions. Until abolition was achieved she proposed there should be a boycott in England of all slave-grown commodities: Sugar from the West Indies was especially targeted, but other goods were also to be proscribed. She organized a house-to-house canvass to ask householders to boycott slave-grown goods. Other Quaker women rallied to the cause and soon female societies were set up to support the boycott, which became known as the 'free produce' movement.[11]

Although there were local women's anti-slave groups in existence when Heyrick's publication appeared, there was no national or metropolitan women's society. Her work soon stimulated organized women to exert pressure on the 'gradualist' male-dominated societies. 'The Female Society for Birmingham, West Bromwich, Wednesbury, Walsall and their respective Neighborhoods for the Relief of British Negro Slaves' was founded in 1825 by Quaker women of Birmingham, prominent among whom were Sophie Sturge and Mary Lloyd, along with Lucy Townsend, the wife of an Anglican clergyman.[12] It became a national network of individuals and local groups and was very active throughout the second half of the 1820s. An examination of the subscription and donation list for its first year (1826) reveals that the organization was not dominated by a small number of 'prominent' names, nor was there a list of titled members enrolled as vice presidents, as was common in many of the male organizations. Reflecting its Quaker origins, the membership was made up of a large number of women members who paid a standard twelve shillings annual subscription. Some also gave an added donation to the Society, but they were all modest amounts, the highest being ten pounds, the most common contribution one pound. Membership was drawn from all parts of England, north and south as well as Wales and Ireland. The majority lived in the towns that were listed in the organization's title, with Birmingham the home of the largest number. As might be expected, many Quaker names of families prominent in other philanthropic causes are found in these lists.[13]

To give themselves their own special interest in the anti-slave movement and also to establish their position as upholders of the domestic and other female interests, the women of the Birmingham anti-slave society took up the particular cause of female slaves and slave children. The sisterhood of all women was emphasized and promoted in its first report in 1826, which stated that its goal was to 'awaken in the bosom of English women a deep and lasting compassion not only for the bodily sufferings of female slaves, but for their moral degradation . . . repugnant to the principles of Christianity'. At this first meeting a resolution was passed stressing the plight of female slaves and their children and asking 'that the lash shall no longer be permitted to fall on the persons of helpless Female Slaves: . . . and that every Negro mother living under the British domain shall press a freeborn infant to her bosom'.[14]

Besides the publicity they spread about the evils of slavery, these women's organizations promoted the 'free produce' movement which supported the boycott of slave-grown products. Such direct action was controversial, especially if successful and the slave owner lost his market. Travelling agents, both men and women, were hired and paid by the women's organizations to organize 'kindred associations' of women and to publicize the boycott by showing that 'those who consume the produce of Slavery are its chief abettors and supporters'.[15] The claim was made in the Birmingham Female Society's *Annual Report* that a boycott would help slaves; it was said that where sugar was declining the slaves were becoming self-supporting: They were given 'plots of ground' where they could raise their own food.

Money was collected not only for the organization itself but also to support charities aimed at relieving some of the distress caused by slavery and related ills. In 1825 fifty-nine pounds was raised by the sale of 'work bags' filled with anti-slavery literature. Of the funds dispersed, twenty pounds was sent to the Female Refuge in Antigua, which was working 'for the relief and protection of young females, daughters of Negro slaves, whose mothers are not in a situation to preserve them from the contagion of ill example'. Money was also given to the London Anti-Slavery Society, the Female Refuge Society, and the Moravian Sunday Schools.[16] The Birmingham Quaker women were also active in a female movement to have their Birmingham coreligionists stop sending money to the National Society because it supported the gradual emancipation of slaves.[17]

During the late 1820s and early 1830s there was a great increase in the number of female anti-slavery groups. By 1831 there were thirty-nine listed in the Anti-Slavery Society's subscription records,[18] and their membership continued to grow. An active anti-slavery society in Sheffield in the late 1820's enrolled many of the town's ladies in the work.[19] In 1833 an Edinburgh Ladies Emancipation Society was organized; it lasted until 1865. In 1846, long after slavery was forbidden in British territories, English women organized a Bristol and Clifton Ladies Anti-Slavery Society which continued until 1861; it was aimed against American slavery as well as an obligatory 'apprenticeship system' that was imposed on freed slaves in some former slave-holding countries.[20]

Public lectures were an important part of the work of the anti-slave societies, meant to inform their own members as well as the general public about the evil they opposed. In addition the members of the women's anti-slave societies personally went on house-to-house visitations to increase support for the boycott of slave-produced goods.[21] Going directly to the public with their cause, talking to the men and the women in the households and leaving literature to reinforce their arguments, they persuaded many to their cause; in fact they roused up such concern over slavery among the ordinary citizens that the government was forced to take heed of public opinion. The women's activities brought them so much prominence that some of the traditional evangelicals in the movement were unhappy. William Wilberforce, for instance, wanted to reduce the women's influence, by limiting the reporting of their direct action in the *Anti-Slave Reporter*.[22]

As public interest over the slave issue mounted and Parliament became the scene of pressures and counterpressures from the lobbyists of both the pro-slave and the anti-slave groups, the women felt there was great urgency in their mission and decided to take more direct action. No longer content with the circulation of 'free market' pledges, the women turned to political action and the organization of public petitions against slavery. Particularly during the great anti-slave agitation of 1833, when Parliament abolished slavery in British possessions, was the women's work effective, so much so that other reforming movements later adopted and refined their methods.

In 1840 the first international conference of the anti-slave movement was held in London. The 'Committee of Arrangements' for this conference decided that no female delegates would be seated: Women would have to attend only as observers, sitting in the gallery, far apart from the working conference. For many of the English female delegates this was no shock because it had become a common English practise to exclude women from such public meetings; however, some English male delegates, particularly among the Quaker and Unitarian members, had hoped for a change.[23] There were also such well-known persons as Sir John Bowring, Daniel O'Connell and Mr. Ashurst among those protesting the decision to exclude women.[24] For the American delegates the ruling was unexpected, and the first day of the conference was taken up with acrimonious debates over this issue, during which Bibles were waved in the faces of women. Joseph Sturge, a Quaker on the organizing committee, treated the matter as a 'procedural one', and ruled that the normal English practise would be followed.[25]

The women were banished to the visitors' gallery, where they were 'railed off'; it became nicknamed 'the Negro Pew'.[26] But not all the American males were willing to accept the decision: One Negro delegate, Charles Redmond, and a prominent white abolitionist, William Lloyd Garrison, joined the ladies in their exile.[27] Garrison became a hero to English women, who long after remembered his stand.[28] The immediate reaction of the male leadership at the convention was to ignore any criticism and make no changes in the role of women.[29]

This incident at the London Convention was widely publicized in the United States as well as England. It was seen by the English traditionalists as a well-merited put down of the pushy Americans. Almost two years later *The Nonconformist* recalled how 'William Morgan in 1840 read the American female anti-slave delegates a lesson about the power that a "Committee of Arrangements" could wield at conferences'.[30] Among those American women who were 'read a lesson' were Lucretia Mott and Elizabeth Cady Stanton, who were so angry at their exclusion that they decided the time had come for equal treatment of women in public life. The incident has been credited as the beginning of the women's rights movement in the United States.[31]

It was also an incident many English women angrily remembered. Louisa Stewart, a Quaker who was to become a leader in the women's temperance movement, reminisced almost fifty years later that 'she felt keenly the barrier raised by social position against any practical participation by women in the stirring movement of the time.'[32]

Looking back in 1931 *The Birmingham Post* stated:

> that the absurdity of holding a Convention in which the chief workers against slavery were present as spectators, not as participators, caused much discussion; and the general movement in England towards the social, educational and political equality of women may in some sense be said to date from that period.[33]

THE ANTI-CORN LAW LEAGUE

The effectiveness of women in rousing public opinion to put pressure on the local and national governments now could not be denied. Utilizing the lessons learned in the anti-slave agitations and propaganda, the fight against the corn laws drew middle-and upper-class women into direct political work. It started in London in 1836, but the main thrust of the movement came three years later in Manchester with the founding of the Anti-Corn Law League. The basic issue was economic, pitting landowners who grew the corn (wheat) and wanted high prices against the new industrial and urban classes who wanted cheap corn – imported if necessary. The League fought for laws that would allow low duties for imported grain if the price of domestic corn rose. It was essentially a movement for cheap bread for industrial workers and became a battle between the new industrial cities and traditional rural England.

It was also a free trade issue, that appealed mostly to the middle class of industrial England. The League, based in Manchester – the center of free trade in England – wanted the newly enfranchised 'ten pound householders' brought into the arena. They also asked property-owning women to create 40 shilling freeholds so that the male lessees could vote for the League's goals.[34] It was a crucial issue for the political leaders of both major political parties who fought a long hard battle over it. The Anti-Corn Law League and its allies tried to make it a popular reform similar to the anti-slave movement, and it was towards this end that the League utilized women in the now traditional manner – house-to-house visitations, distributing literature, and gathering signatures on parliamentary petitions. But because it was a political reform agitation, a free trade issue without the Christian motivations of the anti-slave movement, no evangelical support was given.

With Parliament the primary focus of the League's attention, its workers were much involved in elections, aiming to get Members of Parliament returned who were favorable to their cause. However, the greatest role that the women played in the Anti-Corn Law League was in keeping the movement solvent. After the first flush of enthusiasm, the League found itself fighting against apathy and financial problems. The correspondence between George Wilson, chairman, and Richard Cobden, the nationally known League spokesman, reflects the leadership concern about the League's perilous financial position. The problem of money dominated their discussions in the fall of 1841 when the League was in a particularly bad way. Wrote Wilson to Cobden: 'the Money Question with us, like as it is with Sir Robert, is of the first importance – we must now call the council out and raise funds to pay our debts and carry us over'.[35]

One way of raising large sums was by holding a bazaar, a method which had become very popular for charitable causes; typically these recruited 'ladies or respectable women to attend to the stalls . . . , who are to be recompensed for their attendance by a ball'.[36] So the Anti-Corn Law League decided to hold a bazaar. The first move was to send a printed invitation to the wives of men interested in the movement to see if they would serve on a Ladies Committee charged with organizing the bazaar. The invitation was sent on September 20, 1841, and the response was poor. The contrast with the women's attitudes towards the cause of anti-slave reform was great. Although some Quaker women were involved in the Anti-Corn Law League,[37] the League did not have the emotional appeal of anti-slave reform. There was no women's organization to fight for the repeal. Instead the women were 'helpmates', albeit essential helpmates, in the work. None could vote or hold political office at this time, so they were on the periphery of this political cause.

The excuses the wives gave for refusal to serve on the bazaar committee typify the public postures of many middle- and upper-class women at this time and as such are worth noting. All were invited because they or their families had connections that might make them responsive to the League's message. Many were connected to families of public prominence. Most of the women invited were personally unknown to George Wilson, the organizer of the bazaar. One woman cautiously requested publicity for 'people of rank who have attended League functions'.[38] Some no doubt just did not want to be involved with such a venture, such as Mrs. Bazley who 'uniformly declines to be officially connected with *all* Bazaars' and refuses to 'change her rule'. Lady Fanny Kinnaird wrote that her husband would be a patron but she believed 'politics were not for ladies and that the corn laws have now become purely a party question'. Mrs. MacFarlane wrote that her husband 'would have decided objections to her taking such a conspicuous part . . . '. Mrs. Louisa Shaw refused because her husband's position as a police commissioner made it inappropriate for her to be involved in such activities. Mrs. Beardsall rejected the invitation on the grounds that her name 'has no influence in Manchester'. But the most commonly stated reason for rejection was 'delicate health' which prevented participation in such exertions as helping at a bazaar.[39]

George Wilson also asked 'titled and prominent ladies' to be 'Patronesses' of the Bazaar, but he did not get the response he had hoped for. Most of those approached refused. As one lady wrote, 'it would not be agreeable to me to appear in so conspicuous a situation'. Wilson then wrote to the ardent freetrader and popular public lecturer John Bowring asking him to enlist titled ladies to become Patronesses. Mr. Bowring said he would try but did not believe he would have much luck. Mr. Milner Gibson, the Liberal Member of Parliament for Manchester, was asked to 'procure names of some Ladies as Patronesses', but he also thought it would be difficult, owing to the objectives of the League:

> 'If the object was to build a new church or to propagate the Gospel in Foreign parts I should have no fear of getting the ladies in shoals to assist us but what the 'distinguished' matrons will say when we talk of an anti-corn law Bazaar I cannot say til I try.'[40]

Eventually a Bazaar Committee of 350 women from all parts of the country was formed.[41]

The bazaar fulfilled its sponsors' greatest expectations. Opening on January 31, 1842 at the Theatre Royal in Manchester, it lasted six days and was an immediate success. By the end of the last day, a total of nearly nine thousand pounds was raised, a large sum for a provincial town. The women ran most of the stalls, but men were in charge of selling books. A daily paper, *The Bazaar Gazette*, was published each morning listing receipts of the previous days and giving advice on how to promote the anti-corn law cause.

Later it was decided to hold another bazaar, this time in the capital where the organizers expected an even bigger success. And they were right. This second bazaar, held in 1845 at the Covent Garden Theatre, London, lasted seventeen days. It was an elaborate affair with a daily paper and a postoffice of its own. For this bazaar the women inaugurated a new method of collecting contributions. They divided the city into districts and allotted women their own areas for canvassing. Thus, the whole city was blanketed with collectors.[42] With twenty-seven stalls and an attendance of between eight and nine thousand people a day, this bazaar raised twenty-five thousand pounds for the League, an excellent return for its outlay of 5,713 pounds.[43]

More important for the future than the cause they served or the funds they raised was the way the bazaars brought together a number of women from all parts of the Metropolitan area, women who were to become leaders in social-reform action groups. In modern parlance, they were an important connection in the networking of women activists. Margaret Lucas, Quaker and sister of John Bright, was active in the Ladies Committee for the Bazaar, and held temperance meetings for the women workers while preparing for the bazaar in the Green Room of the Covent Garden Theatre. Her activities bore fruit: At least one of the women attending these meetings became an important temperance worker. Mrs. Louisa Stewart, a Quaker, recalled that she was first introduced to the temperance movement at the London Bazaar. She eventually became a founding member of the Women's Friends Total Abstinence Association in Stoke Newington as well as a national leader in the later British Women's Temperance Association and an active worker in many other women's political causes.[44] Mrs. Lucas herself was a founder of the British Women's Temperance Association and became its president soon after its inauguration in the 1870s.

THE EARLY TEMPERANCE MOVEMENT

The first temperance society formed in the British Isles was a Scottish one and it was a women's association. Organized October 1, 1829 by a Miss Allen and a Miss Graham at Maryhill, near Glasgow, it predates by a few days the first general temperance society in the United Kingdom, also formed in Scotland.[45] But as in the other reform movements, most of the early temperance societies were male-dominated, with boards of vice-presidents made up of prominent men, preferably titled or church-associated. The first national English temperance organization, The British and Foreign Temperance Society, was organized in 1831 with the Bishop of London as its patron and five other bishops as vice presidents.[46] It was a 'moderation' society, proscribing only spirits and supporting moderate drinking of wines. Beer was not limited at all. Other male-dominated regional moderationist organizations were formed in London and Scotland. Apart from a number of Quaker ladies who were usually in the forefront of reforming causes, few middle- and upper-class English women were working in the early temperance movement.[47]

In the mid-1830s a new goal emerged, primarily among working-class temperance reformers. They wanted the complete prohibition of all alcoholic drinks, spirits, wines and beer. Drink they saw as the enemy of the working classes, hurting the economic position of working men in two ways: by rendering the workingman physically and mentally less fit for productive work and thereby preventing him from bettering himself; and by encouraging the dissipation of a workingman's limited resources, thus preventing him and his family from enjoying a comfortable home and other benefits. Ambitious working men organized temperance societies that were as much self-help organizations as anti-drink. These new reformers became known as teetotalers and were completely dedicated to the anti-drink cause. The commitment needed to be total in a society where the traditions not only encouraged the serving and drinking of all such beverages but condemned those that did not.[48]

In the 1830s, 1840s and 1850s, there were independent women's temperance societies organized, mostly in the north, but they were small and usually local in nature. In the North women were an important part of the factory labor force, and many different women's groups were already active. In 1820 a Friendly Society of Women was established at Mellor-Moor-End in the County of Derby, but there is little information as to its success.[49] London was also a place with a large number of working women and so it is not surprising to find female societies there. In Birmingham, a Female Temperance Society was established in 1836 and another at Ipswich.[50] In 1837 in the East of London and in Chelsea women's temperance societies were formed. In all these groups the work of the organization was with women or the home: Women stayed within their sphere.[51]

As in other evangelical organizations, women in temperance reform were prolific writers, especially of works aimed at a female or a juvenile readership. Children were encouraged to read in their Sunday Schools, and there was a great demand for morally uplifting material for children: stories with the right values written at a level that poorly educated children and women could understand. There were always heroes and heroines with whom the reader could identify. A few women like Mrs. Clara Lucas Balfour, who wrote stories and verse for children, earned enough to support themselves through their writings. Mrs. Balfour had married a temperance man, a reformed drunkard who had led her to sign the temperance pledge in 1837. This stimulated her not only to write temperance tales but also to mount the public platform and speak out against the evils of drink. Such activity caused much criticism as she was acting 'beyond the sphere allotted to women . . . outraging the feelings – stepping over the bounds of her sex',[52] but Mrs. Balfour's writing activities made her an early pathfinder for many women coming after. By the 1850s and 1860s increasing numbers of women became known through their writings.

If women wanted to be part of any 'general' reforming organization at this time they had to work, as in the Bible Society, through special 'ladies associations', and even then they were restricted to the usual work for women – home visitation and collecting funds – and had little say in the disbursement of those funds or in the direction of the main body. It was a common practice for the wives of the male members to form a Ladies Committee which then did the day-to-day work often essential to the whole organization.

Not until the 1860s did temperance reformers become aware of the great potential talents under the modest bonnets and ungainly dresses hidden away in the galleries and auxiliaries. The success of their work might depend on the support given by women at all levels of society; but it took the coming of American temperance activists to reveal this truth to their English colleagues.

Part Two

1850–1875: The Sound of the Horn

Part Two
1850–1875: The Sound of the Horn

GENDER SEPARATION

By the 1850s the women in English society were not sharing in the expanded opportunities that their menfolk were experiencing. In fact, they were losing ground in many areas of English life. Their official role in religious life had declined: The Wesleyan Methodists and various other Methodist connexions had moved away from a lay ministry towards a professional one, where women were not admitted unless, as in the Leeds Female Revivalist Chapel, they started their own connexion.[1] Even the Quaker church, with its long tradition of women preachers, was not immune to the growing hostility towards women in the pulpits. In the 1830s the opposition had been so strong that, although there was no official change, fewer and fewer women 'felt the call'.[2] Among Quaker women such a call was always regarded as 'an awful one', not to be disregarded if experienced; now it was not to be sought at all.[3]

The position of women in politics had also declined. By the Reform Act of 1832, women had been eliminated completely from the franchise, with those who had previously held it because of local anomalies now losing it to the standardized ten-pound, male-householder rule. Working-class women united with their male bretheren to seek universal suffrage, but when the men in the 1840s restricted their goal to male suffrage only, working-class women left politics, not to return in any numbers for the rest of the century.[4]

A strong social and economic gender segregation was developing. In earlier times there had always been some exclusions of females but now the separation became so exaggerated that middle-class Victorian society was split into two spheres: the public one for the males, which encompassed work, politics, clubs, sports, and many other activities, and the private or domestic one for the women, which revolved around the family and home. The division most affected middle-class families; but it was this segment of society that came to dominate English public life of the nineteenth century.

Above, the Queen exemplified and extolled its values; below the lower classes imitated it. The life style that has come to be called Victorian was that of the urban, middle classes.

Though many English men and women subscribed to the notion of separate spheres for men and women, not all could practise it. There were more women than men in the population and so not all could have husbands to support them and a domestic sphere to manage. Many had to be self-supporting. Consequently large numbers of women in the lower middle class and the working classes were in the workforce, in a society that told them it was wrong yet gave them no alternatives.

Though trade unions and other working-class organizations were developing to protect working-class employment, they generally excluded women. Jobs in factory, mines and commerce were gender-differentiated, even in places where machines did the work. New jobs were allotted to men while women had to take what the men did not want. Consequently women were employed where the pay was low or the conditions very bad or both.

Middle-class women faced many similar problems when they sought employment. They had to face not only gender discrimination in the work place but also the disabilities caused by their inadequate training. Middle-class education for females did not prepare the girls to enter professions or the workplace at the same level as their brothers. Education, even as it expanded and developed, became increasingly more gender separated, as the new day schools of the middle classes adopted the upper-class single sex model rather than that of the old church school of the lower orders where boys and girls at least attended the same school (though perhaps in different classes). Girls continued to receive a lesser intellectual education than the boys, and improved female education became an important issue for many women.

The gender segregation was clearly manifested in clothing styles. As in previous eras the various levels of society wore distinctly different clothing: Velvets, furs and satins were reserved to the upper classes while fustian, moleskin and coarser fabrics were the lot of the lower orders. But in the nineteenth century the clothing of the two sexes greatly differed in practicality. Whereas men's raiments became increasingly more simple and functional, the opposite occurred with female dress.[5] Women's garments, especially among the middle and upper classes, changed towards the more elaborate and impractical – crinolines and bustles – and the tightly laced whalebone corsets that were the rule for all middle- and upper-class females impeded any physical activity. They also made the wearer subject to fainting fits and other physical ills, which helped support the belief that women were 'delicate'. Needless to say, working women in the mines and in the fields were not dressed in crinolines, nor were they laced into corsets.

THE ANGLO-AMERICAN CONNECTION

While the new Victorian life style was being established, revolutionary technological developments led to closer contact between Britain and the United States. This relationship was to have an unanticipated impact on English society in general and on the lives of the middle-class women in particular.

Up to the first decades of the nineteenth century, there was little communication between ordinary Englishmen and Americans, and American ideas had little effect on English thinking.[6] In fact the opposite was true, with the English influencing the Americans far more. John Wesley was typical of Englishmen who went to the United States to evangelize. At this time the former colony was perceived by many Englishmen as small, inconsequential, and backward – a frontier land. But this quickly changed, for two major reasons: the development by the English of new technologies affecting travel and the emergence of a new egalitarian society in the United States.

Important to Anglo-American relations was the introduction of steam-powered ships to replace the slower, less reliable sailing vessels that crossed the Atlantic. This change led to a sharp increase in the number, speed, and safety of ships travelling across the Atlantic. The development of railways and the advent of the telegraph also increased the amount of contact between the two nations; and because these changes led to a great decline in the cost of travel between the two countries ordinary working Englishmen could and did go on extended visits across the Atlantic, financing such trips, if necessary, by earnings from work in the new world. A large number of these 'immigrants' did not intend to remain abroad; they went partly in a spirit of adventure, but also to make enough money to allow them to return and establish themselves comfortably in their native land. While in the United States these European 'immigrants' were influenced by the new ideas and ways of the young American republic, which they brought back home.

For many Victorian Englishmen the United States was the home of a new egalitarian society based on a mass democracy. During the 1830s and 1840s the former colonies experienced such a growth in radical democratic spirit that the universal franchise was granted to all adult white men, regardless of social or financial status. Open access to official political positions for all male citizens was also mandated. Men and women of all classes in England crossed the Atlantic to study this new open society, often returning with great enthusiasm for American ideas.[7]

At the same time that these new democratic ideas were taking hold in the United States, there was also an upsurge of religious revivalism in the new world. As John Wesley and his colleagues had taken their religious message across the Atlantic in the mid eighteenth century, so now in the nineteenth their American disciples reversed the process as the apostles of a new evangelicalism in Britain. There was a continual stream of American preachers crossing the Atlantic throughout the Victorian period; along with their British disciples they were to be found throughout Britain working in various types of missions in the mid- and late-Victorian period.[8]

For many of these preachers the old Wesleyan goals of personal salvation still held. But the methods of achieving them had now changed. In the United States the new evangelicalism transformed the old Methodist ways into a new type of revival meeting. Organized in public halls, away from the traditional religious churches and chapels, these new services focused on emotions aroused by charismatic preaching and reinforced by a strong but subtle use of music. Following carefully worked out plans of operation – it was a highly organized method of proselytizing – this new revivalism when brought to Britain swept the country, changing the religious practises of many middle- and lower-class English men and women.[9]

For English men and women on almost all levels of society (except the very top and the very bottom), Victorian norms of 'respectability' were the keys to acceptance by their peers. The ideal of the virtuous woman as one who is pious, pure, submissive and domestic,[10] worked its tyranny on many women, who never left their domestic world. But some maverick females who insisted on venturing forth into forbidden territory utilized the emphasis on piety to follow one of the few avenues of escape from the domestic realm that Victorian society allowed them – religion.

To English women who wanted a larger role in public life the important function women had in the new religious awakening was inspiring. Women, alone and with husbands, were organizers, preachers and soloists at public mission services. There was some criticism of their role, particularly of their preaching before 'promiscuous' (i.e., mixed) audiences, which appeared to modest English women and their menfolk as in poor taste. However, not all English men and women felt that way, and there were many public controversies over this issue.

For respectable Victorian society the authority of God took precedence over the demands of man. Thus claims of a divine call or of Christian duty were an acceptable reason for women of all classes with sufficient time, energy and leisure, to run religious missions, or work for any of the myriad of 'Christian' reforms such as temperance or anti-slavery that were so much a part of Victorian life. These activities gave women a chance to develop their talents and learn leadership skills in the public world, and it is not suprising that those so trained provided the early leadership of women's causes. Even though many of them were not feminists, they became the models and the pathfinders for later women activists. Their work sounded the horns that called their sisters to the great collective efforts of the later years of the century.

5 The Two Spheres

Relationships between the sexes were not radically changed for the new urban working classes. Largely of rural origin, they often avoided urban cultural shock by bringing as much of the old village as possible to their new homes and recreating many of the familiar traditions.[1] They also sought jobs where their 'mates' worked and encouraged friends they left behind to join them in their new life. Both men and women in this class had always supported themselves; although coming to the new industrial world did cause some disruption in their lives, it did not create the separation between men and women found among the middle classes. Out of necessity, working-class women had a strong commitment to community and could not afford, even if they so desired, to ignore their neighbors and workmates. They had to help one another in sickness and other difficulties because without reciprocation there would be no one to help them in their own time of need. Survival necessitated pooling resources, and thus not surprisingly many of the poorer chapels and working-class clubs became centers for community self-help projects.[2] While the lot of the working-class woman was not an enviable one in many ways, she did not suffer the physical and psychological isolation frequently the fate of middle-class women.

At the opposite end of the social scale, at the upper levels of society women had their own specific problems and resources, also little changed. Many of those from aristocratic families were part of large extended families with connexions that protected and looked after all their members. For various reasons men and women at this level frequently did not marry. For the men, it was often because they were younger sons and did not inherit. This meant they had to make their own way, some in positions not favoring establishing families: Life in in the army or navy was not conducive to the married state. Nor was life abroad in parts of the Empire where the death rate for Europeans was high a desirable situation for a wife and family. For upper-class women the lack of a dowry could inhibit marriage. The older daughters would have their portions, but, if family resources were limited, the younger daughters would have to stay at home. Sometimes remaining at home was the fate of a younger daughter because her parents wanted to keep her with them at home as a companion in their old age. In many instances single daughters had to look after parents not because of financial necessity but because of psychological needs: Parents came to depend on such support. But regardless of marital condition, women of upper classes were not usually isolated, normally living as a members of a collective household with many familial supports.

In the middle ranks of society the greatest changes were occurring. Here a whole new life style developed that focused on the protection of the nuclear family and its privacy. Interference by outsiders was abhorred; an Englishman's house was his castle. The most prosperous men bought houses in the suburbs where they would have no close neighbors, a sign of success that caused even more isolation for the females of the family. Some men deliberately moved their families to a rural environment while they stayed in the city to work and socialize in an urban fashion. Henry Hunt, the radical Quaker, was one who followed this life style, leaving his wife and six children alone with their servants in a small town while he lived ten miles away in Bristol. He visited the family 'constantly', supporting them and seeing to their welfare, but he did not live with them.[3]

Having so little contact with the outside world, it is not surprising that the middle-class adult women of this era lacked self-confidence and often developed a negative self-image. Many could not handle complex matters or make decisions easily because they had so little experience. Having been kept from adult responsibilities they were like children in the public world. Society and the law treated them as immature dependents, and the establishment – i.e. government, church and other official authorities – preferred to have men responsible for their wives and daughters.[4] To many women this situation was a natural one; women were created 'out of Adam' as helpmeets – junior partners in the family structure.[5]

Female independence was seen as unnatural and undesirable in a wife. Men did not want to share authority in their families. In consequence women cultivated those talents that were appreciated by their menfolk. They were told the welfare of the family depended on them, that the protection of the home was their duty. They also believed they had the best of all worlds, comparing their lot to that of the poor working-class women, who had to carry out heavy physical labor under appalling conditions in order to survive.

In case middle-class women might feel that those in the upper ranks had a better life, it was asserted that only in the middle ranks was to be found a true moral superiority, the basis for the greatness of the English character. They were also told that they should avoid 'false notions of refinement'.[6] Complaining of the way some women 'have lately learned to look with envious eyes upon their superior in rank, to rival their attainments, to imitate their manners, and to pine for the luxuries they enjoy', one popular writer in 1839 claimed that such attitudes had led to the French Revolution.[7] There were stories about dissolute aristocrats who gambled and drank away their resources with resulting suffering for their families. The notorious behavior of the Queen's uncles was held up as typical dissoluteness in the upper ranks of society, not to be emulated by respectable families.

CLUB SOCIETY

Many a middle-class wife had to contend with the lures of the male club for her husband's attention. While the wife stayed at home and looked after the domestic scene, the husband went forth into public life. Typically nineteenth-century gentlemen were members of one or more of the many all-male clubs appearing on the public scene. These clubs were to play a dominant role in the political, social and, to some extent, economic life of the country.

Clubs were not invented in the nineteenth century. There had been informal dinner clubs in the eighteenth century where men (and infrequently women) regularly ate together. Club members usually worked in the city and needed a public eating place, and so formed a club.[8] Gambling clubs for aristocratic males had also arisen in the eighteenth century, but most of the social life in society's upper ranks had been based on the family and its connections. Home hospitality of family, friends, and associates, often of extended duration, at one of the many abodes supported by the family was the normal form of entertainment. In the rather small world of official England, it was essential to maintain close personal associations with those whose influence could be important to the family's success. The English establishment of the eighteenth and early nineteenth centuries was controlled by a small number of high-ranking families. This was a time before political parties in their modern form had evolved to become means of drawing outsiders into official life.

In nineteenth-century England, social clubs developed into a new and integral part of the national life. Membership in certain clubs helped distinguish one's standing in all aspects of society, social, economic and political, and indicated the degrees of acceptance by those who controlled society. Anyone accused of socially reprehensible behavior, such as cheating or involvement in an unsavory divorce or other such scandal, would be *blackballed* – that is, expelled from his clubs. Such a rejection signified that the former member was no longer acceptable. Victorian society did not spell out the nuances of acceptance – if you had to ask then you did not belong. There were other subtle ways of separating one group of people from another: by accent, by education or by the way one held a knife and fork. The English placed great emphasis on what, to an outsider, must have seemed like trivialities in creating categories of acceptability within various segments of society. Clubs played an essential role in this rank-conscious world.

With the electoral reforms of 1832, there came a need for different forms of political organization. In the move from the smaller, personal control of official England to a larger, more impersonal selection of public leaders, new means had to be devised for making this selection. Private clubs were to play an important role in this political determination. Because background, financial resources, and family connections were so thoroughly investigated, to a depth that could not possibly be duplicated politely in a personal way, the complete situation of any applicant was revealed to the club authorities. Membership in some of the elite clubs allowed an individual to socialize with the upper echelons of society. It also created a pool of individuals from whom future leaders of British society would be chosen.

The growth of explicitly political clubs was also an important development in the changing political life of England. The establishment of the Carlton Club for the Tories and the Reform Club for the Whigs in the early nineteenth century allowed control of a public political party by a private club. These clubs acted as a conduit for political activists coming from the open sphere of lower-level politics to the more closed world of the true power brokers. They enabled the forms of open selection to be followed while in reality a more important selection had already taken place. In an age when there was much talk about democracy and equality, acceptable ways had to be devised to give at least the appearance of some social and political mobility while maintaining traditional exclusivity: Clubs were the English way of doing this. (Even if one tended to ignore it, memories of the French Revolution were always there to remind Englishmen of what happens when no safety valves exist for dispersing the accumulated pressure from men's public ambitions.)

Specialized clubs also played important roles in other areas of society. Military clubs for officers were organized according to the regiments with certain Guard regiments having the most prestigious position. Sporting clubs were organized to control racing and other sports; the Jockey Club was one of the most famous, effectively controlling all horseracing in England.[9] Other clubs appeared and disappeared as society's needs changed.

Up until the last quarter of the nineteenth century, political and social clubs were only for upper- and middle-class males. Around them a social life developed from which their womenfolk were completely excluded. A gentleman could spend his time eating, sleeping and socializing at his club, limited only by the time at his disposal. These clubs had premises and facilities open at all hours. With all the comforts of a home and none of the responsibilities, the clubs allowed husbands to escape the sterile environment of their homes without incurring any criticism. In the last quarter of the nineteenth century, working-class political, fraternal, and social clubs (also usually for males only) came into being as imitations of upper-class establishments, though usually on a much more modest scale.

This club system also effectively kept women out of public life by not allowing them to become members. Upper-class women retained some associations with the outside world through their family connections which enabled them to continue working in traditional ways, but middle-class women had few opportunities to develop working relationships so essential for success in the public world. The importance of these clubs – or the lack of them – was not understood until the women finally organized their own societies both political and social. But this did not happen until the late 1860s and 1870s.

RESPECTABILITY

The ascension of Victoria to the English throne led to a new emphasis on rigid manners and narrow morality. The Queen, with her rather extreme reaction to her 'dissolute' uncles' life styles, supported the new society that measured all behavior according to an inflexible standard of public respectability. A growing number of upwardly-mobile families, whose economic positions enabled them to think of themselves as of the 'middling sort', sought to impress on their neighbors and any of their outside contacts that they were well established. The typical middle-class household became dominated by the need for a good public image. To assure their acceptance in this fluid society of the early industrial period, they took their values and norms from whomever they wanted to be identified with, imitating especially those on the level of society above them.

In this Victorian world women became indicators of the family status. The nonemployed wives and daughters were evidence of the economic and social success of the family, and their household's conspicuous consumption showed their menfolk's financial achievement. The area of residency, the size of the house, the number of servants employed were all part of the measure of a family's position. There was a self-consciousness in the way the family behaved, an awareness that their place on the social scale was perhaps held only precariously and tenuously. Often the man's business would depend on maintaining a proper public image – no one would deal with a man tainted with deviation.

In former times, when only a minority of families employed domestic help, male servants were the rule. But they were rarely found in the new middle-class establishments. Female servants were cheaper and more numerous. In this very female world, a new behavior pattern evolved emphasizing a careful separation between the 'family' and the 'domestics'. The frail family women did no work for remuneration, only for charity, social, or religious causes, while the domestics had to disregard their 'weaker sex' identification and work extremely hard, mostly at tasks demanding heavy labor.[10]

Well-to-do merchants and farmers sought to have their daughters trained in the accomplishments prized among the hostesses of the aristocracy. Girls were sent away to schools to be 'finished', or worked with a governess at home. Governesses were cheap and plentiful, theirs being the only occupation a woman of education could pursue. Most girls at this time were poorly educated. They spent their time learning to paint watercolors, play simple airs on the piano, sing popular ballads and provide similar entertainments for their families and guests. They learned to dress in silks and satins and elaborate fashions with intricate hairstyles. Plain, practical clothing was no longer the norm. The dark wool worsteds so common among the middle groups of the previous century were cast aside for more elaborate wear. If families could not afford the real thing, in clothing or furnishings, they bought imitations. At the top were the trend setters and below them at various levels were the imitators, some with the ability to recreate the mode above, but the majority more often having to compromise and make do with cheaper versions or their betters' discards.

One important change for many women in these new aspiring classes was the adoption of *chaperonage*. Taking on the patterns, though not the circumstances, of aristocratic women, the public activities of women were severely restricted. Unfortunately for the middle-class women, they were not compensated with large, extensive private lives which encompassed many homes and family members among whom they could move in comparative freedom. Instead, the private life of a middle-class woman was limited to one small house and a family of few members. No woman with claims of respectability was out alone in public. In the evening she had to be escorted by a male: her husband, her father, or another family member or acceptable substitute. Even during the day or attending a female gathering, women normally had female companions.

The usual excuse for this protection was that women abroad alone were unsafe: Only women of bad reputation – that is, prostitutes – wandered the streets. For men there were no such restrictions. If the wellbeing of men on public thoroughfares or in buildings was threatened by illegal actions, the law was activated to remove any menace. While men had the right to go out when they wanted, the attitude of the law was quite different for unescorted women, who were said to be asking for trouble. Even women who had a legitimate reason for being abroad at night were not protected by the law: Women alone could be arrested and charged with soliciting.[11] The woman's sphere was the private world, and so the rules that controlled her behavior were a private matter, while men in their public world were protected by law.

THE 'INFERIOR' SEX

Middle-class women did not rebel against these restrictions. On the contrary, they often welcomed them as evidence of their rising social position. They also often interpreted these limitations as an indication of the family's concern for their well-being. Without such protection they might be attacked, raped, or in other ways molested by aggressive men who were always at large in a hostile society.[12] The home was the place of safety for females, while outside was a dangerous world.[13] Such fears led to the development of the stereotype of the 'frail' lady. The concept of the weaker sex encouraged ill-health fantasies, with the self-fulfilling consequence that many actually became weak from female disorders. Older women, particularly, often declined into an invalid state.[14]

Women, it was claimed, suffered many mental handicaps. They could not understand masculine subjects such as mathematics, philosophy, and so on. Their brains were smaller, which meant that they could not grasp these serious intellectual matters, and any women who could was a freak. This gave a strong incentive for girls and women to act as if they were intellectually inferior to men, lest they be taken for a 'blue-stocking'. Nourishing this view of female intellectual inadequacy was the inferior method of educating girls. Up to the middle of the nineteenth century middle- and upper-class girls were taught at home by a governess.

While it was deemed good to read and perhaps write a little, because a good Christian woman should know how to read the Bible and other religious works, a governess could supply this learning, and anything further was unnecessary. Motherhood did not demand academic training in mathematics or logic, and any vocational guidance should come from the mother and other family females, not outsiders. This method of education had the advantage of keeping a girl dependent on her family by not allowing her to become familiar with the outside world, which thus increased the feeling of living in a cocoon. Wrote one supporter of this kind of education, when a girl is educated at home she gets the

> opportunity . . . to make the acquaintance of her parents and brothers and sisters. Yet it is those to whom she is bound by family associations of inherited tastes and the similarity of circumstances, who will probably be the companions of her future life, and it is among them that she must win the respect and affection that will secure her their cooperation in whatever work she may take in hand . . . [15]

There were a number of ladies' schools in different parts of England, nearly all boarding schools, very small and very expensive. In 1836 it cost over one thousand pounds for the two years of schooling that most of their pupils received.[16] The education these students obtained was academically no better than that offered for the lower classes in the state-supported church elementary schools, but that did not matter because upper-class parents were uninterested in an academic education for daughters, merely in seeing that they met the right people and lived in a proper environment.[17] These establishments were primarily finishing schools, putting on a social polish that would enable their pupils to marry well and later mix socially with their equals or, one hoped, their betters. The contacts a girl made in school could be important in her adult life.

To reinforce prevailing ideas on the physical and mental inferiority of women, there arose a great deal of pseudo-science, which was widely publicized as physiologically validating these social myths. Women needed care and extra guidance because they were physically more fragile than men. This was because their bodies were weaker and their nervous systems 'delicate'. All kinds of evidence was offered to prove this point, purporting to show, for example, that a woman could not drink liquor like a man because her physique was such that alcohol in large quantities would do irreparable damage. Whereas a drunken man could be saved from his intemperance, a drunken women could never be redeemed.[18] A drunken male was typically chastised with a mild reproof, but a drunken women was thoroughly decried as an abomination in Victorian society.

Such negative ideas that women assimilated about themselves were responsible for some of their greatest problems when trying to play a full role in public affairs. Only strong or supremely confident women, often those whose fathers had encouraged them to become active outside the home, were able to function independently in public life.[19]

6 Economic Disabilities

A popular image of Victorian England portrays a preoccupation with work and industry – and indeed ambitions and professions were discussed and written about at great length. The devil finds work for idle hands, every Victorian child heard. But the greatest aim of the majority of Englishmen at all levels, noble to vagabond, was to live in comfort without working. In nineteenth-century England the lower classes worked because they had no choice; the upper classes played because they had a choice; and the middle classes worked until they had enough money to make a choice. The mark of financial success often was a life given to one's own personal pursuits.[1] Middle-class merchants, especially Quakers and others of a benevolent mind, might retire to devote themselves to charitable works. But many middle-class Englishmen (such as sons of successful industrialists) aspired to comfortable unemployment as a requirement of the life of a gentleman. Attainment of such freedom from the claims of trade or industry made available the expanding opportunities of public life – except to women, for whom they were increasingly closed whether they worked or not.

However, the majority of men and women in nineteenth century England had to support themselves. They worked in order to survive.

SURPLUS WOMEN

In April 1859, the *Edinburgh Review* in discussing the problems of women's employment asserted that more than one-third of the women in England had to be self-supporting. This judgement reflected the growing concern in England, especially among women, about a manifest flaw in the 'separate spheres' society. How could the natural role of women be solely that of wife and mother when there were not enough husbands for all Englishwomen? A variety of books and pamphlets that appeared in the mid nineteenth century attest to the felt urgency of the problem of 'surplus' women.

Underlying the concern was the growing realization that many women who did not marry had no choice: They could not marry if they wanted to. Throughout history there had always been a sizable proportion of men and women who had stayed single for various reasons, but prior to the development of the 'separate spheres' society, the working woman was a normal part of life, and most women were expected to earn at least part of their own keep.[2] Women would mix home duties and outside employment without having to contend with public condemnation. In fact, prior to the nineteenth century, it was seen as the right thing to do. Seventeenth-century Quakers had an official policy of setting up widows in a trade. All such women received financial aid from their fellow Quakers as well as instruction in management and any other help needed to make a success of their business.[3] In the eighteenth century it was a 'universal assumption . . . that to provide work for women and children was a great benefit to the nation . . . .'[4]

Not until the late eighteenth and early nineteenth century were working women seen as a social evil. The ideal of women as mothers – the domestic protectors, the 'guardians of Christian and domestic virtues'[5] – was supported by the evangelical religious movement. Combined with the counter-revolutionary ideology fostered by the repressive atmosphere dominating England during the years of the French Revolution and the subsequent Napoleonic Wars, it helped create the separate spheres ideology.[6] Economically the belief was that if a woman stayed at home and looked after her family, then the man would be free to spend all his time and energy in earning enough to support them all. Politically this gender segregation was promoted because it was hoped that the ensuing isolation of the family in its own separate domestic world, with only church as a connector with the rest of society, would reduce the opportunity for public demonstrations and any other spontaneous outbursts that the government dreaded.

Middle-class women now had to marry or be considered superfluous in a society devoted to the nuclear family. There was no recognized place for a woman who did not have a man to support her. But according to the official census of 1851, more females than males were born, and the females survived infancy better than males. Whatever the causes, there were 400,000 more females than males in 1851.[7] Furthermore, according to an article in the first issue of *The English Woman's Review* in 1866, the problem was exacerbated by the number of men who did not marry and thus left even more females without husbands.[8]

Some men could not marry because of their employment. The armed services on all levels did not encourage marriage and, especially among the lower ranks, often forbade it. Even when by law a soldier could marry, his commanding officer would frequently refuse permission. Wives and children were a nuisance to the military as well as an extra expense.[9] It was a responsibility that the authorities preferred to avoid if at all possible. The middle-class public was unwilling to pay the allowances of married soldiers, so they, too, supported the military hierarchy's opposition to marriage in the ranks.[10] Wars also killed off many of the young English males. Those who died in India, in the Americas, during the Napoleonic Wars, or in other of the numerous conflicts of the nineteenth century did not return to marry. As the ambitions for Empire grew, so did the number of British troops enlisted in the army and navy, many of whom were sent overseas.

In the mid nineteenth century many English men and women emigrated to the colonies or to other foreign lands, including the United States, to seek their fortunes. Emigration increased due to the cheapening fares and a publicity campaign that told, often erroneously, of the lands of milk and honey to be found across the seas. Schemes were organized to send what was called surplus population to the colonies. Although some of the emigrants went as family groups, there were a number of single men seeking their fortune who felt their prospects were better if they went alone. These emigrations further diminished the pool of potential husbands for single women at home, few of whom had any opportunity to emigrate themselves because few jobs for single women existed in the colonies.

There were also many men who, for a variety of reasons, chose to remain single. Some perhaps were misogynists, and others were homosexual and rejected the normal family pattern. A number of men felt no need to marry, especially if they did not want children. An English middle-class male, if he did not want to wed, could have all the advantages of marriage along with those of bachelorhood. Frequently a bachelor would have an unmarried sister or other female relative to run his domestic establishment. Servants would see to the domestic comforts, while a plentiful supply of other females would supply the many delights that the Victorian males, married or unmarried, often sought. The ample supply of women for this underside of Victorian society was assured, because there were few alternatives for large numbers of single women within respectable society.[11] Consequently, even if there had been parity in numbers between the sexes, with so many bachelors there would still be many unwed females.

EMPLOYMENT OF WORKING-CLASS WOMEN

For most working-class women, a life devoted to the domestic world was unreal. Whether married or single, these women had always had to support themselves. Marriage did not have the same meaning for them as for middle- class women. A married woman would sometimes live at home with her parents and not with her husband. Husbands were often away, traveling around looking for work. It was common for even skilled journeymen 'to go on the tramp' and take work in any place they could find it: Working-class women learned to live without their men for long periods of time.[12] Therefore, it made sense for a woman to stay with her family, who would give her support while she was without her husband. Sometimes the wives and the children would travel around with the husband, but that was usually only for the poorer families. A working woman stayed at home where she had a job and a family and a community of other women that made up her world. Men, even living at home, gave their prime loyalties and time to their 'mates' – their male companions.[13]

Working-class marriages were sometimes not legal or religious, but simply fully accepted common-law unions. If a woman was economically independent and unconcerned with middle-class respectability, she might find many advantages in staying legally single: Her man could not legally beat her, he had no right to her earnings, and any children of the union belonged to the mother. Only towards the end of the nineteenth century when changes occurred in the legal status of women was there an increase in formalized marriages among the working classes. The real change for working-class women came with motherhood. The birth of children made her and the females of her family responsible for the support and care of the babies. Fathers did not generally concern themselves with their offspring, especially in the early years.

Working-class women, like their middle-class sisters, had a problem with employment. Whether spinsters, widows, or wives, these women had to take care of themselves. They needed employment; but many of their traditional employment opportunities disappeared as a new urban life style arose. Most of the better jobs in the developing urban society were taken by men, who kept women out of them and out of the trade associations through which they might have found new opportunities. In the middle of the nineteenth century, few employed men were inclined to be generous about admitting new groups as competitors for limited employment openings.[14]

Traditionally the English retail trades had been dominated by women. The early shops had been small affairs often run out of the homes of craftsmen and other local workers where they sold the goods they made. Their wives were in charge of these retail sales and ran the shops. This was convenient because there were few fixed hours for selling and the women were available for sales whenever there was a customer. Some wives expanded the range of goods for sale, making a profit on whatever they could sell. A few grocery shops set up in the center of town or on busy streets did not at first affect most of the women's small local establishments. Then cooperative societies organized retail stores for the benefit of their customers, which took away some trade from the female merchants. When some goods, such as clothing, furniture, draperies, and hardware, were moved out of homes and into larger, more professional retail businesses, few women ran the new establishments.[15]

One area of retailing which did not lend itself to this kind of change was the local food store, which continued to be run by women out of their homes, particularly in working-class districts where most of the working class families needed to buy food every day. They often bought just enough for the meal ahead because they lacked the storage space or facilities to keep excess food. Pantries or 'cold cellars' which most middle-class homes had for food storage were not available to the poor. Even if by chance they had the room for storage they rarely had the money to buy ahead – many of them had little enough to eat at each meal. Consequently, the food store had to be close and open for business whenever working people needed it. Many women working away long hours could not shop until they returned home. Neighborhood shops, run by a local woman, were open at all hours and never really closed. Furthermore, many of the customers could not afford to pay their bills regularly and needed credit, which the local shop would grant – allowing its customers to 'put it on the slate' until payday.[16]

Women were also the most common sellers of beer. The first beer houses were set up in regular homes where the housewife brewed her own. She often started by making beer for her family, as was common in traditional society, and when her reputation for good brew became known, or when she required extra income, she sold beer from her home. Later special rooms were set aside in the home for the sale of beer and from these developed the modern beer houses, which were unregulated by the government until the 1830 Beer Act. By that Act beer house keepers had to be licensed, and many of the first license holders were women.[17]

By the mid nineteenth century, as many of the retail establishments were moving out of homes and into establishments organized specifically for retail goods, women not only lost their proprietorship of such businesses but also the employment they provided. In the new shops men were hired as sales assistants for the reason, it was argued, that women could not do the heavy work of retailing – carrying heavy bales of cloth that a retail fabric store had to handle, for example. But, as Victorian reformer Josephine Butler pointed out, women were at this time working as porters and coalheavers without much public outcry, and a large number of women – 43,964 according to Butler – were employed as outdoor agricultural labourers.[18]

Even if the shopkeeper wanted to employ female labour, many women preferred to buy from men, as the proprietor of one draper's and mercer's shop found out when he hired some men to work along with women. The women customers ignored the female assistants and preferred if necessary to wait in order to deal with the men.[19] *The English Woman's Journal* published an article asking women to give their business to women retail clerks when they went shopping.[20] Some of the lack of support women gave to each other's work was a manifestation of the widely held female belief that men were actually superior to women, and that this superiority was expressed in the service that was given in the shop.

Large numbers of working-class women were employed in the lowest jobs in tailoring, known as 'slopwork', as well as the other needlework. Slopwork was the piecework in sewing that came from a wholesaler or some middleman. Both men and women worked in this trade but, as there was constant pressure to reduce very low prices even lower, only those with no alternative did slopwork, and they usually were women.[21] Matchmaking, nailmaking and other jobs, many of which were done at home, also employed large numbers of poor women, all paid by piecework at the cheapest rates. They had to work hard mostly in appalling conditions in order to survive. Workers in these 'sweated trades' were unprotected by factory laws of the mid nineteenth century; when middle-class women became more assertive on the issue of protection for employed females, these trades were the objects of the most complaints.[22]

Most of the new industries of the 'industrial revolution' – iron and steel, for instance – employed few women. However, women found new opportunities in the Lancashire cotton mills; and factory employment continued in expanding local industries like the Staffordshire potteries and the Yorkshire wollen trade.

Some jobs paid well but were looked down upon as unacceptable to the community. It was important for girls to be employed in respectable or fashionable jobs. Many girls, especially in the more ambitious working families, were concerned with their future, and marriage was part of that future. They wanted to be sure that they were perceived by their community and prospective in-laws as being respectable, much of that perception being tied in with their employment. There was such great competition for respectable positions that these jobs were usually poorly paid. For example, in one study made of women's work in 1906, it was found that warehouse work was more desirable than factory work even though it was much lower paid. In the last decades of the nineteenth century, clerkships became desirable, and many working-class girls were therefore kept in school in order to qualify for such positions. But this was only for those who could afford to stay off the job market for a longer time and also be able to choose a lower-paying position.[23]

One field where many of the working-class women found employment was in elementary school teaching. In the decades before state Board Schools were set up, the government gave increasing support to elementary schools run by churches. From 1833 on, Parliament gave state funds to the Anglican National Society as well as to the nonconformist British and Foreign School Society to support their schools. Most of these institutions hired unqualified men and women, many of whom came out of working-class backgrounds, as teachers.[24] There were few standardized tests either for the teachers or the pupils, and conditions in these schools were usually quite poor – partly due to the general indifference towards church-run education on the part of both parents and children. The schools were often seen as bastions of anti-working-class sentiment by lower-class families, many of whom did not view schooling as immediately important. Time spent at school was time not devoted to earning money to help the family. Teaching in such a hostile atmosphere was often disagreeable and stressful, not to be desired by 'gently reared' middle-class females.[25]

Most male pupils believed there was was little advantage gained by schooling; but their sisters, in being deprived of it, lost the opportunity to learn valuable skills for future employment. In the second half of the nineteenth century there was a rapid opening of clerical positions in both business and government. (The post office had expanded enormously, with its penny post in 1840 and the introduction of the Post Office Savings Bank in 1861.) Many women, both in the middle and lower classes, could not be hired because of their poor skills in writing and arithmetic. Special classes were successfully introduced in London in 1850 to improve these skills and for nearly forty years helped women become more employable.[26] Only in the last decade of the century did the regular education of girls improve so that these special classes could be dropped.

A major problem facing working-class girls was the lack of apprenticeships. Many trades forbade the articling of girls, often because of male opposition to female competition. In the 1820s and 1830s, a period when many women were seeking work in the city and competing with men also looking for employment, the male tailors in London went on strike a number of times with the object of keeping women out of their trade.[27] But even if the trade consented to accept women, and very few did, the families of the girls were rarely willing to pay the cost of an apprenticeship. They did not want to invest their scarce resources in training that would not help the family and might possibly go unutilized if the girl were to marry a man in another field. And even at the end of apprenticeship training, women workers faced long hours and low wages.

A frequent women's complaint was unequal pay for the same work. It did not seem right for a woman to be paid less than a man for the same work. Sometimes this situation was avoided by gender segregation: Some jobs were only for men, while the lower paying ones were reserved for women. In the 1830s the Owenite socialists called for equal pay for equal work, but they were unsuccessful. One reason was the prevalence of the 'family wage' concept that men had to provide for a whole family and, therefore, must earn enough for all. This emphasis on wages to maintain the family had universal support among the working class, many of whom believed, with reason, that wages automatically drop to the lowest level possible: A family man who accepts a wage that supports only himself forces all wages to fall to that level, and his family will be unsupported. In 1833 the British and Foreign Bible Society reduced wages for their women workers on the grounds that 'women can manage on less'.[28]

During the nineteenth century the male worker was learning to organize; many a worker believed that a union, or some combination of workers, would help him improve his situation. But in the end the paramount agency for his protection had to be the national government. It is not surprising, therefore, to find that much action by the working class, from the beginning of the nineteenth century to the end, was aimed at extending the franchise to all working men, then using their votes to force Parliament to regulate working conditions and give protection to the workers. Working-class women, on the other hand, while active in the fight for universal enfranchisement in the early nineteenth century, by the middle of the century had withdrawn almost completely from political activities. Increasingly the working man saw women as competitors and rejected cooperation between the sexes in the labour unions and in the fight for universal suffrage. Consequently, women were unable to get union protection or the vote. Exacerbating the tensions between male and female labour was the use of female labour as strikebreakers, actual or threatened.[29] Laws formulated and passed by men 'to protect' females often placed women at great disadvantage when competing with men for jobs.[30] When women's unions began to appear they were mostly led by middle-class women, who had the time and the skills needed for such organizations.[31]

In the rural areas, as to be expected, women worked very hard. They labored in the fields, often at jobs that were heavy and dirty. It was especially true of the farm labourer's wife and daughters. All had to work, and a man's chances of being hired were greatly improved when he had a wife and children who could help during harvest or whenever there was extra work to be done.[32] Here there was little talk about 'female delicacy' or 'separate spheres'; the family's survival depended on all members, small children as well as large.

But it was in domestic work that the majority of both rural and urban working women found employment. Not only did the number of domestic positions increase enormously as large numbers of families no longer did their own family chores but hired others to do them, but females replaced male servants.[33] Male butlers, footmen, chefs and valets were still common in the higher levels of society, but in the middle classes females largely replaced them. Housekeepers, maids and cooks were the most common positions, but many women were also employed in auxiliary domestic positions such as needlewoman, laundrywoman and so on. Whereas in the late eighteenth century a footman always used to accompany any woman of standing, by the nineteenth century he had been replaced by a maid.[34]

Working-class servants had no special status as members of the 'weaker sex'; their 'frailties' were unrecognized by society. They had to work for a living, often in hard and dirty jobs for long hours, doing much of the heavy labour that the middle-class home depended on. Women had to carry the heavy coal scuttles from cellars up long stairs to rooms throughout the house to feed fires that heated the rooms. Women also did the heavy job of washing the family's clothing and heavy bedding – not a job for a frail female. Working-class men also supplied the labour necessary to maintain middle-class existence. In the nineteenth century the notion of two separate spheres was inappropriate for the lower-class labour market where both men and women had to work.

Because servants were required to manage their employers' households day and night, living in was obligatory. There was an acknowledged hierarchy in the domestic field, as rigidly adhered to as that of the outside world. Positions of butlers, cooks and housekeepers were at the top. These usually paid well and went to people in service all their lives. They saw their work as careers and spent much of their time and energy training on the job, showing their competence to their employers and others who could get them promoted. It was common to call the women in senior domestic positions 'Mrs' as a courtesy title. Parlour maid and ladies' maid were also considered solid positions and in the middle ranks. At the bottom were the scullery maid and the boot boy.

All this ranking was carefully observed in the servants' quarters where they ate and lived. The differences in position were evident not only in the salaries paid but also in the servants' living conditions. The lowest group was housed in the meanest places, while the upper servants had comparatively better quarters. The privileges of the upper servants were the envy of their underlings and would often include extra tea and beer rations as well as the choicest bits of food in the 'below stairs' eating room. The larger establishments generally had a more rigid and organized form of separation among the levels of service.

There were also a large number of people who worked for the family but lived outside. Sometimes they came in to do their work in the family home and then returned to their own domicile to sleep, while in other cases they would do their work at their own home or in public washing facilities. Laundry work was heavy and hard. Standing over hot tubs, using strong lye soaps that got the dirt off the clothes and took the skin off the hands that used it, was not a pleasant occupation, but it allowed many women who did it to live home with their families. (There was great concern among some middle-class reforming ladies over the conditions of these laundry women, particularly about the great quantities of ale they consumed while working in such hot and unpleasant conditions.)[35]

Large numbers of sewing women were also employed by the middle- and upper-class families. While many of the women from these families prided themselves on their needlework, most of it was purely decorative. Every girl had to learn to sew, but embroidering 'samplers' was often all she achieved. Lower-class sewing women were hired to mend linens, draperies, and other family fabrics. At this time all material was expensive and so sheets were darned and tears repaired, ideally with such small stitches that the damage would be undetected. Personal clothing had to be made, repaired and altered when needed. Before the advent of the sewing machine, hand sewing required countless hours of labor under generally poor conditions – often in ill-ventilated rooms by candlelight.

Although working-class women all expected to work, many, particularly at the poorest levels, had to support their families alone. A large number of unskilled male laborers in the nineteenth century were killed or injured in industrial accidents, thus leaving a family to be supported by the mother. Some fathers left their families, sometimes to find work and othertimes just to escape the great poverty. Frequently they never returned. In a society without any social services the mothers had to take full responsibility for the family and it was not uncommon for the children to be sent to the poor house or to an orphanage when the mother could not carry the burden alone.

EMPLOYMENT AND EDUCATION OF MIDDLE-CLASS WOMEN

For middle-class women the problem of employment was a more complicated one than for their working-class counterparts. Usually having more family resources than the poorer women they were often able to afford some type of training. Typically dressmakers and milliners were from middle-class backgrounds. These occupations were, according to one observer, the most mixed in terms of class. The majority of such workers in London, which according to the census of 1841 included over twenty thousand females (and one hundred and seventeen males), came from the country. They were the daughters of 'clergymen, military and naval officers, surgeons, farmers and tradesmen'.[36] These women had served an apprenticeship in the country before coming to the capital to work. The 'prestige of London' in clothing fashions would be a boost to their business if they returned to open an establishment in their hometowns. But once articled they became part of the working population and lost any claim to gentility or equality with their middle-class customers.

For middle-class women without a trade or the means to establish themselves the economic picture was bleaker, especially for those who had to be self-supporting. The only careers open were those of teacher, governess, or companion, all of which were badly paid because of the fierce competition for openings. An advertisement in the 1860s for a governess between 20 and 30 years, 'no foreigners', with a low salary had 250 responses.[37] Another for a nursery governess that offered no salary, only room and board as recompense, received over 300 replies.[38]

A few women supported themselves and sometimes their families by their writings. Women produced a great number of the books and articles that Victorian society so loved. The great upsurge of publications of all kinds, from children's readers to adult 'elevating' works, created a market for the work of some women writers, but this was not an occupation for many. We have previously encountered Mrs. Clara Lucas Balfour, a successful writer of temperance literature[39] Also unusual is the story of Marie Jane Jewsbury, the daughter of a cotton mill owner in the early nineteenth century, who when her father experienced financial disaster successfully supported herself and her four young brothers through the sale of her writings.[40] But few women had both the special talent and the opportunity for publishing commercially profitable material. Clearly, then, there was a great need for 'respectable' work for ordinary middle-class women, as Josephine Butler, among others, recognized in the 1850s.[41]

There was a growing belief in the mid nineteenth century that education was the key to success at some levels of the industrial and urban society. Traditionally training in many fields had been gained through apprenticeships or other kinds of on-the-job training. This changed in the nineteenth century when an increasing number of occupations became professionalized and preparation came to be based on a solid academic foundation, followed by a carefully organized professional training. Controlled by formal licensing, or examination, standards were established by law for each profession. Those without professional qualifications were not allowed to practise at all. As positions gained acknowledgement of professional status, and concomitant prestige and financial rewards, they became more attractive to the dominant groups, with the result that females and others without public power were squeezed out on the grounds they had no proper training. In this way the male medical profession took over that most feminine of natural functions – childbirth: Middle- and upper-class families hired male practitioners to supervise the delivery of their offspring, while the lower classes retained the traditional, and less expensive, female midwives.[42]

Education was following on the heels of politics in the nineteenth century as an area of prime national importance. Apart from the economic issues, there was another fundamental problem: The governors of England were ignorant. With the movement towards a mass democracy, the British found it imperative to educate all levels of society. All citizens should have some learning.[43] In the first reformed Parliament of 1833, the government acknowledged the importance of schools to the nation as a whole and indicated that some kind of government involvement was called for; at this time the first state appropriation for education was made.

Most educational experts agreed that the starting point for reform of the system was in teacher training. Girls' schools in particular needed better trained teachers.[44] Female academies were all private and without any official control over curriculum or the qualifications of the teachers. Most of them were proprietary establishments started by single women who had a small competence to invest and needed a steady income. Frequently these proprietors would organize a school in their own homes and then, if successful, hire other young women to teach some of the classes. It was poorly paid employment with bad working conditions. The teachers lived on the premises and usually had to supervise the pupils at all times. We have no figures as to how many schools for girls there were in England at this time; any estimate would have to take into consideration that schools came and went rather rapidly. Rarely did a school continue past the first founding generation. In 1836, in the fashionable town of Brighton, there were over one hundred schools for young ladies.[45]

For the working classes there were the elementary schools which the churches organized, but their teachers were no better trained than those who taught in the private girls' schools. Recognizing this deficiency, in 1840 the Church of England, with financial help from Parliament, set up the first teacher-training college in England.[46] Within five years twenty-two Anglican training colleges were established, but for male teachers only. In response supporters of female education and training began public agitation for improved training for women too. The first move came again from the Anglicans. In 1848, Queen's College was opened in Hartley Street, under Anglican sponsorship, for the specific purposes of training governesses;[47] it quickly became closely associated with King's College, whose male professors gave the women, suitably chaperoned, most of their instruction.[48] The following year another college, Ladies College, was opened in Bedford Square, London. It was officially nonsectarian, though much of its support came from Unitarians, who were particularly devoted to education.[49] In 1855 a college for working women was also started but it does not appear to have been successful and soon disappeared.[50]

These developments could not stifle continuing doubts about the quality of education. Education itself was still thought to be unnecessary for the working classes, of relatively little importance to landowners, and superfluous for women. In the 1850s the industrial middle classes, lower and upper, continued to press for a better educational system. This segment of the population was having increased influence on the government, however, and by 1858 had persuaded the government that something should be done. Just what, was unclear to those in authority; therefore the government in typical fashion resorted to a Parliamentary Commission, under the Duke of Newcastle, to inquire 'into the present state of popular education in England'. Nothing much came of its work, except that 'payment by results' was adopted: Schools were to be paid according to the number of their pupils who could pass a stipulated examination.[51]

A few years later, in 1864, the Taunton Commission was formed, to investigate the prevailing educational situation again; the initial focus on the boys' education was eventually widened to include that of girls. At this time few English men and women, even the professionals in education, knew much about school conditions. When the headmistress of a school was asked if the education of a girl should differ from that of a boy in a family of the same social rank, she replied that she had little knowledge of boys' education and did not know what is 'the proper education for a boy', noting that for both boys and girls, 'serious study is considered unnecessary and unsociable' by parents and others.[52]

By 1864 the education for girls was largely unchanged and still had little academic content. Mary Frances Buss told the Taunton Commissioners that for the middle classes good schools were very scarce. There were not enough of them, and those that existed had few good teachers. Once in school it was hard to get the girls to study, as they had little motivation to gain academic success. Their parents did not appreciate education and did not keep their daughters in school very long.[53]

The main problem was that society itself was unclear on what it wanted from women's education. The 'separate sphere' ideology required middle-class women to be the guardians of the home, devoting their time and energies to family life. But such a small protective, restrictive world was not what an increasing number of active women wanted or could have. Consequently, the 1860s saw a growing movement among prominent upper- and middle-class women calling for a better training for women in all academic subjects. Some of these women demanded that a university education be available for qualified females.[54] In 1865 the Cambridge local examinations were opened to women and in 1869 a college for higher education of females was inaugurated at Hitchen Harts.[55] The 1870s saw a number of women's colleges established[56] and these institutions were to become, as perhaps many of their critics suspected, breeding grounds for a new wave of female activists. Their graduates were to spread throughout the land and lead other, less educated women into broader fields of purpose. (They were also to give the lie to the old belief that no man wanted a 'blue stocking' for a wife.)

ECONOMIC DEPENDENCE

A major barrier to most middle-class women challenging the norms of the time was their economic dependence on their male kin.

The main problem for married English women stemmed from their position under the common law: When they married, they ceased to have an independent existence and became 'one' with the husband. But it was not a partnership: The man controlled the woman, and all her property was his. This did not cause much of a problem in the preindustrial society because there had developed in English law a way of protecting an upper-class woman's property when she married. Under the law of equity, a system of legal marriage settlements was established by which a legal contract might place a woman's property in the hands of appointed male trustees before the marriage. This meant that the husband could not get control, nor could he force his wife to give him control, while the trustee stood in the way. On the death of the woman the property usually went to her children or, failing that, reverted to her family. Thus, any man hoping to take advantage of an heiress' fortune would find it protected if her family had drawn up settlements before marriage. These contracts were common among the upper class with property to protect. They were also the greatest cause of wife beating in in the early eighteenth century, according to the applications for a legal separation in London at this time. Husbands, it appears, resented having wives with independent wealth. It lessened their power over spouses and many men beat their wives trying to get control of their money. Usually they were frustrated by the legal protections her family had imposed.[57]

Generally, however, this applied only to the upper class and some of the upper middle class. The vast majority of married women, especially in the lower middle class and working classes, had no such protection. Of greater import to the middle-class and working-class married women was the law by which any money acquired by the wife after marriage, whether by inheritance or her own labour, automatically belonged to her husband. There were some well publicized cases. One of the best known was that of Caroline Norton, whose estranged husband took the earnings she made through her successful writing career. While husbands did not need their wives' agreement in decisions a wife could have no independence without her husband's consent.

To get Parliament to rectify this situation an early feminist meeting was called in December, 1855. Meeting in the home of Barbara Smith in Blandford Square, London, a group of women formed the Married Women's Property Committee. This committee included women from many different parts of society: Quakers and Unitarians as well as Anglicans; respectable conservatives, along with not-so-reputable radicals. These women worked to draw up and circulate petitions supporting a Married Women's Property Act. Fanning out from London into other parts of the country, they developed a network that was to be important in future women's work.[58]

The Married Women's Property Committee did not achieve its goal of getting Parliament to pass the act; but many members, now they had taken the first step to public life, turned to other feminist concerns, especially the problem of women and work. They moved from Blandford Square to Langham Place, their headquarters for a number of years. The Langham Place Circle, as these women were called by their contemporaries, were 'advanced women', active in many causes. Barbara Smith and some of her associates in the Committee established in 1858 the *English Woman's Journal*, a paper which sponsored an employment register for women. It was quickly discovered that there was great need for help in this area, and so in 1859 employees of the *Journal* founded the Society for the Promotion of the Employment of Women.[59] They successfully organized their own printing firm, the Victoria Press, run by women and often for women. A number of girls and young women were taken on as apprentices and then as journeymen.[60] The Victoria Press was in business for many years, printing for the *Journal* as well as for other women's organizations.[61]

The initiatives of the Langham Place Circle made no more than a small dent in the problem of economic independence for unmarried English women. In the 1860s the country as a whole was unwilling to abandon the two spheres ideology. Though it recognized that some women would remain unmarried, it tried to handle the problem of 'surplus women' by calling them 'redundant.' Women who were unmarried and therefore unable to fulfill their true destiny of being wives and mothers, were 'redundant'. England, it was stated, had many redundant women. What to do with them? One popular solution was to get rid of the problem by sending them away to the colonies, where they could do useful work as teachers and nurses and, perhaps, eventually become wives to the single men who were leaving England in large numbers. The colonies in Australia and New Zealand, in particular, were expanding in the mid nineteenth century because of the promise of cheap land; families and single men went off in the hope of eventually owning their own farm. Female emigration societies were formed for all classes of women. The Queen herself gave approval to this effort by lending her patronage to one of the societies. At Langham Circle a Female Middle-Class Emigration Society was established by Maria Rye to send some of the surplus women to New Zealand and Australia.[62] For many decades there was some disagreement in women's ranks on this issue. When in 1888 a former president of the British Women's Temperance Association offered to give a lecture to the membership on California, where she was going to live, she was rejected on the grounds that 'emigration is not in accordance with the objects of this association'.[63]

A MONEY ECONOMY

There were exceptions to the general dismal picture. Many of the women leaders in the second half of the nineteenth century, with other women from affluent families, were beneficiaries of a new role of money in the economy. In previous times only a few females could have personal control of property; now, as the nineteenth century progressed, a number of women inherited their own fortunes. In contrast to real property, money is flexible and easily divided. Only in such traditional ways as the granting of dowries would a landed family pass to others some of its substance. But money can be shared out through bequests, annuities, and other financial tools without any substantial power loss to the family. Consequently, daughters and younger sons, particularly from the industrial middle classes, gained by being included in such inheritances and bequests from fathers, uncles, and others who usually knew how to protect funds from legal attachment by husbands or other outsiders.[64]

Such financially independent women funded many projects of interest to women. Married and single women with control over their own funds used them to finance political parties, reforming societies, journals, religious missions and other public ventures. Women's causes and journals were particular beneficiaries. There are no separate figures for funds controlled by females, but the sums, mostly from commercial and industrial ventures, were great. One indication of the growing wealth of independent women was the business started by one woman, a Miss Amy E. Bell: She was a successful stockbroker. Unlike many women who go into unconventional employment, Miss Bell's family was not in stockbroking. From a family of surgeons and public servants, she came to work in finance because she developed a great interest in it; although not allowed to have a seat on the Stock Exchange, she had her own office and a female clerk. She did have some male clients but most of her customers were women. She noted that 'one of the pleasantest features about my work is the number of interesting, able and cultured women with whom I have made acquaintance'.[65]

As it did for their fathers, brothers, and husbands, this type of financial support enabled women receiving it to live independent lives. They were freed from the economic pressures that forced the majority of society to conform to 'respectable' patterns of behavior: Rich ladies were allowed far more latitude in conduct than poor women. Though such women were few in the middle of the nineteenth century their numbers and influence on English society were to grow substantially through the last decades of the Victorian era.

WOMEN IN PUBLIC LIFE

Many women, even successful ones, accepted the notion that women were inferior to men and condemned vehemently any female who tried to rebel. Mrs. Gaskell, the writer, was one of these.[66] The lack of self-esteem in middle-class women, encouraged as a sign of modesty, was a great handicap in the world outside the home. It was 'feminine' to be insecure in oneself and one's judgements. Told over and over that a woman's natural function was to be wife and a mother and that they were physically or psychologically unfit to function independently in the public world, they came to believe that any woman doing so was an unnatural woman.

Some of these anti-feminists saw their own position threatened by any attempt to change the role of women. They had a stake in the maintenance of the *status quo*, particularly the older women who had spent a lifetime defending the accepted norms. Not to deny these standards would be to say they had been wrong all their lives and had taught their daughters wrongly too. They were unwilling to believe that their life styles were erroneous or their lives a waste. There was also the practical problem that changes could disrupt their lives and leave them worse off.

Eventually these conservative women began to lose their influence as increasing numbers of women came into public life. Reality was not in accord with theory and the majority of women, for whatever reasons – and there were many – could not stay immured in adult adolescence. Women were part of society and had to make contributions. Also, increasing numbers of women, married or not, had to earn a living.

Because of the legal disabilities of married women, not surprisingly some financially secure women preferred to remain single and set up their own establishments, either by themselves or with other women. Nevertheless, the greater number of independently wealthy women did prefer to marry and have families. A question often raised is whether the majority of the women active in political and reform movements were single. An examination of the membership rolls of many women's organizations in the late nineteenth century shows that more were married.[67]

It is not surprising to find that middle-class women, as the ones most affected by the two spheres doctrine, led the fight for change. Unlike the upper- and working-class women who had life styles built on their own customs and traditions, middle-class women had no past to give them social direction. They were the ones who had no recognized place in public life.

It would be impossible to find a typical woman that fits all the criteria for a public woman. The old question 'do the times make the man, or the man make the times' has no answer. As among men, some women leaders were born, but many were made. Some women from prominent families took their places in the forefront, while their sisters from the same families avoided public life. Some women were by nature suited to lead, having the intellect and health needed for such work, while others preferred to retire and think of themselves as in delicate or poor health. Some leaders, like Sarah Robinson, succeeded in their work despite bad health.[68]

The motivations of the women reformers also differed. Many saw a troubled society in need of altruistic betterment. The temperance reform attracted many conservative women who were more pragmatically concerned with the problem of excessive drinking among all classes. The anti-Contagious Diseases movement recruited women who felt a solidarity with women on all levels. But as happened in the past, it was particularly evangelical religion that drew many English women out of their homes and onto the public platform, risking their reputations and their positions in society in order to help save the souls and bodies of their countrymen and women.

7 Religious Revival

In the first part of this book, we have seen the important contribution of women to the evangelical movement of 'methodists' in the late eighteenth century. While these female activists came from all classes, the majority were from the lower levels of society. By the time the various methodist churches had become organized, the women had lost their place in the leadership ranks and had mostly retired to teaching Sunday Schools, and other less influential roles. Only a few local evangelists continued to preach in the 1830s and 1840s. Consequently, when the enthusiasm of the Wesleyan revival had died down, the position of women in the churches did not appear to be fundamentally changed. In fact, there was some negative reaction towards women's work in places where they formerly had official support. The Quakers, for instance, questioned the appropriateness of female leadership within their church and discouraged it.[1]

During the mid century, while the women of the Langham Place Circle and elsewhere were pushing for better economic opportunities for women and devoting themselves to what we would call consciousness raising of the 'advanced' segment of English society, other Englishwomen were seeking to expand their church activities. Many in this group were conservative and, on the surface, do not appear to have been pioneers in the cause for equality. But in a very subtle way they altered the social perception of women's role in public work and widened the limits of toleration of female behavior. They showed respectable citizens that ladies could be useful to society, while allowing the ladies themselves the opportunity to try new challenging tasks. This helped build their self-confidence. Working within the religious establishment and fighting prejudice every inch of the way, these women ostensibly adhered to the rules of proper female behavior but used Christian duty as a means of penetrating public life. First emerging from their allotted domestic sphere to 'save their sisters,' an accepted noble endeavor, they then expanded their work into other Christian reforms. They benefited from the peculiar British situation in which an established church had to compete, on increasingly equal grounds, for the loyalty of a critical citizenry.

DENOMINATIONAL RIVALRY

Although the Church of England was the official church, part of the establishment, and supported by state-imposed taxes, in the mid nineteenth century it no longer enjoyed the support of the country as a whole. It was regarded by many as redundant and was fast becoming a minority church, with the majority of church-going Britons attending the rapidly growing nonconformist establishments.

In the eighteenth century, the established church was the dominant religious force as well as a part of the government: All other churches and chapels were outsiders to the establishment. The Anglican Church did not have to answer to its lay members at all but was responsible to a national hierarchy that was usually uninterested in local affairs. It was run locally by parish priests and their curate, all ordained men. For centuries 'taking Holy Orders' fundamentally separated the priest from the layman in the Anglican church; the layman had little role and even less authority. The power of the parish priest could not be challenged by those in his parish, nor could any organization, religious or lay, be connected to his church without his permission. Furthermore, in many English parishes the social gulf between the priest and the ordinary layman was wide because they belonged to different social classes.

The position of parish priest was not usually strenuous, nor did it demand special talents. Priests were not chosen because of their personal gifts, but because they had the right background and connections. Up until Victoria's reign there was no professional training for parish priests. They typically were educated in academic subjects at Oxford or Cambridge and then 'took Holy Orders'. They were expected to learn on the job.[2] Consequently, many parish priests were not particularly effective pastors, nor were they good preachers, but they were gentlemen. They could copy their sermon from a published collection drawn up for such use and then read it at Sunday service. They did not have to memorize it, and it needed no particular relevance to the congregation.

The popular assessment of these Sunday sermons was that they were soporific. The guiding principle for religious talks (and action) in the Church of England was that they must be 'in good taste,' appealing to the intellect, not the emotions. The priest was not attempting to convert the nonbelievers. No threats of hellfire and damnation were to be found in the genteel atmosphere of the Church of England.

Self-doubts about this role of the established church arose with the publication of a religious census in 1851 which documented the great shift in population and in church-going in England. Population was moving from South to North as well as from country to city. Lancashire and

Yorkshire, formerly sparsely populated farming counties, became new centers of British industry, with its factories and resultant cities. Previous to the industrial development the largest towns in these counties were ports and market towns. Now, in the late eighteenth and early nineteenth centuries, mushroom growth made some of the former villages rivals and then successors of the metropolises of former times, as rural dwellers moved to the new urban areas to find work.

Like immigrants everywhere they had to adjust to completely new ways of life, as if they were foreigners in a new land. Their local religious institutions were transposed but most did not last very long.[3] If the immigrant sought to replace the Anglican village church with its urban counterpart, he was sure to be disappointed. A major problem was the great shortage of Anglican churches in the new towns. Parishes could only be created or expanded with the consent of Parliament, which was reluctant because it would cost money. Paying for new churches would require increases in the Church rates; and this burden would fall mostly on the shoulders of the new middle class, many of whom as members of competing nondenominational churches would be hostile to supporting a church from which they received no benefit. In fact, many in this group were fighting against existing church rates and for the disestablishment of the Anglican church.

The nonconformist churches, whatever their origins, were generally careful, once organized, to smooth their rough edges. They wanted to fit in and be respectable, to be part of the establishment. They followed and imitated the ways of the Church of England and let it set the pace. While laymen (and women) had played a crucial role in their development, the nonconformist churches and chapels setting up permanent organizations very quickly established professional ministries separated from the lay world. They also looked less and less to the conversion of the unconverted and turned their time and energies to the protection and development of chapels and congregations already established. Evangelicalism was muted as enthusiasm declined. Emphasis was placed on protecting those already in the denomination rather than in spreading The Word. Each church was careful neither to poach on the preserves of other churches nor give them aid.[4]

As we have seen, women were the great losers in these changes in evangelical religion. When lay preaching was rejected so were women. No females in the mid nineteenth century were ordained, nor were they admitted as professional preachers in any of the nonconformist denominations. But changes were to come with the development of a new religious atmosphere in the 1850s and 1860s.

A GROWING FEMALE INVOLVEMENT IN THE CHURCH OF ENGLAND

The Religious Census of 1851 confirmed the fears that most Englishmen did not go to church; subsequent investigation showed that the working classes, particularly the poorest ones, typically had no connection with organized religion at all.[5] It was also revealed that there were not enough places for the people in existing urban churches, even if they wanted to attend. But the truth was that most English men and women were no longer interested in attending the established church regularly, for many reasons. Rent for pews and the atmosphere of the churches themselves were barriers for many, particularly in the poorer working families, who did not have proper clothes or money to put in the collection plate. It was difficult for many to accept sitting in 'free' seats in the back of the church without psychological injury. The majority of religiously affiliated urban middle class and prosperous working class gave their allegiance to the nonconforming churches.

Publication of the Census of 1851 led to much soul searching on the part of the Anglican hierarchy over the problem of bringing the Church closer to the people. Some of the gulf between laymen and clerics, they decided, could be bridged by the use of laymen, but not laywomen, in a minor way. In 1860 nonordained men were officially allowed to become lay readers in the church and eventually got the right to preach.[6] Other roles were found for laymen that would make them part of the 'official' hierarchy. To bring it closer to the population, the Church decided to support various nonreligious, ameliorative reforms that it would sponsor and control. In this spirit, the Church of England Temperance Society was created as were other domestic supports such as the Mothers Union, started by a clergyman's wife in 1876 and quickly adopted by parishes throughout England.[7]

Entry into the domestic realm – the women's domain – was facilitated by a massive nineteenth century shift of social values: Religion was becoming less 'otherworldly' and more 'thisworldly' and all churches were expected to see to the physical in addition to the spiritual needs of their members. In competition with the ever-expanding nondenominational churches, the established church now had to perform social work, recruiting workers from among its own members. Because there were not enough men with the time, desire, or expertise, women made up the larger part of these workers. Church funds were often low and the services of women were often free, or at least cheaper than men's.

Women were seen as the main bulwark of the Church of England against the spread of evangelical churches in the second half of the nineteenth century. Women were for Crown, Church, and Country and could be depended on to support these foundation stones of their society. Unlike a growing number of successful businessmen who resented priests telling them what to do, women were used to men, ordained or not, having authority over them. Furthermore, many nonconformist churches were now completely male-oriented. Their values were important to the careers and public behavior of upwardly mobile men but of much lesser importance to the domestically bound women, whose success was based on their menfolk's. Many women found the Church of England, with its new social concerns, increasingly answering their needs: It focused on the values of the whole society, not just on those affecting male members. Consequently, women became viewed as a segment of the population loyal to the established church.[8] And their involvement in church work soon led them to seek an official, active role for females in the Church as well as a voice in its councils.[9]

Traditionally women had always been active in parish work but they did not have any official position. A clergyman's wife was expected to support her husband's work within his parish, particularly in its bearings on the domestic lives of his flock. She visited the families of sick or recently bereaved parishioners and gave whatever personal help she could. Cottage readings, a popular way of bringing religion into the lives of the people, were traditionally run by the women in the clergyman's family. Wives and daughters of the parish priest were often the only lay workers in a parish[10] and were expected to work in both the day schools and Sunday schools active at this time. It was not unusual for a clergyman's wife to identify completely with her husband and to believe that she and her husband had a true partnership. Many a Protestant woman who felt she had a religious vocation could only express it through marriage to a man in Holy Orders.[11] It was common, therefore, to find clergymen's wives as the originators of various social efforts, most born out of personal involvement with the amelioration of poor parishioners. Mary Sumner, for example, a clergyman's wife, started the Mother's Union in 1876,[12] while Mrs. Wightman organized a Workingmen's Hall and Temperance Association in her husband's parish.[13]

In many parishes women were the faithful workers in the Sunday School movement. Middle- and upper-class women had frequently done volunteer work in the schools, teaching as a 'Christian duty' those of less fortunate circumstances who could only go to school on the Lord's Day.[14] Teaching children or other women was seen as socially acceptable work for respectable females. When one wealthy young lady wanted to fill her time, she started a school and her father paid for the building and all its expenses. It is interesting to note that she worked with her sister but none of her brothers. They did not see teaching as a masculine occupation.[15] Male teachers were from the lower classes and had no prestige, while female teaching, if unpaid, was just an extension of their domestic role as caretakers of the young. By 1862, according to Bishop Mackenzie, 300,000 females taught Sunday School in England and Wales.[16]

But not all women could marry priests in order to follow their religious vocations. Neither did they want to restrict their efforts to teaching in Sunday Schools. A growing number of unmarried, wealthy, and some not so well-to-do women wanted an official position within the Church of England. A start was made in the 1840s when the high church group known as the Tractarians encouraged setting up celibate female orders within the Anglican Church. The first Anglican sister took her vows in 1841 and others soon followed. Modeled on the Catholic Sisters of Charity, the Anglican sisters established schools and worked in hospitals, nursing the sick during ever-recurring epidemics.[17] They also worked in prisons, continuing the mission of such well-known women as Elizabeth Fry. They appointed their own superior, their 'Episcopal Visitor', and thus avoided the control of the local bishop.[18] Though they gained the respect of all who knew their work, they did not command public attention as much as the more widely known institution of lay deaconesses.

The institution of deaconesses was established in England during the great discussion of the problem of 'redundant women' generated by the 1851 census report of an excess of females in the population. A revival of the old deaconess orders from the early church of the scriptures seemed to be a worthy and useful method of drawing unmarried women into the service of the Church of England. It was proposed that single women live together in homes. They were to be similar to Roman Catholic sisters' orders in that single women would do community work within a defined structure.[19] The Anglican deaconesses were given official sanction as well as the active support of many respected clergymen. William Pennefather, an Anglican priest, organized a training centre for deaconesses which became known as the Mildmay Deaconess Home, one of the most famous of the diaconates in the Church of England.

Given widespread publicity in secular books and journals as well as in church circles, the Mildmay deaconess movement captured the imagination of many single women. No vows were taken, an important point for many Protestant supporters, sensitive to the 'romanish practises' coming into the Church of England. The women who joined could leave at any time, but there were two groups of women: the permanent members expected to stay barring any unexpected impediment, and others who were recognised as temporary, coming for varying lengths of time to work in the missions set up by the permanent deaconesses.[20] These women tended to local needs and organized outlying missions in other districts. A mixture of the religious and the secular, their programs included mothers' meetings and sewing classes as well as Bible study groups and prayer meetings. In order to help the women of one district the Mildmay deaconesses in 1867 paid sixty sewing women to work five hours a day, five days a week, but the funds soon ran out, even though the pay was modest. They managed to get more money but only enough to hire the women for three hours a day at sixpence a day. This was the only support for many of these women and their families, apart from parish relief.[21] These deaconesses also organized 'penny dinners' and asked local wealthy men to buy tickets to give to the indigent.

The widespread appreciation shown for the efforts of these women no doubt encouraged many to do similar work. There were certainly enough destitute families who needed Christian charity of a practical kind. Local parish churches, if they had the money, would hire individual women missioners to work. There were many lower-class, single women – widows and spinsters – who were respectable but had to earn a living. It was from this group that the London Female Bible and Domestic Mission recruited its workers. Started by Ellen Henrietta Ranyard in 1858 with seven Biblewomen, by 1867 it employed over two hundred. They earned a salary of ten shillings a week for five days of five hours of work. They were officially nonsectarian but in reality were closely connected to the established Church.[22] Lady superintendents, who were appointed to supervise the workers, were all unpaid. Their supervisory duties included distributing wages, running missions rooms and managing their workers. The Biblewomen, as they were commonly called, were located in metropolitan London.

After an official three-month training course, Biblewomen began by selling Bibles, mostly to poor families. They also came to do many other jobs which today would be considered 'social work'. Soon it was perceived that there was a greater need in their parishes than for the distribution of Bibles or for the untrained family help that was available. In 1868 the Biblewomen developed a nursing division where they received three months of extra training before being sent to work in the hospitals and lying-in institutions. They also did home nursing among the poor. Eventually this nursing work came to dominate the organization. When the founder, Mrs. Ranyard, died in 1879, leadership passed to local parish priests, although up to that point the whole movement had been developed and run completely by women.

Now with the assumption of power by the priests, the Lady Superintendent system declined and a Ranyard Council, controlled by men, took over. At this point the name was officially changed to the London Bible Workers and Nurses Mission.[23] Eventually the Ranyard Nurses broke away from the Mission and, as an independent organization, became part of the general nursing system.

For many females in the nineteenth century the greatest problem was unwanted pregnancies: Here was another community service that the established church could take up. Many young, unmarried women found themselves pregnant, not because some lord had seduced them, nor because they were victims of an employer or his son as popular rescue literature would have it, but more often because they were courting and went too far. These women had few places to turn. Most of them were respectable, but unlucky in their choice of friends. Their families, particularly if they were making claims to respectability, would not want them, and their communities shunned them. It was to aid these women that some lay members of the Church of England in the 1860s and 1870s organized charities in London. They sponsored homes for unmarried or deserted mothers, looked after the women, and saw that the babies were cared for.[24] It was a very successful effort that was later taken up by the Salvation Army. It was work for women and by women, and it comported well with the traditional charitable role of the church while not taking the women workers far from their allotted 'domestic sphere'.[25]

The Anglican Church had its own versions of popular, nonsectarian reform movements. The Church of England Temperance Society was started in the late 1860s, though it became widespread in the 1870s.[26] Its Women's Union assumed many duties along with its particular concerns with the problem of women and drink. Laundrywomen, who worked in a hot steamy atmosphere and consequently were great drinkers, became a special project for the union along with the barmaids who sold the drink and who were often exploited by bar owners. Its nontemperance work included visiting the sick and organizing prison missions. At first it enrolled many upper-class and middle-class women in its local branches, but later working-class women joined.[27] The Church Army, another church body working with the ordinary people, was a late nineteenth-century Anglican imitation of the Salvation Army. Other Anglican women's missions were organized in the second half of the nineteenth century but most of them were limited to one or two parishes.

Much of the mission work of the Church of England was generated quite modestly and without much thought to future developments within the local parishes by individual men and women who saw a need and tried to fill it.

Despite pressures against them, some women emerged as leaders in diverse fields, particularly in such fringe areas as temperance reform. Mrs. Julia Wightman was a notable example.[28]

Other Anglican women engaged with less fanfare in similar but more locally oriented mission work. Some went into rescue work from a sense of Christian duty, others for more secular reasons; but regardless of motive, they worked hard and made a solid contribution to the welfare of the most depressed segments of English society.[29] One of the most famous of these was Lady Henry Somerset. She set up her own mission to aid the local poor, thereby inaugurating a very active public life.[30]

RELIGIOUS REVIVALISM: A NEW AWAKENING

A different kind of contribution to the development of public roles was made by women in a more controversial activity. As we have seen, women preachers, popular in the late eighteenth century, had in the early decades of the nineteenth century became a threatened species. In the 1860s they reappeared but with a difference: They were now middle-class preachers working in halls as star performers.

In England in the late 1850s and 1860 there developed a new religious mood that came to be known as 'the second evangelical awakening'.[31] This new enthusiasm opened opportunities for women once again to ascend the pulpit and preach to a mixed audience. Much of this religious spirit came from across the Atlantic, brought by American missionaries who found fertile ground in Britain for planting their message. They came with a system of evangelizing that had been worked out, tested and refined in their homeland, not as amateurs but as professionals possessing the talents and skills needed to draw in and, more importantly, hold an audience with a message of salvation for believers and damnation for sinners. They led interdenominational missions, widely publicized, in areas where they had support from some local ministers. Some came by invitation, only requiring that a local committee of influential citizens make local arrangements. Because of the nonsectarian nature of these religious missions they were often held in nonreligious buildings; temperance halls were popular.[32] Carefully organized and widely publicized, the missions usually stayed in one location for a period of time, ranging from a few days to a few months.

One of the innovations introduced by the Americans was allowing women to preach at their services. At first wives who had come to England with their preacher husbands acted as helpers not preachers, restricting their work to all-female gatherings although they might be preachers in the United States.[33] This changed when one woman, a famous preacher in her own right, came to England and addressed mixed audiences.

Mrs. Phoebe Palmer had made a great name for herself both in the United States where she preached and wrote popular evangelical books, and in England where her reputation had spread and her books had found a ready audience. The daughter of a Yorkshire Methodist, in 1835 she had started weekly prayer meetings for women in her New York City home. These interdenominational meetings proved so popular that in 1839 they were opened to men. A mixture of laymen and ministers, men and women, congregated on equal terms to promote personal holiness. Word of the meetings spread throughout the United States and across the Atlantic where they were emulated.

In 1859 Phoebe Palmer and her husband, Dr. Walter Palmer, decided to come to England to evangelize. Phoebe Palmer was aware of the prejudice against women in the pulpit in England so she did not preach but 'talked' to the people, not from the pulpit but the communion rails. Her husband read portions of scripture and at the end he was the one to call for the sinners to come forth. A local preacher gave the prayers and led the congregration in singing hymns. But it was Mrs. Palmer who was the star event and drew in the crowds; she was popular and feted wherever she went.[34] For four years the Palmers worked in Britain – from June, 1859, to October, 1863 – criticism following them because of Phoebe Palmer's 'talks'. According to her critics, her work contravened St. Paul's injunction for women to be silent in the churches: Though she called her addresses 'talks', she was actually preaching. Because of the controversy the Palmers were denied the use of Wesleyan and Primitive Methodist chapels.

Between 1862 and 1866 the altercation continued. Arguments on both sides appeared in the English newspapers, particularly in the North where the Palmers had been very active. Both men and women were drawn into the dispute over whether women should be allowed to preach. Some of the defenders of women preaching supported John Wesley's view of exceptional call: that some special women (or men) called by God should be able to preach.[35] Many examples from the Bible were given as evidence of scriptural acknowledgements of this call by women. Popular among the supporters of the women was the old view that the first coming of Christ had made sex irrelevant: 'we are all one in Christ'. For many women, including Catherine Booth, who together with her husband William Booth founded the Salvation Army, this was the Christian position. She entered the controversy when her letter in defense of female preaching was published in a journal.[36]

Catherine Booth was herself a preacher – one of a large number of Englishwomen who emerged during the revivals that the Americans inspired.[37] Emulating their American sisters, some of them preached at religious services, while others gave addresses in public auditoriums, in town halls, theatres, and assembly rooms.[38] They were immensely popular and filled the halls. No doubt the public came to hear them because of the novelty, but many returned because of the message. To offset some of the criticism these women preachers were careful to comport themselves as 'ladies'. Dressed modestly, usually in black dresses, they talked in ladylike tones, careful not to display signs of 'female hysteria', consciously avoiding being labelled as 'shrieking sisters'.[39] They came from many different religious backgrounds, some Anglican, others nonconformist. In the years 1859 to the late 1870s, there were many such women, the majority working locally without developing a star reputation or receiving mention in the national papers. There were about forty who received a great deal of publicity in local, national and religious journals.[40] Socially they were mostly from the middle classes, of very respectable backgrounds.

Although some lady preachers developed national reputations and received invitations to preach throughout Britain, they did not continue their religious or preaching careers much beyond the 1870s when the revivalist fervor declined. For the majority, this was impossible, even if they wanted to establish themselves more permanently. Only a handful had the money, the opportunity, the ability and the support to establish their own churches. No established chapel or sect was going to make a female its permanent preacher. Of these stars only Catherine Booth appears to have developed further in her religious work, working with her husband in organizing the Salvation Army and encouraging other women to join and preach as Salvationists. Without special circumstances no doubt Catherine Booth would have been today just as unknown as the rest of her sister preachers of the 1860s and 1870s.

Women preachers were generally very conservative, but they became pioneers in female speaking on the Victorian public platform, and as we shall see, their work was to encourage other women. As women of the Victorian era who had so much societal and family pressure on them to shun public exposure, their belief in God's protection and their sense of doing His Will gave them the self-confidence essential to good platform work. These lady preachers of the mid-nineteenth century[41] unwittingly performed an important service for feminists and the other women who were to follow them in public life. While not fully accepting them Victorian society became accustomed to women as public speakers. These preaching ladies showed how successful women could be in public oratory. They became models for other women with no special call who were less certain of their personal talents.

INDEPENDENT MISSIONS

In the 1870s and 1880s there was a great deal of publicity and excitement over the dreadful lives endured by those dwelling in the slums and the need for Christian ladies and gentlemen to help them. Gladstone himself, motivated by his Christian beliefs, went into the streets at night to help prostitutes. Other individuals and groups set up missions and personally worked among the poor or paid others to do so.

In 1883 this concern heightened to near public hysteria. First the Rev. Andrew Mearns published a pamphlet 'The Bitter Cry of Outcast London', which made 'a great stir among the public' and caused 'slumming' to become 'the fashionable occupation' of the season.[42] Soon after, W. T. Stead published his well-known series about the white slave trade, 'The Maiden Tribute of Modern Babylon'. This sent a 'thrill of horror' through the country and led to a new popular concern about the 'two Englands' Disraeli had written about decades before.[43]

If ladies wanted to work away from home and still retain their claim to 'respectability', the easiest way to do it was through charitable works, particularly among the less fortunate women who lived in the very poorest areas. One of the ladies who had the means, motive and opportunity to set up her own mission was Lady Henry Somerset. After a failed marriage and subsequent rejection by her social circle, she opened a mission hall in Ledbury where she personally worked.[44] This led her into more public work. Early in her career she went to the East End of London to address a meeting on the inequality of wealth in England with John Burns as a fellow speaker. She felt a little 'shy' about her role because she was as yet quite unused to speaking publicly.[45] Later she was to become one of the finest orators on the British public platform.[46]

Lady Henry Somerset's sister Lady Tavistock, strongly influenced, she claimed, by Catherine Booth's writings, yearned to do good works. She was experiencing 'this great new blessing of joy and peace in God' and she intended 'to sit at His feet til I do hear His word and then go and do it I hope'.[47] But Lady Tavistock, more mindful than her sister of public opinion and the pressures of her class, contented herself with setting up socially acceptable and, at the time, fashionable 'ladies prayer meetings' for upper-class women in London during the 'Season'.[48]

The prayer meetings brought to England by American evangelists were popular among all classes. Business people found that a lunchtime prayer meeting helped them through the day, while women found parlour prayer meetings acceptable to the most conservative families. Some of these prayer meetings were organized by ministers and some by laymen. They were easy to set up, needed no special facilities, and could be led by any man or woman with no special training. They were adopted by many women's Christian groups who saw them as an institution particularly suited to women at home. They also became a means of making female associations devoted to secular reform acceptable to many very proper Christians: The British Women's Temperance Association, for example, made prayer meetings an important part of its activities.

THE GOSPEL TEMPERANCE MOVEMENT

Following on the heels of the revival spirit generated by the American evangelists in the 1850s and 1860s came another movement, also from across the Atlantic, in the 1870s. Combining both religion and temperance, the Gospel Temperance movement drew into its fold not only the traditional Protestant mission workers and supporters, but also the temperance faithful.

Gospel temperance received its start in America when evangelical religion combined with 'moral suasion' temperance. Men and women were called on for personal rejection of alcoholic beverages, because it was morally and socially evil. The movement got its greatest impetus from the Women's Whisky War of 1873, started when some women in Hillsboro, Ohio, distressed by the drunkenness in their families and town, decided they had had enough. They organized prayer meetings in the streets, in front of the most notorious taverns, and managed to force them closed. With news of this success, women in other American towns organized to do the same.

In August 1874, while attending a National Sunday School Assembly, women from the Whisky War held a national women's convention to discuss the drink problem. Meeting in Cleveland, on November 18 to 20, 1874, they founded the Women's Christian Temperance Union. A charismatic woman, Frances Willard, was first elected as corresponding secretary and then, in 1879, as president. In 1874 the WCTU joined with another temperance organization, The Reform Club and Blue Ribbon Association, to create the gospel temperance movement. Utilizing the talents of both male and female advocates, the movement spread throughout the United

States, with Francis Murphy and 'Mother' Stewart among its most visible leaders.

The Gospel Temperance movement was officially brought to England from the United States in 1877 by a Londoner, William Noble. Eventually Gospel Temperance Mission Halls were established in many parts of the country and from 1880 to 1885 England was gripped by a temperance fever that rose and fell continuously like the temperature of a sick man. Finally, by the end of the 1880s the movement burned itself out, but not before millions of English men and women had been recruited. Though some of these new adherents stayed on to fight the enemy of drink, others went on to work of a wider scope.[49]

In contrast to the American experience, British women did not lead, nor did they specifically identify with this new gospel temperance thrust; British women supplied none of the leading national missionaries, although individual women did important local work. With a revived public attention to mission work in the late 1860s and early 1870s, it was given a new respectability which eventually led to the public recognition of many of these local missionaries, female as well as male: Agnes Weston was made a Dame of the British Empire, and Elizabeth Ann Lewis, a well-known local missionary, was honoured by her town.

Mrs. Lewis's recognition was of particular importance to the many temperance women who laboured, often unknown and certainly unsung by the 'establishment', national or local. Many of their names are lost and their exploits unrecorded. But not Mrs. Lewis. She captured the imagination of northern English men and women when her story was told in a series of articles in a local paper, later collected and published as a book.[50] She also became involved in a great controversy leading to a law suit, when her enemies accused her of financial impropriety. She won the suit after an expensive and painful battle.[51] Her enemies had mounted the attack because her work had reduced business for the drinksellers in her town.

Elizabeth Ann Lewis was a woman from a temperance family, who, with the help of a supportive husband, set up her own mission. As a child her father had taken her to the outdoor temperance meetings he organized and addressed, but she was not actively involved until she was thirty-nine years old and married. It was when a Gospel Temperance mission came to her hometown of Blackburn, Lancashire, in 1882, that she began this work. The mission, a typically itinerant one, was to operate in the town for a specific time and then move on. Local men and women were recruited to help, to encourage their associates to attend, and to provide a residual corps of workers to carry on the mission's work. Mrs. Lewis, one of those who volunteered, found herself wanting to continue the work when it ended.

With funds supplied by her husband, she rented a hall, hired an assistant, and set up her own permanent mission. She organised a programme of house-to-house visitation and set up activities in the hall to promote temperance as well as evangelical Christianity. Her first audiences were drawn in by old-fashioned experience meetings.[52] Reformed drunkards went on the platform and recounted their experiences as drinkers, then told how they were saved, and finally described the benefits of salvation. Some of these men – for in England they were always men[53] – would embellish their accounts with lurid details sure to thrill the audience and thus make some of them local celebrities, assuring an invitation for repeat performances. The performances of the reformed drunkards soon drew in crowds, and Mrs. Lewis's mission became a success.[54] In 1910, when the royal family visited Blackburn Mrs. Lewis was presented to them.

In Cardiff a Miss Tilly (later to become Mrs. Cadot) started a mission for foreign seaman in 1878. Twenty-five years later the mission was still flourishing, having received important help from local philanthropists, male and female, who enabled Miss Tilly to supply non-alcoholic refreshments to the seamen as well as carry on Christian mission activities.[55]

In Bristol in the 1870s, a Mrs. Terrett started another gospel temperance mission with its headquarters at her Mission Hall. It was an era of 'armies'. Mrs. Terrett called her mission the 'White Army'; she was its 'General' and her husband its 'Lt. General'. Companies were established through the south of England led by 'colonels', 'majors,' and 'captains' with total abstinence required of all her 'soldiers'.[56] These armies were saving souls for Christianity, the spiritual counterpart of the armies defending British power abroad.

There were many religious armies in late Victorian England, but the most famous was, of course, the Salvation Army. Founded by Catherine and William Booth it was one of the few religious organizations of the period to acknowledge women as equals and encourage them in leadership positions. Many working-class women were recruited and trained for public work, and the most talented were given organizational duties and promoted to the upper ranks. In the Salvation Army many women acquired valuable skills that were not often found among females in any segment of English Victorian society. In that way this organization added greatly to the women's fight for equality.[57] Catherine Booth, although she was no proponent of women's secular rights played an important role in asserting the spiritual equality of women;[58] and by her actions and writings she, like other leading women of her day, became a role model for women who wanted to repeat her successes in other fields.

The great majority of women who ran their own missions remain unsung except in local histories, many of them already lost. Few today know of Miss Watson's successful Gospel Temperance Mission in Newcastle in the late nineteenth century,[59] or of the women in Pendleton, a small village near Manchester, who started a women-only Gospel Temperance mission in 1890. It met every Monday night for two months.[60] Often only by chance do we learn about the members of this great army of women who worked in all areas of the Gospel Temperance movement.

WOMEN AND THE CHURCHES

The efforts of the Church of England to bring the Church closer to the people were successful. By 1880 they had reversed the drift away from the established church and started to win back some fallen-away sections of the population. The Methodists continued to flourish but now turned inward and created their own separate world focused on the local chapel.[61] The discord between the churches, sects and even religions was muted in the late nineteenth century, but this was because all religions were challenged by a plethora of laic organizations, forerunners of the coming secular age.[62]

But for all the support and work women had given to the churches, especially to the established religion, their position in the halls of religious power had not changed. By 1890 they were no more included in the decision-making of the churches than before. In some ways, analogous to the political realm in the post-1832 years, their position had deteriorated. Whereas formerly custom only had prevented their participation in Church of England councils, in 1892 by decree they were denied any right to be involved.[63] When the Church Congress met at Folkestone that year women could only participate through a separate women's meeting. It was the same for the Baptist women at a Missionary Congress: They met separately from men. *The Woman's Herald* commented drily: 'We are, of course, aware that whenever money is being raised, the aid of women is heartily welcomed by men and no awkward questions as to their sphere and domestic duties are brought forward.'[64]

The official view of women in the established church remained unchanged. As the Canon of St. Paul's, the Rev. H. P. Liddon stated: 'The social position of women is fixed by the natural laws of God, and not by any human and arbitrary conventionalism of later date.'[65] Thus, for all their 'good works' and support of the church, Anglican women found that they still had no official part in Church policy. In the words of one of the foremost Anglican historians, Brian Heeney:

> until the twentieth century women occupied virtually no positions of leadership or responsibility in the official life of the Church at any level . . . They were excluded both from spiritual leadership and from secular management. Women's sphere in the late Victorian Church was decidedly subordinate, limited and controlled everywhere by the authority of men.[66]

Though the religious situation seemed discouraging to many women who wanted a voice in their churches, the effects of the evangelical revival of the mid-nineteenth century were significant outside the churches. Eventually it would bring lasting change to the role of women in the British temperance movement and attract into public life other women who, without the religious component, would not have ventured into public activities. For the women already working within the English temperance movement, it gave an opportunity to emerge and organize their own reform.

8 Reform Leadership

From its inception women were active in the British anti-drink movement but, as we have already seen, in a very limited role.[1] They laboured either quietly and without official positions in the mixed societies, or organized into special female auxiliaries charged with working only among women and children. Particularly in the various juvenile temperance groups were women active in the local groups. It was a woman, Anne Jane Carlile who together with a Baptist minister, Jabez Tunnicliffe, founded the Band of Hope, the largest of the juvenile groups, and it was women who were the backbone of this movement. One prominent male temperance advocate asserted that the bands 'never fail if women are involved'.[2] The Band of Hope was a truly British contribution to the temperance reform and, conforming to standard British practises, men filled its official positions at all levels: city, county and national. In other juvenile organizations, too, women were the workers in the field, not the leaders.

Women were also to be found in a few widely dispersed and isolated female groups that functioned locally. Though attempts were made to draw them together in some type of union, they remained separate. On May 27, 1853 the London-based National Temperance Society,[3] one of the most important supporters of women in temperance, held a conference of between forty and fifty ladies. A ladies' committee was set up which, in announcing the formation of a temperance society, issued an 'Address to the Women of England'. Six thousand copies were circulated to all known female groups, with the result that 'communication opened up with Temperance women throughout the country'.[4] Officers of this Ladies Committee Temperance Society were elected, some from the provinces, and branch societies were formed in 'London, Liverpool, Birmingham, Gloucester, Canterbury, Chichester, Stroud, etc.'[5]

Though a number of branches were said to have been set up in England by this society, most only functioned intermittently, and eventually all but one faded away.[6] At least the Birmingham Ladies Temperance Association, which heeded the call of the address in 1853, was still in existence more than fifteen years later. It did the work the National Temperance Society had hoped would be done, interesting the educated classes in the temperance cause; clergymen, medical men, and Sunday School teachers were especially targeted. The Birmingham Association also sponsored temperance work among invalids and hired missionaries to promote teetotalism among working men and women.[7]

On its first anniversary, in May 1854, the central association of the Ladies Committee Temperance Society in London appeared to be thriving. More than 200 came to celebrate at a meeting presided over by Mr. L. Heyworth, a Member of Parliament. On its second anniversary, this society put out a report but appears to have had no meeting. Almost immediately after the report was issued, due to circumstances that are unknown today, the Ladies Committee Temperance Society was dissolved and faded into obscurity.[8] The decade of the fifties was a very slow period for all parts of the temperance movement.[9]

JULIA B. WIGHTMAN: A TEMPERANCE PATHFINDER

One important consequence of the National Temperance Society's ladies' meeting of 1853 was that the famous temperance advocate Mr. J. B. Gough, who had come from the United States to tour Britain on a 'temperance mission', was retained to address two meetings on the ladies' behalf, one held in London in April, 1854, and the other in Gloucester soon afterwards. He also addressed 2,000 women in Glasgow.[10] Mr. Gough was responsible for 'converting' a number of influential upper-class English men and women to temperance. (Lady Jane Ellice and Mrs. Margaret Parker of Dundee were both converted to total abstinence by James B. Gough.)[11]

Even though Mr. Gough involved a number of English women in the temperance cause, it was an English clergyman's wife who was to have the greatest effect on women in temperance in the 1860s. Mrs. Julia B. Wightman started out like many other clergymen's wives; her first meeting in 1858 was a Bible reading. Like many others before her she also visited the poor and the sick in their homes. She changed her work after she read *English Hearts and English Hands*, by a well known mission worker Catherine Marsh. This book 'opened up new ideas to me *in the method* of working', wrote Mrs. Wightman, and she felt 'stirred' to follow the example of Miss Marsh.[12] Mrs. Wightman did not originally want to promote temperance. She confessed that she had not been personally attracted to the movement, thinking that its pledge was for the weak-willed; but teetotalism, she had concluded, 'arose from the *necessity* of the case'.[13]

She visited the poor and the sick and then, trying to do more for the women, started cottage prayer meetings just for them. She expanded her activities by organizing a workingmen's group, and then established a hall with an associated temperance society for both men and women. She was criticized by some clergymen for allowing women to sign the pledge.[14] Of great importance when she exercised authority was the deference she was given by the working men. These lower-class men regarded her as being socially above them – in the class of her clergyman husband.[15]

Eventually the work of Mrs. Wightman became so well known that she was encouraged to write about it. The first edition of 2,000 copies of her book *Haste To The Rescue*, published in 1859, was quickly followed by a second edition of 4,000 and a third, two months later, of 8,000. Altogether 26,000 copies were officially published in fourteen months. (A pirated edition was published in the United States.)[16] Ten thousand copies were printed in a cheap edition for the National Temperance League which were sent to the clergy of the Church of England.[17] Mrs. Wightman and her book were credited by the Reverend Henry J. Ellison, historian of the Church temperance movement, with helping create an interest in temperance among Anglicans that led to the creation of the Church of England Temperance Society.[18]

In the introduction Mrs. Wightman acknowledged that it was written for 'the educated classes' and had a single object, 'the stirring up of every heart to more earnest and prayerful effort to rescue those who are placed by God in a less favoured position . . . '. In its conclusion Mrs. Wightman wrote:

> Women of England, if no one else will take up this subject as it deserves, will you do so? . . . Oh, stand not aloof from this cause for any puerile reason! SOULS ARE PERISHING . . . . By your hearty, loving, and steady influence you will get multitudes in all classes of society to banish this hateful poison, alcohol, in every form.[19]

Part of Mrs. Wightman's importance in influencing other women stems from her status as a clergyman's wife, to most Britons eminently respectable. She always included religion, prayers, and Bible readings as part of the agenda of her meetings, but, at the same time, was careful not to take on an ordained man's role. Even so, one woman told her she would make *chartists* of the lower classes by her work.[20] Criticism also came because of its public nature. In the 1850s it was 'considered an unwomanly thing for a woman to occupy a public position'.[21] But once Mrs. Wightman overcame personal qualms about her work, she never hesitated. The money from her book she used to build a Working Men's Hall in 1864, still flourishing almost twenty years later, according to *The Temperance Chronicle*.[22]

Mrs. Wightman started her work at a time when there was a great evangelical revival in England and so the public mood was more receptive to Christian rescue work than it would have been in the 1840s.[23] It was also a time when there was a great distance between the classes of the community. Her sympathetic biographer, the Rev. Fletcher, describes her 'patronizing spirit and kindly condescension'.[24] Such an attitude towards the working classes would not have been tolerated half a century later, especially from a woman.

A CALL TO LADIES

Meanwhile in London the National Temperance League, as the National Temperance Society was now called, concerned at the lack of success of their attempt in 1853 to set up a national ladies temperance organization, decided in 1860 to try again. This time they directed their efforts at the upper classes with the hope that the 'ladies could be induced to forgo their glass of wine'. The National Temperance League appointed a Mrs. William Fison as its main organizer. A well-known author, she wrote at least two books, *Hints for the Earnest Student* published in 1850 and *The Secret of a Healthy Home* published in 1862, as well as a number of tracts and articles dealing with both temperance reform and sanitary reform. She had also set up local ladies temperance groups in Dublin, Bath and other towns.[25] She was a very talented woman, particularly skillful in running Drawing-Room meetings and *conversaziones* – social gatherings very fashionable at this time.

A meeting took place in London in July, 1860 inaugurating the Ladies National Association for Promoting Temperance, which was to organize Drawing-Room meetings. It was also to work with such established groups as the Prisoners' Aid Society, the Temperance League, the Ladies Sanitary Association, and the Elizabeth Fry Society. In this effort Mrs. Fison, during its first year, held over one hundred meetings throughout the country and she was a major force in founding twenty-two branches of this Ladies Association.[26] The Ladies National Association was active for a number of years, but in 1866 Mrs. Fison died and so did much of the association's work.[27]

By the middle of the nineteenth century Drawing-Room meetings were becoming popular as upper-class women for various reasons joined reforming movements. This kind of meeting was seen to have several advantages. Admission to them was by invitation only, unlike public meetings open to all; the organizers could target those ladies they wanted to influence by restricting their invitations to the desired group. They convened in the afternoon and were generally for ladies only. This was important for both those who came to talk and those who came to listen. Many ladies were willing to address or attend a private all-female meeting, but would not do so at an open 'promiscuous' (mixed) public meeting. Some women got their first experience in public speaking before these small drawing-room gatherings.

In London in 1862 an International Temperance and Prohibition conference was held. Only one woman was listed as an official delegate, a Miss Chapman representing the Band of Hope and Abstainers Union of Frome. She was apparently the solitary female delegate , even in the section devoted to juvenile organizations, and no woman was listed as an officer of this or any other section. To be sure, Mrs. Clara Lucas Balfour, the veteran temperance writer, lecturer,[28] and editor of the *Juvenile Abstainer*, who had also written many popular children's temperance stories, was listed as a speaker, one of six, on the Band of Hope program. She contributed a paper and, though she had originally planned to come and read it, a male substitute did it for her. In the general discussion that followed the papers in this section, the discussants talked extensively of their experiences while working among the children, but in the printed report of the conference only men's comments were given; whether Miss Chapman or any other woman spoke up, we do not know – there was nothing published about mothers and daughters, only about fathers and sons.[29]

In the whole conference only four papers, out of a total of seventy-five, were given by women. One, a paper by Charlotte H. Ferguson of Preston, had the topic of 'Women's Work in the Temperance Reform'. It was mostly a very traditional view, covering all the acceptable tenets. She discussed the women's 'social and domestic relations' as the proper locus of female activity as they worked for the temperance reformation. She also gave the then traditional view of temperance workers that women were the victims of male intemperance, and had the role of protecting the children from the damage inflicted on a family by a drunken father. The role of women as instructors of youth in the home and the Sunday School was also discussed.

In one respect this paper went further than many temperance supporters would have liked by asserting 'the imperative need of women's societies, managed by women' to work with women. Mrs. Ferguson called on 'temperance women everywhere to band themselves together in societies that they might labour together in a field hitherto hardly cultivated';[30] she argued that women have a natural aptitude for rescue work because they have the 'natural wise simplicity of a loving heart', though many are held back by 'paltry conventional trammels'.[31] She told the convention that a woman 'may use her influence in countless ways, and without the slightest outrage to the natural retiringness of her disposition'. Finally this temperance advocate called on women to help with local prohibition by persuading their menfolk and other voters to help candidates who supported the 'Permissive Bill'. Though they did not have the vote women could have a strong influence on those who did.[32]

Two other papers were given by women at this conference, one by Mrs. Fison of the Ladies Association on 'Sanitary Laws the True Basis of Temperance Work', very much to the point of her concerns with both the sanitary and the temperance reforms. She had the year before, in 1861, spoken before the Social Science Congress and the British Science Association. The fourth paper, by Miss Florence Hill, dealt with the liquor trade, which she called 'The Unholy Alliance'.

ROLE MODELS

In 1867, just two years after the death of Mrs Fison, the National Temperance League again attempted to attract ladies into the temperance cause by arranging a series of afternoon meetings for them. But now, without Mrs. Fison, the League needed to have a good drawing card to encourage those not previously involved in the cause to volunteer. The best way, the League discovered, was to provide what we would now call role models for the women, showing what other women had done before – women from ordinary backgrounds who had found personal rewards in their temperance missions. Thus, in 1868, on May 26, the League held a conference in London at which well-known temperance women were asked to give papers on their work. (The collected papers were later published as *Women's Work in the Temperance Reformation* and circulated among women's temperance groups.)[33]

Three hundred ladies came to the City Terminus Hotel, London, for the gathering, which started with a silent prayer.[34] After an introduction by Mrs. S. C. Hall, a well-known authoress, twelve papers were given, by some of the best-known women in temperance. Mrs. Balfour, writer and worker for the Band of Hope movement, who was to become the head of the women's temperance movement soon after it was founded in the following decade,[35] gave the first paper. She argued that the vice of intemperance is in three ways different in women than in men: Women's drinking is less a social vice because women are often secret drinkers; a woman is reclaimed with greater difficulty; and intemperate women are judged more harshly by society. These were all standard views of the time, although the second was later disproved by the experiences of the 'Asylums for Inebriates'.[36]

Mrs. Sarah Stickney Ellis gave the next paper. She was orginally a Quaker who became a member of the Congregational church when she married a missionary of that faith. One of the first women to write on women's social role and the author of a number of books dealing with women's behavior, Mrs. Ellis also ran a school for young ladies and became a great supporter of female education. A thirty-year veteran in the temperance reform, she aimed her paper at women charged with the care of children and told them to ask themselves, 'What have I done with those opportunities which God gave me with the young?'

Mrs. Wightman contributed an account of her experiences, from her start in Cottage Bible readings. She described organizing the workingmen's hall in her husband's parish, at a cost more than four thousand pounds. She also spoke about her work in setting up temperance refreshment rooms on market day so that the farmers and their wives could have an alternative to the local public house. The impact of Mrs. Wightman's book *Haste to the Rescue* on a large number of women was clearly revealed at this gathering.[37] Here, just nine years after the book's first appearance, four out of twelve women recounting their personal experiences credited Mrs. Wightman's book with inspiring them to begin their own temperance societies.[38]

For instance Mrs. Lucas-Shadwell, who had sent a paper to be read by her husband, wrote that after she had read *Haste to the Rescue*: 'The thought arose, is there anyone whom *I* can rescue?' Living in a rural area, she created her own temperance society of over three hundred members at the time of this conference. Another speaker from a rural district in Shropshire, Mrs. Lumb, said that she too was influenced by *Haste to the Rescue* to become a teetotaler and join the temperance movement. She started a temperance hotel and refreshment room at the local railway hotel after she had raised 1,300 pounds to buy it. There she arranged for sleeping accomodations as well as a recreational hall, and the hotel became a center of local social life. It also had a reading room and large lecture hall, which could be made into a coffee room and a commercial room when not in use. Prayer meetings as well as temperance meetings were held there.

Miss Hatford Battersby, another speaker, was influenced by *Haste to the Rescue* as she believed many others were. She was already doing temperance work, but after reading the book she altered her philosophy and methods of handling excessive drinking, now deciding that 'it had been Gospel Temperance that was really needed': A religious approach to intemperance was more effective than the traditional secular one.[39]

She followed Mrs. Wightman by organizing a temperance society in the schoolrooms of a parish where the vicar, though not himself a teetotaller, gave his support to her efforts.

Miss Sarah Robinson, popularly known as the 'Soldier's Friend', although not present at the original meeting wrote a paper for the resulting volume. She, too, stated that she started in mission work only after learning of Julia Wightman's experiences.[40] Like Mrs. Wightman she was an Anglican, but without a direct connection to the established church. Her special concern was religious and temperance work among the soldiers in the British Army at her Mission Hall in Aldershot. Another paper included in the volume from a worker not present at the conference was by Mrs. Sturge of Birmingham, a member of a well-known Quaker family prominent in many public causes. Her topic was the Birmingham Ladies Temperance Association, a survivor of the 1853 organizing movement that continued to flourish because it enrolled members of many religious denominations.[41]

The conference was a great success and the book it sponsored received wide circulation. It prompted many women to ask themselves, like Mrs. Lucas-Shadwell, if they could do anything to help in temperance or other rescue work. Many of the speakers, role models themselves, went on to greater achievements in temperance and other reforms with many other women who saw an opportunity to help those less fortunate than themselves. The decade after that conference was an important one for women in British public life, especially for those in the temperance movement.

WOMEN MISSIONERS IN ARMY AND NAVY: SARAH ROBINSON AND AGNES WESTON

Miss Sarah Robinson, one of those who sent a paper to the 1868 London conference, had already become a model for many temperance women, and was nationally famous for her work among the soldiers. In 1862 she had met an officer's widow, a Mrs Daniell who was planning to do mission work among the soldiers. A staunch Christian evangelical, Mrs. Daniell unlike Miss Robinson was not personally a teetotaler nor a temperance advocate. In 1863 Mrs. Daniell opened a mission hall with Miss Robinson as her assistant. But Mrs. Daniell was a cautious woman, and, to avoid any criticism over her female leadership, put her 'Aldershot Mission Hall and Soldiers' Home' under male authority. As a result Miss Robinson left the mission and returned home.[42] Soon she was working in other military posts promoting teetotalism among the soldiers.

When Mrs. Daniell died in 1871 Miss Robinson returned to Aldershot where she took over the Mission Hall and its work. Under Mrs. Daniell, the Mission Hall had been run on very narrow lines, with the work being 'too religious and too sectarian to be widely appreciated by the soldiers'.[43] When Miss Robinson took charge she continued the Bible teaching but muted the evangelicalism. But her most important role was in the field. With the financial help of the National Temperance League she outfitted and ran a mobile coffee canteen for troops on manoeuvres.[44] Selling nonalcoholic refreshment she helped promote temperance among the troops. Both her Bible lessons and her teetotalism made her an object of hostility among some of the troops but she obtained the support of the army hierarchy. Her work was officially acknowledged by the army when the Secretary for War formally visited one of her canteens, leading to a spate of publicity in English newspapers.[45]

In 1874 Miss Robinson and her associates raised seven thousand pounds to pay for a Soldier's Institute at Portsmouth. Portsmouth was the official port of embarkation for British troops going for service abroad; there the soldiers had to leave behind all those not 'on the strength' of the regiment, mostly wives they had married without permission, and their children. Frequently these dependents were destitute with no place to go; Miss Robinson's Institute took care of them. It also took on responsibility for dependents of soldiers killed abroad.[46] The Institute helped wives and families who came to Portsmouth to greet arriving soldiers, and aided returning sick and wounded troops on their way to a hospital in England.[47] All this work was essential at a time when army reforms were a public issue, but the Army was not yet funded to provide the social services. Eventually they were taken over by the Army when the need became too great for private philanthropy. In the meantime Miss Robinson and her workers were saving the taxpayers a great deal of money and the army a lot of trouble. So famous did this Institute become that the Duke of Cambridge, who was the Commander-in-Chief of the British Army, and the Prince of Wales both visited it.[48]

No doubt Miss Robinson was accepted by the military establishment in part because 'she endeavours to make men contented with their profession . . . . She said "my influence has often decided men to remain in the army and serve God there".'[49] Her personality must also have contributed to her success with the army hierarchy. A bold, brash, energetic woman might have been in fact or perception a threat to those in charge. But Miss Robinson was an unassertive woman who spent most of her life with a 'body encased in steel', in constant pain from a damaged spine.[50] Miss

Robinson was too self-conscious on the public platform to be a good speaker and she avoided speaking whenever possible.[51]

Miss Robinson's naval counterpart was Agnes Weston, also an Anglican who went into anti-drink work through the influence of another woman – in this case an unmarried friend, a Miss Wintz[52] – and the urging of her evangelical parish priest, the Rev. James Fleming. The daughter of a Bristol barrister, Agnes Weston went into lifetime missionary work that had a profound effect on a large segment of the Royal Navy.[53]

Never a drinker, Agnes Weston joined the temperance movement and signed the total abstinence pledge to encourage others to abstain.[54] After a first missionary post in Bath, in the early 1870's she moved to Devonport where she worked among the young boys in naval training. Hearing about her activities, the National Temperance League invited her to work with them, which she did. Beginning in 1873, together they set up a number of 'Sailors' Rests' which were to serve as alcohol-free centers for navy men.[55] Supplying a place for them to sleep and a center for their recreation, Agnes Weston also organized prayer meetings and temperance talks.

Navy authorities supported her work: She was very much an 'establishment' figure who, like her Army counterpart Miss Robinson, did important work for the service. Drink was a terrible problem for sailors at this time, because many were lonely ashore and tried to fill the void in the public house. Furthermore, when released from a ship after a voyage, sailors frequently had large amounts of money – accumulated pay – in their pockets, which made them targets of unscrupulous schemes and attacks. In order to prevent this and encourage financial responsibility, Miss Weston and her workers set up banking services for sailors and their families. She became a national figure identified with the Royal Navy and for her work was made a Dame of the British Empire. Her story was told in her autobiography, *My Life Among the Bluejackets*.

During her career Agnes Weston controlled a large business organization, which by 1905 was worth more than a hundred thousand pounds. It included 'Sailors' Rests' in three towns as well as other assets. Her appeals for funds were always successful: Up to World War I the public gave over one million pounds – over one thousand at a single Drawing-Room meeting – for her work.[56] She was accused by one sailor of 'lining her pocket,' but there was no evidence of this. Many enemies, particularly among the drink sellers, were constantly looking for an excuse to bring her into disrepute and cripple her temperance work, but this never happened because she was always careful handling funds.[57] An accountant audited her books and she published balance sheets every year.[58]

The stories of Mrs Wightman and the Misses Robinson and Weston were widely publicized by the temperance movement, which was extremely sophisticated about publicity and lost no opportunity to exploit the activities of anti-drink workers in furthering their reform. These women, all very respectable, became much admired examples for middle-class girls and women seeking a larger role in society than the strangulating domestic one. Of immense importance to many women economically dependent on others was the financial support the temperance movement was willing to give to almost any respectable group doing temperance work. Many temperance organizations encouraged women to work actively in the field so long as they did not bring the movement negative publicity.[59]

However, although the National Temperance League was in the forefront of any effort to encourage women to take a public stand for temperance, they appointed none to their official governing bodies. On the executive of the National Temperance League were to be found many prominent, establishment Englishmen, including a number of Anglican clergymen, but no women.[60]

Part Three

1875–1900: The Great Shout

Part Three
1875–1900: The Great Shout

THE FRANCHISE

In pre-nineteenth century England the franchise theoretically was given on a representative basis; those who had the vote were to use it in the interests of the whole community. In the unreformed Parliament the franchise was tied to places and certain segments of the population according to past priorities, and once given it was never taken back. As a result, many areas had the franchise that no longer could justify it; these *rotten boroughs* had declined over the centuries and lost their populations but not their representation. There were also recently populated areas, such as Manchester, with little, if any, representation. The system was justified on the grounds that those who had the vote were 'trustees for the general population';[1] in this way Parliament could be said to represent all of Britain in its collectivity.

Despite its anomalies, the old Parliament was in many ways more representative of the English population than the reformed Parliament of 1832. In its unreformed state more diverse sections of the population were directly represented: Poor householders in Preston with the 'Scot and Lot' franchise[2] and property-owning women in various parts of England had the franchise.[3] There were no stated gender prohibitions or rigid national property qualifications in the old Parliaments; these came with the 'reformed' House.

By the suffrage based on property and gender, the franchise became a right connected to a man's investment in the society. However, when votes were allotted in this way voters could no longer be reasonably viewed as 'trustees for their neighbors'. The whole basis on which the franchise was granted had been altered. With this departure from ancient tradition the barriers to other changes were weakened, especially changes in the amount of property required for the vote. Ten pounds was merely an arbitrary amount put into the 1832 Reform Bill without any historical or rational significance.

When property became the primary basis for the franchise the gender restriction was seen by many as discriminating against women property owners; Henry Hunt argued this in petitioning Parliament on behalf of a Yorkshire woman of property.[4] The 1867 and 1884 Reform Bills successively reduced the importance of property as 'lodgers' became eligible to vote. Even so, women were still firmly excluded, the last major segment of the adult population to be denied a vote on the grounds that they were represented by others.

A NEW FRAME OF REFERENCE FOR WOMEN

The exclusion of women from the franchise took on new importance as the women themselves began to acknowledge discrimination against them. Up until the middle of the nineteenth century women in Britain did not see themselves as having separate concerns from their menfolk: Women and men of similar rank shared the same interests and perspectives, and social status was more important than gender. Now economic, political and social developments were setting men and women apart. The doctrine of the two spheres which assigned to women a strictly domestic role, marginalized them economically and excluded them from political life. After their husbands and sons had been admitted to the franchise the women were left with a feeling of inferiority, of being 'second class' citizens without a voice in their own destiny.

The men talked of 'the family' as a social unit, but the family was a legal autocracy with the father having ultimate control over the person and the property of all the members. Men could legally beat their wives as well as appropriate any monies their spouses had earned. Middle-class women in particular, unprotected by legal settlements, became aware that they were dependents with no more economic and political rights than their children. Furthermore, the power that the men gained was used to further their own interests and not that of the community as a whole, or so many women came to believe.

So began the realization that there was a 'Woman Question' – a cluster of issues revolving around the role and position of women in the family and in society. Just as there was talk in the late nineteenth century of the 'Irish Question' and the 'Drink Question', so was there debate on the Woman Question. The phrase itself was unpopular among many English women. Unlike the term 'feminism', which implied a positive commitment to equality between the sexes, involvement with the Woman Question could come from a positive or negative position on women's rights. However, the emergence of the Woman Question signified an awareness that in nineteenth century England men and women could have distinct interests, economically, politically, and socially; and that dependence of women on men could be disadvantageous if the two interests came to diverge. Such divergence was indeed occurring economically, as 'surplus' women in need of employment were shut out of many professions and businesses – even from those in which they had traditionally worked. And, as we shall see, it was for many women epitomized politically and socially by the Contagious Diseases Acts, which took away the civil rights of certain women in order to protect the well-being of a group of men. But most fundamental, women came to believe, was their exclusion from the franchise.

THE KEY TO ALL REFORM

In the nineteenth century Parliament was increasingly viewed as the great agency for change. All groups seeking protection or advancement had to find a means of influencing the national government. The most direct was to elect sympathetic Members of Parliament, but this required the franchise. After the Reform Act of 1832, which enfranchised only upper- and middle-class males, there was unhappiness among excluded women and working-class men. Agitation for further reform was strong throughout the forties, dropped somewhat in the fifties, then surged again with renewed urgency in the 1860s. Working men, because they wanted the economic protection that the vote would give them, made it clear that they would continue their demands with great insistence; both Conservatives and Liberals knew that an inevitable expansion of the electorate would have to include them, especially in urban areas. Women too wanted a voice in Parliament, but lacked organization and lobbying skills, and above all the clear sense of their distinctive interests that working-class movements were developing. Women were decades behind in pressuring the government for the franchise.

In 1867 the first suffrage society for women, the Kensington Society, was formed by the Langham Circle, the London-based group of women dedicated to equal rights.[5] In that same year John Stuart Mill presented a women's suffrage petition to Parliament, making a major speech in the House of Commons in its support. Nothing official came of these efforts and the 1867 Reform Bill enfranchised only working-class males. From this time on, however, women's suffrage, both in local and national elections, was an issue that would not go away. In the 1860s, 1870s and 1880s, women's suffrage was just one of the many issues that made up the 'Woman Question', but later it came to dominate all women's organizations. Like working men before them, women came to accept the franchise as the key to all reform.

As in all public policy issues, there were many people uninterested in the matter, but activists wanted to force the question on all the public, believing that when injustices to women were revealed and understood, a national movement to rectify the situation would follow. Their first move was to draw into the agitation women already involved in public affairs: They were the natural leaders for less liberated women. Women's groups thus became targets for penetration by evangelizing suffragists. The women in the temperance movement confronted this issue as did the women in the political associations. All women had to take sides; and those who refused to support the demand for suffrage found themselves increasingly isolated from the mainstream of women's activities.

By the 1890s the continuing lack of response by the British government to the needs of women activated many formerly uncommitted women to take up the suffrage cause. The scattered voices of the women of the 1860s and 1870s were amplified in the 80s and 90s into a great shout that before long was to bring down the walls of political exclusion.

9 Speaking Out

The leaders of female reform movements of the 1860s and 1870s had the enormous task of bringing women out of their isolated, parochial world into the mainstream of national public life. Unlike men who were away from home in their workplaces or clubs, middle-class women had no easy access to the larger world; they were effectively imprisoned by the prevailing rules of etiquette. To bring them from obscurity into visibility an active network of women was needed; and this was created by a handful of dedicated women working in various organizations.

One important tool was the official journal. In the last quarter of the nineteenth century, each woman's organization gave top priority to establishing and sustaining a journal that was circulated to the membership and not only educated them in organizational matters but gave them a sense of being part of a larger group – no longer isolated and unimportant. The consciousness-raising of these publications was essential. Many women had come to accept their lot as the *natural* condition of women: God and nature had placed them in a separate sphere from men. Challenges to existing conditions usually occur only when problems appear;[1] a major role of these journals was to publicize issues affecting women and provide women's perspectives on their resolution.

It was also important to show that women had the ability to organize, run, and write for their own papers, particularly as the early papers, even of women's organizations, were edited and run by men.[2] The need for a regular publication owned and run by women for women was a lesson the American women had emphasized to their English sisters.[3] The experience women gained in this work proved a significant asset in promoting women's issues.

Especially in the last two decades of the nineteenth century, there was a proliferation of journals devoted to various women's issues. The Ladies National Association opposing the Contagious Diseases Acts in 1870 began to publish and distributed its weekly, *The Shield*. The British Women's Temperance Association started its *Journal* in 1883; it played a prominent part in the organization.[4] The *Women's Penny Paper*, started in October 27, 1888, originally covered a variety of women's issues, but in 1891, its name changed; it became *The Woman's Herald* and represented the prosuffrage faction of the Women's Liberal Federation. In 1893, *The Woman's Herald* became the organ of the temperance women and the following year was renamed a second time as *The Woman's Signal*. It was finally disbanded in 1899 when it lost its financing. There was also the *Woman's Gazette*, a journal of the Women's Liberal Federation, that lasted from 1888 to 1891. *Wings*, another important women's temperance journal founded in 1892, was issued monthly until 1925. It represented the Women's Total Abstinence Union – a strictly temperance organization. The breakaway Women's National Liberal Association set up its own publication, the *Quarterly Review of the Women's National Liberal Association*, which lasted from 1895 to 1918 (when the two Liberal branches amalgamated).[5]

No doubt there were many women who read one or more journals regularly, but compared to the number of women in the total population their readership was never great. Many women, even middle-class women, had no money for such luxuries, especially if their husbands did not support the cause; and there were others who were not great readers. But those women who lived in the towns and cities in the late nineteenth century had other sources of information. Perhaps the most important was the public platform.

ONTO THE PLATFORM

Traditionally, great oratory had been reserved for the pulpit. Preaching in church, or even, in some cases outside, was the most important means of communicating with the common people, who usually were not literate. Politicians before the Reform Act of 1832 did not go to the public, did not need to be good speakers, and generally were not. Not until the early nineteenth century do we find the public platform becoming the 'main engine of propaganda'. According to Lord Asquith, Liberal leader and Edwardian prime minister, it was the Anti-Corn Law League in the 1830s that pioneered the use of the platform in 'a systematic and continuous way'.[6] Cobden, Bright, and W. J. Fox, all of middle-class origin, were brilliant exemplars of this political oratory. Later, in the 1840s, the Chartists developed great speakers and used the public platform to promote their cause, finding that the best way to reach mass audiences was through large public meetings and attention-getting demonstrations. In the 1850s and 1860s the anti-drink movement organized great meetings, hiring such popular orators as James B. Gough to bring in the crowds.

Except for a special handful of women all the known speakers at this time were men. Before the 1870s few women would talk on the secular public platform. To do so they had to face many gender handicaps, the most important of which was the strong prejudice in nineteenth-century Britain, of both men and women, against women speaking in public.

Women were often at the forefront of evangelical movements, but even as preachers had faced great hostility. Though John Wesley allowed women to preach if they had an 'extraordinary call' from God, women in the pulpit were often only barely tolerated; once a sect became established and a professional class was organized to run it, women were forced out. It was so, as we have seen, in the Baptist, the Congregational and the Methodist churches. Women preachers were unwanted by the hierarchy in most organized churches until the twentieth century. And at the same time that the secular public platform evolved in the early and mid-nineteenth century there was a decline of women's political activism.[7] Except for a small number active in Chartism and the early and mid-nineteenth century social reform movements, women were generally absent from public life. Not until the last three decades of the century were their numbers greatly increased.

First lured out of their domestic world by social reform movements proliferating in early nineteenth century society – particularly anti-slave and temperance reforms – early women activists believed they were doing God's work. Even so, it was a rare woman who would mount a public platform and speak to a mixed audience. Only a handful, like Clara L. Balfour and Anne Carlile,[8] were willing and able to do so. When Harriet Beecher Stowe came to England on an anti-slave speaking tour, her brother read her speeches before mixed audiences while she herself sat quietly on the platform.[9]

In the 1850s and 1860s female evangelists from the United States opened a new era for women on the British platform. They, too, believed they were called by God to do His work. After these pioneers had breached the walls of public hostility against women preachers, a few brave middle-class English women followed their example The decision to gain the public platform usually came only after much anguish and self-searching. Catherine Booth made her first appearance in the pulpit in 1860 but only after months of 'inward conflict and reluctance' and the persuasion of her husband.[10] She told her listeners that she had 'by her silence, been disobeying God, and was resolved to do so no more'.[11] A woman speaking in public on a secular or religious platform was still a rarity even at this time.

CONVENTIONS OF THE PUBLIC PLATFORM

Most secular public meetings were organized according to a set formula that followed a traditional pattern. There were beginning exercises consisting of opening remarks and passage of a resolution of welcome to special individuals present. Then the business of the meeting was discussed and resolutions and amendments proposed and passed. Any special speaker would at this point stand up and give his address. When he had finished, there were closing exercises. A vote of thanks to the speaker had to be proposed and passed. Other resolutions of thanks to members of the platform party, especially if any notables were present, were adopted. Occasionally the audience would send up three cheers to show its appreciation for some special visitor or member of the platform group. Only then was the meeting brought to a close, in an orderly and sober manner.

Public meetings were not for entertaining but for educating those who came. The audience came to a meeting to be identified with the cause. Only in special cases was the speech of a star orator the main drawing card. Usually the platform party was selected with the hope they would draw to the meeting respectable public support for a cause espoused. Therefore, it was important to get someone of high social rank on the platform and preferably as the main speaker.[12] The chairman of the platform party was responsible for keeping order and seeing that the speakers attended to business.

This system worked to the disadvantage of women. The first problem was getting onto the platform. Members of the platform party had to be acceptable to the rest of that party. More than one man must have echoed the words of the Rev. Mr. McNield, who presided at a meeting where women appeared, reluctantly he said, because he 'was not clear in his mind about women appearing upon public platforms'.[13] But by 1875 when this remark was made, although such appearances were still condemned, they were less daring than in the 1850s, when only a rare woman would risk her good name and that of her family by appearing on a platform.

Further hurdles were the skills of running a meeting. Even for those with a natural talent for public speaking, there were many techniques essential for a successful platform career to be learned, and rules of public debate to be mastered. Newcomers had to learn the etiquette and traditions of platform work: setting up the business discussions, proposing resolutions, making amendments, and so on.

The speeches themselves were performances governed by custom. Most important perhaps was the way a speaker handled the audience. In Britain the audience continuously interacted with the speaker through various traditional responses. Shouting 'Hear, hear', as well as clapping and cheering showed the approval of the audience, while cries of 'Oh, oh', 'Shame, shame' and hisses indicated its disapproval. Calls of 'Time, time' and the stamping of the feet meant 'We are tired of you.' 'Question, question' meant the speaker had wandered from the topic, and 'Order, order' was a demand to silence unparliamentary language. If the audience felt that a speaker had talked too long, it would shout 'Chair, chair' to get the chairman to exercise his authority to get rid of the speaker.[14] Another popular method to get a long-winded speaker to terminate his peroration was for someone on the platform to pull his coat tails – this was one custom that women did not appropriate.[15]

This two-way communication between audience and speaker was important for a successful meeting. Speakers had to be sensitive to the mood of their audience and able to interpret its calls. Thus, if the speaker appeared to forget the audience, 'taps of heels' brought it back to mind.[16] In the United States audience etiquette was quite different, it appears. There audiences listened politely and undemonstratively; if they did not like the speech they just quietly departed. (The visiting English actor Kean commented that 'such an audience would extinguish Etna'.)[17]

FIRST RUNG ON THE LADDER

When Florence Balgarnie said in 1889 'I do not think that women speak as well as men. Women are, at present, but on the first rung of the ladder', she was indicating the tremendous advance women had made by even getting on the ladder of public speaking.[18] By this time more and more women were taking this step and while few were polished speakers, in the same league as the best of the male orators, many were learning and practising the craft. So many were volunteering to speak that the British Women's Temperance Association reported on it at their executive meeting of January, 1888.[19]

For women without previous exposure to public speaking, mounting a public platform for the first time to address a mixed audience was a step of gigantic proportions. Because many women gave their first speeches without any training and simply learned from their mistakes,[20] their initial efforts were traumatic occasions few ever forgot. Mrs. Humphrey Ward, the anti-suffrage leader, was terrified when she first spoke in public.[21] In 1890, when she was thirty-nine years old, she had agreed to speak in support of a Settlement Hall. Fortunately for her platform career she was a natural speaker and within two years of her platform baptism went on a speaking tour of England.[22]

Frequently the first speech was unplanned. Many women speakers took their initial steps onto the platform when some emergency arose. This was often caused by the nonappearance of a scheduled speaker: Any possible replacement was then pressed into service, even a complete novice. One veteran woman activist later recalled a temperance meeting in 1874 when the two well-known visiting speakers failed to arrive. The organizers were going to cancel the meeting but one of them – the only one with experience – quickly organised a platform program selecting speakers from among the women present. '"*You* (turning to me) must propose the first resolution, and you (to another lady who is now one of our best speakers) must second it . . . " Thus she assigned us each our work and herself set up the example by clearly stating why women should not touch drink . . . With knees that knocked together and trembling voices which almost refused to utter our thoughts, we followed the example thus nobly set us . . . '[23]

Florence Fenwick Miller, a medical doctor and well-known speaker on all women's issues,[24] had a similar initiation. In 1873, while still a medical student, she attended a public meeting with her father. When the opening speaker did not appear, the organizer, knowing her strong opinions on the topic, asked her to open the debate. Her father encouraged her to try. (Had her mother been with her, 'she would not have permitted my speaking', Dr. Miller wrote.) As a schoolgirl she had practised her public speaking skills when she ran an evening nursery church for the local children while her mother was at the real church service. Florence had been 'passionately religious' as a child and her sermons delivered from the kitchen steps were 'deeply felt, whatever they may have been otherwise'.[25]

Annie Besant also first practised public speaking in private sermonizing. As a young adult she had a great desire to see how it felt to preach. But that was in 1873 and she wrote: 'I saw no platform in the distance nor had any idea of possible speaking in the future dawned upon me. But the longing to find outlet in words came upon me.' She then declaimed to an empty church. Recalling the experience years later she wrote: 'I shall never forget the feeling of power and delight – but especially of power – that came upon me as I sent my voice ringing down the aisles . . . [26] She became one of the finest speakers of her day and one of her male listeners commented that 'the flaming fire of her eloquence must consume every man and woman who listened to her'.[27]

Mrs. Millicent Garrett Fawcett, one of the foremost speakers in British public life in the nineteenth century, made her first public appearance at the annual meeting of the British Association in 1868. Here she read the speech of her blind husband Professor Henry Fawcett. Mrs. Fawcett went on to make her own first speech in that same year when she addressed a women's suffrage meeting attended by John Stuart Mill, an early advocate of the women's cause.[28] At this time she wrote out and memorized her address so that she 'could have said it backwards. But I was terrified at having to speak'. Twenty years later she told an interviewer that she was not happy on the public platform and that she 'never liked speaking'.[29]

One of the most effective leaders of a reform movement, Mrs. Josephine Butler,[30] was fortunate to have her first controversial public speaking appearance carefully orchestrated by a young male colleague, Professor James Stuart. He chose a meeting of sympathetic railwaymen at the Mechanics' Institute in Crewe for her start, to which he escorted and introduced her. She knew she was breaking strong social taboos by addressing the audience, but her natural speaking talent emerged and she was a great successs.[31]

Like Mrs. Butler, some women were fortunate enough to have a gift for public speaking. One of the earliest women politicians was Lady Sandhurst. Born into a Conservative family, when she married a Liberal she became a Liberal herself. Elected to local office but then unseated on a technicality, she was an important public speaker for the cause of women in political life. Commented one journalist, 'When she begins to speak her special capacity for public work is shown at once. Her voice is deep, an incalculable advantage for a speech maker.'[32]

Mrs. Wynford Philipps, president of the Westminster Women's Liberal Association,[33] used to recite and teach elocution. As a girl she had wanted to go on the stage but as 'a ward in chancery' she was forbidden to do so. Joining the temperance movement, she made her first public speech on its platform. She was asked to become a lecturer for a national temperance association but instead married a politician and became a leader in the Women's Liberal Federation as well as a member of the executive of the Central National Committee for Women's Suffrage. This activist believed that women's problems with public speaking came because they tended to give up after a few attempts: 'Speaking is no easier than any other art,' she wrote, seeking to recruit others to the public platform.[34]

Men had the great advantage in the many opportunities available to them to practise speaking. Various clubs were often opened to male speakers who would address the members and receive criticism: Robert Walpole, for instance, was invited to rehearse one of his major House of Commons speeches before the Kit Kat club.[35] Men also enjoyed the facilities and help of debating societies that flourished in nineteenth-century England. For beginning women speakers there were sometimes drawing room meetings which provided a platform before other women.[36] In the late 1860s and early 1870s the only mixed group that accepted women and men as equal members was the temperance organization the Independent Order of the Good Templars.[37] The Good Templars focused on training its members, both female and male, for speaking in public on the anti-drink platform. Because of this work the Good Templars produced 'many good women speakers'.[38]

But for many upper- and middle-class women their first experiences in public speaking came through teaching in Sunday Schools. Particularly for upper-class girls, teaching the local children once a week was often their only useful work and for many it was the only break in a rather dull upbringing.[39] Laura Ormiston Chant, who became a well-known public speaker, started teaching Sunday School before she was fifteen. Lady Battersea's mother had a school for girls built in the local village where her daughter taught straw plaiting.[40] But even with this limited opportunity, such teaching was an important step toward speaking before a completely strange body.

Quaker women had an advantage over other women because they were not required to sit silently during religious exercises. In Friends' Meetings, unlike other religious services, all participants, male and female, were expected to speak if the spirit moved them.[41] The speech in such a situation was of a traditional 'sing-song' pattern which Quakers affected in their eighteenth- and nineteenth-century meetings.[42] Nevertheless, speaking out at meeting encouraged them to do so before others and gave them practise in organizing their thoughts while on their feet.[43] Perhaps for this reason many female Friends were among the best-known public speakers. Eliza Mary Sturge, for example, from a famous Birmingham Quaker family, made quite a reputation for herself as a public speaker when she spoke on women's rights in the 1870s. (She became the first woman elected to the Birmingham School Board.)

For most English women whose upbringing had taught that it was unnatural for women to speak out the psychological barriers against public speaking were great; only a dedicated or very strong-minded woman would do so. A female Tory candidate for the School Board in Bristol agreed to stand on condition 'she should not be asked to make a speech'.[44] Another Tory woman, a Miss Bignold 'unlike many Tory women spoke in public'.[45]

The Countess of Carlisle was a leading woman activist with little natural ability on the platform who nevertheless became an impressive speaker through a dedication to self-improvement and hard work. She told an audience of women, 'If you care enough about it you will forget your bashfulness and go and speak.'[46] For her, 'political ardour overcomes my diffidence'.[47] The Countess gave her first public speech in 1891 in support of the temperance reformation; she was encouraged by James Whyte, the Secretary of the United Kingdom Alliance, the prohibition organization. Her insecurity was revealed in the correspondence between them. Answering one letter from the Countess that expressed her misgivings about her speech at an anti-drink women's meeting, Whyte felt it necessary to reassure her: 'Whoever told you that our ladies' meeting was stale, flat, and unprofitable misinformed you', he wrote. 'Yours was, in my opinion . . . a "notable" speech.'[48] The Countess continued speaking, overcoming her own nervousness. She believed women should be forced to think and act for themselves: 'Self reliance is not easy; we shall need every incentive to achieve it.'[49]

Fortunately for the women's movement some women, after learning public speaking techniques themselves, were willing to help others improve themselves on the platform. Lady Henry Somerset became a brilliant and impressive speaker, but only after she learned to overcome a terrible stage fright that she suffered whenever she stood up to speak. She worked hard to improve her platform presence and eventually became a master at handling a crowd.[50] Much of her knowledge she got while in the United States, from the Moody School for Evangelists in Chicago, which she attended in the early 1890s.[51] There, according to her American colleague, Frances Willard, Lady Henry Somerset 'gained mastery of herself in Public address'.[52] However, Frances Willard was being modest because she herself tutored the Englishwoman in public speaking.[53] Returning to England, Lady Henry Somerset passed on her knowledge to other Englishwomen in the workshops she organized as part of the annual conference of the British Women's Temperance Association and also at other meetings around the country. Her students were taught

> how to serve on a committee, how to take the chair; and were guided through the mazes of the amendment to the amendment. They were also taught how to speak at public meetings, what not to wear on a platform, how not to tire an audience by shrill or monotonous voice, and the importance of avoiding the mannerisms of most parliamentary speakers.[54]

Of great importance to platform women was dressing for the role. The women preachers of the late 1850s and 1860s affected 'a certain decorum in their dress and manner when preaching'.[55] Conservative black dresses were the standard, partly to avoid distracting the listener from the speaker's words but also to indicate to the audience that these women were speaking to promote their cause and not their femininity: The words were more important than the speaker. The black dress for women took the place of the black robes that male teachers, preachers, lawyers and judges wore for public speaking in Victorian England.[56]

Lady Henry Somerset stressed that conservatism in dress was not incompatible with attractiveness. She placed great emphasis on appearance, asserting that if speakers 'wear ugly clothes they are positively hindering the cause they wish to help . . . By giving due care to these outward things we provide real pleasure to others.'[57] She always wore a black silk dress and advised others to dress similarly.[58] One deviation from normal public practise that Lady Henry Somerset allowed herself was speaking 'bareheaded'.[59] According to one writer, she had 'discovered that the weight of millinery does not assist the brain in the deliverance of public addresses'.[60] A few other well-known women speakers, including Lady Carlisle and Mrs. Eva McLaren, followed her in this.[61]

Some public women were never able to overcome their anxieties on the public platform. Prominent among them was Catherine Gladstone, wife of the Prime Minister and president of the Women's Liberal Federation, who had tremendous stage fright whenever she made a public speech.[62] Miss Bryson, a gospel Temperance worker, reported that 'I have grown less timid in addressing meetings . . . '.[63] Miss Robinson, the 'Soldier's Friend',[64] when she was on the platform 'handled her subject discreetly for fear of giving offense', reported one colleague.[65] Perhaps this was because early in her career, in the 1850s when she had been a church worker organizing and speaking at Cottage Meetings, she had been called before a church meeting and forbidden to speak any more in public. She had defied this edict and continued to speak, and in consequence was not allowed to take communion in her parish church.[66]

'Speaking from a platform was a very emotional issue in the nineteenth century', writes one historian; it was considered 'immodest, indecorous, unwomanly and unbecoming for a woman to speak in public'.[67] The opposition could be violent: In 1871 Mrs. Peter Taylor and Mrs. Fawcett were forcibly prevented from speaking at a public meeting.[68] Commenting on the hostility at her first public speech in 1873, Florence Fenwick Miller wrote, 'Speaking in public was the very head and front of our offending'; women 'were mocked for "shrieking for their rights".'[69]

Further intimidation came from the threat of male violence against women on the public platform, particularly in the 1860s and 1870s, if the cause being espoused was an unpopular one. The perpetrators knew that society would not punish them – the women would be blamed for 'asking for it'. In the 1870s Josephine Butler in her meetings against the Contagious Diseases Acts[70] and the women of the British Women's Temperance Association promoting temperance in their early public meetings[71] had to take precautions to avoid such violence. When the American Eliza Stewart went to Scotland in 1874 to speak for temperance reform, a disruption of one of her meetings was planned but thwarted by her supporters.[72] Reminisced one of her Scottish helpers, 'it was the rarest thing for any woman to speak in public in Scotland'; 'only one or two of our sisters had the moral courage to brave the existing prejudice by speaking from the platform.'[73]

Besides the problem of hostility from males, women speakers had to contend with anger and ridicule from other women. Beatrice Potter, (later to become famous as Beatrice Webb) as a young woman decided she would have to speak in public. Nervous about the prospect she decided to learn from observation of successful women speakers. She chose Annie Besant, by then a famous orator; but her reaction was a negative one: 'To *see* her speaking made me shudder. It is not womanly to thrust yourself before the world', she wrote in her diary.[74] Hostility towards 'platform women' was evident in the article 'What to do with our Daughters', by a Mrs. Rentoul Esler. She wrote, 'It is so human to regard woman from the spectacular point of view, that age in her wears some aspect of the ludicrous. An old woman in the pulpit, on the platform, in legal wig and gown, would evoke laughter. It is inevitable. Average human nature is not sympathetic . . .' Such writings reinforced the low self-esteem of many women.[75]

AN 'UNWOMANLY' TRIUMPH

Herbert Asquith, the Liberal leader and Edwardian prime minister, reflecting on the ending of political discrimination against women, wrote in 1920:

> Perhaps a more potent cause [for the change] was the opening of the platform to female oratory. Long before the militant excesses of the 'Suffragettes' the cause of the enfranchisement of women had found, among the sex, advocates who could hold their own on the platform with the best of male speakers. In the 'eighties and 'nineties there was an imposing and constantly recruited array of such standard bearers and missionaries. Mrs. Fawcett, Lady Frances Balfour, Lady Henry Somerset – to name only a few – not only displayed extraordinary gifts of persuasive dielectic [sic] and moving eloquence but they achieved

what their mothers, and in those days the large majority of 'their sisters and their cousins and their aunts,' would have regarded as unseemly, because an 'unwomanly' triumph.[76]

In 1870 '"platform women" were quite a new phenomenon for the people',[77] but during the next twenty-five years the transformation was so great, both in the number of women speakers and in the public's response to them, that many women remarked on it. In 1888 the *Women's Penny Paper* claimed 'speech making is now rapidly becoming a matter of course among women . . . Princess Sophia distinguished herself . . .' when she made a speech to a Greek deputation. The Queen's daughter taking on such a role was quite an encouragement for other women making the attempt. This journal stated 'there are certain types of women who can plead a cause better than any man excepting rarely gifted orators'.[78]

The American Eliza Stewart, who first visited Britain in 1874 and then returned to Scotland in 1891, noted a great difference in many of the women temperance workers. In 1874 they had, 'with timidity and shrinking, carried out their role', but in 1891 'these ladies were carrying forward their business, reporting their several associations with work accomplished, reading papers on various topics and discussing questions with much parliamentary dignity and dispatch'.[79] By then women were also reading papers before the conservative mixed Church Congresses; the naval temperance advocate Agnes Weston[80] was the first woman to read her own paper at one of these meetings.[81]

Florence Fenwick Miller, veteran of many feminist causes, noted similar changes between the early 1870s and the 1890s. She wrote, 'I have sometimes wondered what I should have done in life had I been born half a century earlier, for I was certainly born a speaker.' In the 1870's, she wrote, a woman who tried to have a public voice was mocked and called 'unsexed'; she was told she was a 'shrieking sister'.[82] But by the 1890s the women had so persisted that the changes in public sentiment were 'extraordinary'.

This alteration in attitudes can be traced within such organizations as the British Women's Temperance Association. In October 1883, it had difficulty in getting a 'prominent' woman to preside at its annual meeting. Lady Hope was first asked, but she wrote that she prefers 'work of a less public character'.[83] Then the Association asked Lady Elizabeth Biddulph to preside, but she, too, declined on the grounds of 'it being too public a position for her to take'.[84] But three years later, when asked again to preside at an annual meeting, Lady Elizabeth agreed.[85] So quickly did she become a public personality that in 1889, when the Association was looking for a new president, Lady Elizabeth Biddulph was the first suggested as a candidate.[86] A few years later, after having spoken on a number of public platforms, she became president of the Women's Total Abstinence Union. In 1897 Lady Elizabeth completed her public 'coming out' by giving a speech before the International Prohibition Convention at Newcastle upon Tyne.[87]

Throughout the nineteenth century, all organizations experienced a shortage of women speakers; demand outran supply. When the British Women's Temperance Association first organized, among the first requests it had to answer were from some wanting a woman to speak to a meeting. The minute books of the British Women's Temperance Association as well as those of the Women's Liberal Federation verify the shortage of speakers. The latter in its second year tried to overcome the shortage by asking its 'local associations to help train their own members to do their share'.[88] One advantage conferred on local affiliates by membership in the Federation was the availability of woman speakers from the London headquarters to address their public meetings at least once a year. Even so, because of the shortage of women speakers they were asked to have only 'one outside woman speaker per meeting'.[89]

The Women's National Liberal Association, a breakaway group that rejected women's suffrage and other parts of the women's movement, could not attract enough women speakers to its ranks. The few that they had were 'overtaxed by the number of invitations they receive' and they advised their members to accept the offers of male Liberals to speak at their meetings.[90] Lady Byles, one of the leaders of this Association, to encourage more women to go on the public platform suggested that the local groups recommend that their members read Mr. Dell's book *On the Art of Common Sense of Public Speaking*.[91]

By the time women began to move into purely secular, political work – the Primrose League and the Women's Liberal Federation and its two Liberal rivals, Women's National Liberal Association and the Women's Liberal Unionist Association, as well as the various suffrage societies – the stereotype of the 'shrieking' sister had given way to one of the dedicated worker who should be listened to. Advertised speeches by women drew in large audiences, many of whom came originally out of curiosity but stayed on to cheer. All the leading politicians by the 1890s had to take seriously women's demands for a greater say in the country's decision-making process. Florence Fenwick Miller was right: The change in public feeling was truly remarkable, much of it due, no doubt, to the expertise some women had developed in platform work.

10 'This Revolt of the Women'

> 'We know how to manage any other opposition in the House or in the country, but this is very awkward for us – this revolt of the women. It is quite a new thing; what are we to do with such an opposition as this?'[1]

THE CONTAGIOUS DISEASES ACTS

For over two decades before the 1860s there had been attempts to introduce the European continental system of state regulation of prostitutes into Britain. An Association for the Control of Prostitution by Government Regulation was organized to support this work, but until 1864 all efforts failed. However, with growing demands in the early 1860s for military reform, especially for improvements in the health and general conditions of soldiers, many English politicians changed their attitudes towards the regulation of prostitution.

The British army was an important instrument of the Victorian government, but it had not fared well in the Crimea, mostly because of the soldiers' poor health. Of greatest concern to government was the large increase in venereal diseases in the ranks of the army and the navy. According to the official view, the natural sexual appetites of the men could not be appeased in the normal way, because soldiers were not allowed to marry; they were expected to resort to sexual relations with any available female, usually local prostitutes.

Riding on the crest of this concern for the health of soldiers, the regulationists, as the proponents of state vice control were called, managed to slip the first regulatory law through Parliament with little public notice, by giving the bill a title similar to one used for earlier acts passed to prevent contagious diseases among animals.[2] With the Contagious Diseases Act of 1864, eleven military and port towns (later raised to eighteen) were to have their prostitutes regulated. All women in these areas suspected of being prostitutes were to be registered as such by the police, who wanted to (and sometimes did) interpret the law as meaning that 'any woman who goes to places of public resort and is known to go with different men should register'.[3] Such discrimination against women was accepted by the authorities because they believed women were responsible for perpetrating the social evil of selling their bodies for material gain, while men were merely satisfying a natural need.[4]

In 1866, a second Contagious Diseases Act was passed allowing the police, with no real evidence, to pick up any woman suspected of being a prostitute, and bring her before a magistrate who could then order a medical examination and registration as a prostitute. If found infected with a venereal disease a woman could be incarcerated for three months – later extended to nine months. A special police force outside the control of the local authority was authorized to enforce these laws. No men at all were to be examined.

At first there was little opposition to the laws; their application was only in a limited area and affected few individuals. The regulationists congratulated themselves on the passage of an important public health measure. Opposition came only from those of the minority who viewed the measures as medically ineffective and worried about the creation of a special police force with much authority and little oversight.[5] But these few were soon joined by others, particularly members of the Society of Friends, who argued that the laws protected immoral behavior: The state had no business increasing its safety by regulating a social evil and thereby making it more attractive. The Friends and their allies utilized religious connections to form a network of associates and their meeting houses as centers for agitation alerting England to the terrible evil they saw inherent in the Acts.

But they were, in these first years, a few voices in the wilderness opposing a strong lobby that had the support of the medical profession as well as the majority of the British establishment, including many in the Anglican Church and the armed services. Among the newspapers, *The Times* was strongly in favour of the Acts and published nothing against them; the *Daily News*, a radical newspaper, was a major critic.[6] Some support for regulation also came from men who themselves travelled to the designated towns for the sexual services of the registered prostitutes, believing they were safer than unregistered women.[7] Although there was no evidence to show that the laws made any difference, many people accepted the regulationists' contention that there were fewer sexual diseases in the controlled towns.[8] But the greater part of the general public was unaffected by the Acts and therefore indifferent to them.

Change came in 1869 with the passing of a third Contagious Diseases Act which increased the number of towns to be regulated. There was growing discussion in official circles of extending the system of regulation to the north of England and other non-military areas. This proposed increase in police authority generated a wider range of criticism of the laws and what was first just a low grumble among a few members of the population grew into progressively louder criticism, until it finally erupted into a great roar. Excessive police authority was a development that many Britons watched for and resisted. The abolitionists, as the proponents of repeal preferred to call themselves, likened their work to the freeing of the slaves: the slaves in this case being the prostitutes, now without civil rights and under the absolute control of the police.

In 1869, the Social Science Congress was asked to take up the matter of the Contagious Diseases Acts at its meeting in Bristol. When it refused the abolitionists set up their own conference in Bristol, parallel to the Congress. While it was a great success and the meetings were crowded,[9] women were excluded from most of the deliberations that followed, although women attended and some spoke at the gatherings. No doubt the men felt some of the topics were not for ladies' ears, and that their discussions could be freer in their absence. Led by Quakers, Unitarians, and Freethinkers, these men set up an organization to fight the Contagious Diseases Acts, which they called the National Association for the Abolition of the Contagious Diseases Acts. At first an association for men only, it later allowed women to join. Branches were formed in the provinces, especially in the midlands and in the north,[10] and, although never very large in numbers (fewer than 800 members even at its peak in the mid-1880s), it was a zealous group committed to the eradication of what they believed to be a state-sanctioned evil.[11]

THE LADIES NATIONAL ASSOCIATION FOR THE REPEAL OF THE CONTAGIOUS DISEASES ACTS

Meanwhile, in Bristol a number of women, both Friends and non-Friends, had planned a conference to promote the education of women. Like the abolitionists' conference it was to be held at the same time as the Social Science Congress; many women would be attending the Congress, both as participants and as wives of participants, and would therefore be available. Miss Mary Carpenter, one of the leaders, invited women activists from all over the country.[12] One of the topics discussed was the extension of the Contagious Diseases Acts; many women heard for the first time the case against these Acts and their anti-female character.[13] Concerned over these new laws and their possible extension, some women decided to organize a female association to oppose them. For many this was their first venture into public life.[14] Because the topic was so socially sensitive – one that could bring much opprobrium on the heads of any who would take it up – the women organizers decided that their leader must be carefully chosen. They wanted a married woman of impeccable reputation and with establishment connections. Elizabeth Wolstenholme, a Quaker and veteran supporter of women's education and a founder and secretary of the Northern Schoolmistresses Association,[15] suggested that one of her colleagues in northern women's circles would be the ideal candidate. With her colleagues' approval, she contacted Josephine Butler, and asked her to lead the women's movement.

A mother of four children, Josephine Butler, of Liverpool, was married to an ordained Anglican, the principal of Liverpool College. Her own family was from the landed upper classes in the north. She was a cousin of Earl Grey of 1832 Reform Bill fame, and her father had likewise been a reformer, and ardent supporter of the anti-slave movement.[16] Mrs. Butler had personal connections throughout the British establishment and her husband, though not of such elevated rank, was a friend of William E. Gladstone and had his own links in Oxford and Anglican circles. Furthermore, Mrs. Butler was president and one of the founders of the North of England Council for the Higher Education of Women, through which she became known in northern public life.[17] She had also been active in rescuing prostitutes in Liverpool, and, with her husband's help, set up a refuge for destitute women.

Josephine Butler accepted the invitation to lead the women abolitionists and became the head of the Ladies National Association for the Repeal of the Contagious Diseases Acts, inaugurated in the early days of 1870. She proved to be an inspired choice, developing into a charismatic leader. One of the most effective women speakers of her day, she had in addition a tremendous natural political skill that was nurtured and refined through her public work. Important also for the movement was her religious conviction that she was doing the Lord's work by fighting against this evil legislation. Her faith gave her great personal comfort as she faced the anger and condemnation of many other women, who felt no respectable woman would acknowledge knowing anything about prostitution. Some of her own friends and colleagues, both male and female, became hostile when she took up this work.[18] In 1871, when she came to Sheffield to speak, she met such strong prejudice that 'no woman could be persuaded to accompany Mrs. Butler on the platform except Mrs. H. J. Wilson', reminisced one writer two decades later.[19] (Mrs. Wilson was the wife of a well-known Parliamentary leader in the anti-Contagious Diseases fight.)

One Member of Parliament, Sir James Elphinstone, publicly declared that 'he looked upon these women who have taken up this matter as worse than the prostitutes'.[20]

In December, 1869, Harriet Martineau drafted a *Solemn Protest* against the Contagious Diseases Acts for the Ladies National Association. An active woman writer aligned with many feminist causes in the mid-nineteenth century, Miss Martineau was one of the few voices opposing the state regulation of prostitution from the beginning. She wrote many letters and articles against attempts at regulation throughout the 1860s. By the end of that decade she was in her sixties and had already withdrawn from public activity, but the enactment of the later acts brought her out of retirement to revive her agitation; her articles and letters from the earlier 1860s were reissued as pamphlets.[21]

The *Protest* which Miss Martineau wrote was published in the *Daily News* on December 31, 1869, signed by Josephine Butler, Florence Nightingale, Elizabeth Wolstenholm, and 124 other women. It called for the repeal of the Acts on the grounds they were discriminatory and denied customary legal rights to a class of women, singling them out for particularly cruel and degrading treatment. Under these acts the police, without proper evidence, could pick up any female, which was contrary to English legal traditions – indeed, it was said to be the first legal gender discrimination in the area of civil rights. The protestors claimed that the Acts 'punished the sex who are the victims of a vice, and leave unpunished the sex who are the main cause'. In addition, these laws promoted immorality, because 'the path of evil is made more easy to our sons and to the whole of the youth of England'. Finally, the protest condemned these acts because they were ineffective – 'the diseases which these Acts seek to remove have never been removed by any such legislation'.[22] The first two complaints about the Acts – their social injustice to women and the immorality of a government regulating vice – many women saw as major offenses, more than sufficient to warrant working for their repeal.

Though a small minority initially, Mrs. Butler and her allies were aided by a growing number of men and women, also willing to risk their own good names in a fight for social justice. The men's and women's associations, though kept quite separate, were close allies. Within a few years the anti-Contagious Diseases Acts movement was made up of the National Association and the Ladies National Association, with branches in the provinces as well as a few independent regional and local organizations. All worked together, constituting an important nationwide network. Some churches such as the Friends had their own organizations but cooperated with other groups and were important in the fight. In 1872, many leaders of the working classes, such as Joseph Arch, Henry Broadhurst, George Howell and others, held a joint public meeting with the abolitionists and spoke out against the C. D. Acts, as they were popularly called.[23] One result of this agitation was the creation of a Working Men's League for Repeal. Despite the number of branches the total membership of the Ladies National Association was very small. In one of its early years, with 57 branches it had only 811 subscribing members.[24] But the strength of their commitment compensated for their lack of numbers.

For the first four years of its existence the anti-Contagious Diseases movement was not very effective. The general public regarded the abolitionists as a handful of fanatics fighting for an obscure cause. Their lack of prominent support enabled opponents to discount their efforts, and their lack of publicity in major journals largely kept their efforts from being noticed by the public. Publicity was the life blood of any cause in nineteenth century England. The movement's need to draw more workers into the fight was an imperative that no reforming cause could ignore, especially in the later decades of the century. In a mass democracy, governments respond not only to the quality of the opposition, but to its quantity. Consequently, every opportunity to hold a public meeting and get the public's attention was exploited. The movement collected signatures on petitions drawn up and presented them to Parliament and individual M.P.s in an effort to get the laws repealed. One such petition in 1871 had the signatures of 250,283 women.[25] How much good such efforts did, no one really knew, but they added to the publicity and made the promoters of the petitions feel useful to the cause. Unfortunately, many newspapers, including the powerful *The Times*, refused to print anything critical of the Acts, and the press in general was unfriendly towards the cause, and particularly towards the women.[26]

JOSEPHINE BUTLER'S LEADERSHIP

The first successes for the anti-Contagious Diseases movement came in by-elections. Josephine Butler and a few of her most dedicated women from the Ladies National Association worked with male colleagues against the election of candidates known to support the Acts. In 1870, when General Sir Henry Storks, a strong Liberal supporter of the state regulation of vice, stood at Newark, he was opposed by such forceful abolitionist efforts that he withdrew his candidacy.[27] He then went on to stand at another by-election in Colchester but was defeated: The opposition by abolitionists had helped split the Liberal vote, and victory went to the Conservative candidate.[28] These were small victories, but, as a result of the attention the anti-Contagious Diseases movement gained in these elections and in other political activities, the government in 1870 set up a Royal Commission to investigate the workings of the Acts.

In 1871, Mrs. Butler went before the Commission to give testimony. Many of its members were in favour of the Acts and particularly hostile towards the Ladies National Association because of its political activities.[29] With only a few days notice for her appearance, Mrs. Butler was unable to prepare her testimony well and consequently failed to answer some of the searching questions put to her by commission members. But her religious devotion appears to have impressed the members.[30] Josephine Butler was an effective leader, in part because she learned from her experiences. From her appearance before the Royal Commission, she learned the importance of always being well-prepared and supporting beliefs with facts.

In 1872, Mrs. Butler and her allies were again at work in a by-election at Pontefract, opposing the candidate H. C. E. Childers, a former First Lord of the Admiralty who had supported and administered the Contagious Diseases Acts in the naval stations.[31] The women's association worked closely with the male abolitionists, who were required to protect the women from potential violence on the part of opposition-paid bullies. At Pontefract, when the women held their meeting, someone set fire to the loft in which they were gathered.[32] Despite their efforts Mr. Childers was reelected, but with a lower majority than expected.[33]

The threat of physical harassment was often present at public gatherings where women spoke, but particularly so when addressing such a socially sensitive problem as venereal diseases – considered by many as improper for ladies. When she spoke at Glasgow, two hundred medical students rioted and forced Mrs. Butler to abandon her meeting;[34] and in Colchester Mrs. Butler was chased by a mob and forced to hide in the storeroom of a sympathetic Methodist grocer.[35] No doubt some of those committing the violence were encouraged by the indifference of the establishment towards the fate of females who involved themselves in social 'filth'.

But a great change in the image of the movement in mid-1870s was caused by two events. The first was Mr. James Stansfeld's conversion to the anti-Contagious Diseases cause. A prominent Liberal politician and former cabinet member, Stansfeld in July 1874 became vice-president of the National Association for repeal. With such a man as a leader in the Parliamentary fight against the Acts, the newspapers could ignore the abolitionists no longer. *The Times* was unhappy that such an important statesman should be allied to such an 'hysterical crusade'.[36]

In 1875 a second event with wide-ranging repercussions gave validity to the fears of many about the dangers of allowing the police uncontrolled power, and drew the general public into the Contagious Diseases issue. In Aldershot, one of the regulated towns, a respectable actress and widow, Mrs. Percy, for some unknown reason had drawn the enmity of the police. They were determined to punish her and her teenage daughter, and exercise control over them. With no evidence both women were accused of being prostitutes and ordered to register as such and be subjected to a medical examination for venereal diseases. Mrs. Percy objected and appealed for help by writing to a national newspaper, giving the facts of her situation. The letter went unpublished and nothing was done. Mrs. Percy, then, to help protect her daughter, deliberately created a scandal by committing suicide. The national outrage that ensued was further fueled by the newspaper publication of Mrs. Percy's letter, which had surfaced after her death. The abolitionists took advantage of the situation to demonstrate against the Acts and keep the issue in front of the public. The Butlers took the Percy daughter into their home, and looked after her until she could fend for herself.[37]

From 1875 on, the anti-Contagious Diseases movement grew rapidly and enlisted men and women from all classes and all parts of the country. For the next eleven years abolitionists worked steadily for repeal of the Acts, with Josephine Butler and her female assistants playing a substantial role in the movement's success. The women set up conferences, first in Britain and then on the continent of Europe, to fight against state regulation of vice. Mrs. Butler proved to be a great speaker whose logic and passion were instrumental in moving many of her listeners to join her cause. Her leadership strategy was also masterly. Utilizing her limited resources effectively, she organized her crusade like a general planning a military campaign. With her loyal band of dedicated women she travelled throughout England and the continent.

Her organizational genius was demonstrated at the International Congress held in Geneva in 1877. From the beginning Mrs. Butler had to stand firm on the equality of the sexes at the Congress. Some of the Swiss male hosts insisted that ladies be barred from certain sections of the proceedings. In a letter denouncing this move, Mrs. Butler wrote that the English male delegates would boycott the conference if this exclusion were imposed:

> I believe there is not a man among them who would attend the Congress if a public announcement should be made of the exclusion of women from any part of the deliberations. Our gentlemen here would look upon such a public act as an abandonment of principle. It is precisely this peremptory exclusion of women by statesmen and others from all

> participation in council and in debate on such vital questions which had led to the present terrible wrong to Society by the passing of these oppressive and God-defying laws.[38]

The Swiss withdrew their limitation on women's activities at the congress, which then took place with the full support of both male and female abolitionists from Britain and other countries. Five hundred and ten delegates came to Geneva from fifteen countries. Some were ministers from various evangelical churches who condemned all state regulation of vice on the grounds of morality. Among the delegates were medical doctors who believed state regulation was ineffective in curbing diseases and not a true public health measure, as other medical men had claimed. Lawyers battling the legal injustices of such regulation were also present. Regulationists, too, had their supporters, adding to the excitement of the debates.[39]

The congress had five sections, each of which had its own papers, discussions, and resolutions. Voting on the resolutions was probably the most important part of the Congress as these resolutions were the delegates' final agreements. Throughout the proceedings Mrs. Butler organized her few troops so that all sections were covered and all the English delegates participated to their maximum effect, particularly in the balloting. As Mrs. Butler recalled:

> We always anticipated that when the final resolutions should come to be voted upon, then would be the real war, and so it was. On Thursday morning the voting began. Our faithful bands of ladies worked and watched in their different sections quite splendidly. First we had a considerable conflict in the Social Economy Section. Then came the voting in the Legislative Section, in the smaller Hall of the Reformation, which was densely crowded. The discussion lasted three hours.[40]

From early morning to late at night the delegates met, debated, and voted. Some sessions started at 6 a.m. and continued into late evening; at each the English women kept watch to see that the English perspective was fully represented. So tired at one point were these women that when Mrs. Butler's son went into a session to monitor the proceedings, he saw 'A long row of ladies, all sound asleep'. Only one, Mrs. Bright Lucas, at the end of the row, was awake. She was the 'watcher' whose duty was to wake the others whenever there was a vote. She was 'wide awake, with eyes shining like live coals'.[41]

A SUCCESSFUL WOMEN'S CAMPAIGN

Although the women's anti-Contagious Diseases movement was small, its place in the history of the women's movement is a large one. It was the first organization of women to take up a women's issue – an issue on which the interests of women and men had clearly diverged. The government had protected the men at the expense of women, thus giving the lie to the claim that male voters and politicians could protect the interests of the female population. Clearly some women had been reduced to second-class citizenship in order to serve male needs. For many Englishwomen it was now evident that only by active political pursuit of their own interests would they be able to enjoy the same protections as their menfolk.

At home and abroad Mrs. Butler and allies spoke to mixed audiences, shocking many women but encouraging others to enter public life and speak out for many causes. She was an effective speaker and attracted large crowds to hear her addresses. According to one male colleague, 'she has a voice of great charm and softness and intense but subdued earnestness and perfect simplicity in her style of speaking such as only the most accomplished orator possesses'.[42] One of her biographers calculated that in one year Mrs. Butler 'addressed 99 meetings and four conferences and travelled 3,700 miles' in her campaign against the Acts.[43] But she achieved her goal. After sixteen years of hard politicking the women and their male colleagues saw victory when in 1886 the Contagious Diseases Acts were repealed.[44]

Although the impact of the campaign of the Ladies National Association was great, its total membership remained small: in the mid 1880s, its peak years, never more than 1,000 members and probably considerably fewer.[45] Thirty-three women served on the executive board, respectable well-to-do middle-aged women, a number of them widows and some childless, but others like Mrs. Butler, married and with children at home. Nevertheless, they all had the time and the money to devote to the cause.[46] Mrs. Butler spent all her money on the work, and when her husband retired because of ill health, she and her family were supported by gifts of money from friends until eventually his old friend Gladstone awarded Mr. Butler the Canonry at Winchester.[47] Various members of the Society of Friends also helped pay Mrs. Butler's expenses.[48]

Among the women on the executive of this association were two of John Bright's sisters: Mrs. Bright McLaren of Edinburgh and Mrs. Margaret Bright Lucas. The former was drawn into the movement when her sister-in-law, Mrs. Jacob Bright, 'opened her eyes' to the issues surrounding the Contagious Diseases Acts. This led Mrs. McLaren to become involved in other women's issues.[49] The initiators of the women's association, the Quaker women of Bristol – the Priestman sisters and Miss Margaret Tanner – remained faithful to this cause, although active in other feminist causes also. They were particularly hardworking in the women's suffrage movement and in the Women's Liberal Federation.[50] Miss Wolstenholme, the lady who originally proposed Mrs. Butler as their leader, married and, as Mrs. Elmy, continued her work for the anti-Contagious Diseases Act movement and other educational causes. She too was active in the women's suffrage movement. Another executive member, a Miss Isabella Tod of Belfast, whom Josephine Butler called one of our 'most ablest and certainly the most eloquent' of the women workers,[51] became a founder of the Belfast Women's Temperance Association and a leader in the Women's Liberal Unionist Association. The names of the women and men mentioned by Mrs. Butler in her *Reminiscences* are those names to be found in many other reforming causes, especially the ones dealing with women's issues.

Although organized and run by women, the Ladies National Association had many men supporters. In the early days one of them anonymously gave the Association one hundred pounds, earning him the special gratitude of the women whose resources at that time were 'meagre'.[52] Without men's support Mrs. Butler and her assistants would have fared less well, particularly in activities where physical violence was threatened. Though a few men in the National Association disapproved of women's involvement in such an cause, they were not many.[53] Mr Henry Wilson, a parliamentary leader in the anti-Contagious Diseases Acts campaign, was a strong supporter of women's rights.[54]

The links between the Ladies National Association and the temperance movement, both in Britain and the United States, were strong. Margaret Bright Lucas, one of Mrs. Butler's workers at Geneva, became a longtime president of the British Women's Temperance Association. Josephine Butler early in her public career, when she was doing rescue work in Liverpool, had joined the International Order of the Good Templars and signed the teetotal pledge.[55] In the 1890s after the goals of the anti-Contagious Diseases Acts movement had been achieved, she became a superintendent of the World's Women's Christian Temperance Union purity department and influenced the American temperance feminist, Frances Willard, to fight against the state regulation of vice in the United States.[56]

In 1896 an attempt to revive the state regulation of vice in India showed many English women the need for constant vigilance on this issue. Through subsequent decades it was frequently reiterated by women's groups that such regulation was offensive to women. In 1910 at a meeting of the Executive Committee of the Women's Liberal Federation, it was stated that the issue of the state regulation of vice was of such great importance to the Federation as to be almost on par with the women's suffrage issue; candidates for political contests were examined as to their views on both issues before the Liberal Women would give them support.[57]

Josephine Butler did not see herself as a feminist: She did not want to change the separate spheres doctrine.[58] The reformer saw the anti-Contagious Diseases Acts movement not as a part of a women's movement but as one for both sexes: 'I never myself viewed this question as fundamentally any more a woman's question than it is a man's,' she wrote.[59]

As we shall see. her work fueled great debate among women on organizational strategy. The successes of the Ladies National Association were cited in the early 1890s by the faction that fought to limit the work of the British Women's Temperance Association to one issue, that of temperance alone.[60] Opponents wanted it to take a stand on all women's issues.

What is not in doubt is that Josephine Butler and her Ladies National Association helped to promote women's rights by indicating how they were being eroded by pressure from the masculine church, military and medical establishments. More than any other organization in the 1870s and 80s, these women represented a female viewpoint on an issue that was important to women. Josephine Butler trained many of her assistants in platform speaking and platform politics and these assistants, in turn, played a vital role in training other women within their movement and helping them gain the self-confidence necessary for effective political work. These skilled veterans also joined other organizations where they taught and encouraged more women to enter into public activities.[61] It is in large measure due to their example and influence that in the 1880s and 1890s, a growing number of women took up the Woman Question with great enthusiasm.

Another important consequence of this women's campaign was its illustration to the country's political leaders of the effectiveness of women working in public affairs. In the 1880s both Conservatives and Liberals recruited women for political work; the Primrose Dames quickly became effective workers highly valued by their Conservative leaders, and the Liberal women were called to action by Gladstone himself.[62]

Josephine Butler and her small band of women of the Ladies National Association for the Repeal of the Contagious Acts played a significant role in gaining a public voice for the women of late nineteenth-century England. But before the women achieved an officially recognized political role, they had to learn to organize a mass movement and disseminate their knowledge more widely. And they needed to train more women in organizing and speaking at public meetings and demonstrations than the few from the Ladies National Association. These things they accomplished through their temperance efforts. If the movement to repeal the Contagious Diseases Acts was the organizational nursery of the British women's movement, then the temperance movement was their primary school.

11 A National Temperance Movement

THE GOOD TEMPLARS

A women's national temperance movement finally took hold in Britain in the 1870s after decades of false starts.[1] It owed its birth partly to the work of the London Temperance League, but more importantly to a newcomer to the British temperance world, the Independent Order of Good Templars. An American fraternal organization, the Good Templars (as it was popularly called) was brought to England in 1868 by a returning English workingman, where it quickly caught hold among the respectable working classes. Even a few middle-class reformers joined. All members had to be pledged teetotalers and committed to fighting the use of drink wherever possible. It was an aggressive association and encouraged its members to take controversial stands in the fight against alcoholic beverages. Within a few years the Good Templars claimed a membership of over 200,000 in Britain.[2]

For British women the Good Templars was of special importance; it was the first national organization to accept women members on the same basis as the men. Women were encouraged to take an active role and could vote and stand for election on par with male members. The Order gave them the opportunity as well as the training for leadership; some women rose high in its ranks and then moved on to a wider world, promoting the cause of women as well as that of temperance. Furthermore, the gender-neutral policy of the Good Templars attracted to its ranks women already fighting current discrimination.[3] Such activists became an important nucleus for training other women, especially working-class and lower middle-class women. Throughout the 1860s and early 1870s women joined, worked, and trained in the Good Templar Order, and in the late 70s it became the midwife to the British Women's Temperance Association.[4]

Of great importance in the organizing of women were the connections that the Good Templars had as a *national* order, with its far-flung membership linked together through a network of branches. Members in one part of the country could learn what their fellow members were doing in other parts; this was especially important because the English temperance movement was mostly a local phenomenon and the actual anti-drink work was carried out in the town and city organizations. Moreover, because it was more difficult for women to travel around, the Good Templars' conventions – county, national and international – presented unique opportunities for women, both as members themselves or as relatives of members, to meet and exchange ideas with women from different parts of Britain and even, in a few cases, the United States.

TEMPERANCE NETWORKING

Although efforts were made to create networks of women's temperance societies throughout Britain in the 1850s, 1860s and early 1870s, as we have seen they had little success.[5] Women's groups came and went with great rapidity. They had no basic support group to keep the local branches alive and in contact with one another. A few isolated groups survived but became local phenomena. Not until 1874 did this situation change. Then gospel temperance, uniting religion and temperance, motivated many 'conventional' females to enter into the public limelight, women who without it would have stayed at home.[6]

The first women's city unions were created in Ireland. In Belfast, a Ladies Temperance Union, originally established in 1863 during one of the recurrent organizing campaigns for women in temperance, was reconstituted in 1874 and renamed the Belfast Women's Temperance Association.[7] In the same year, in a separate effort, a Dublin union was also formed. Each of these Irish associations aimed at uniting various women's temperance groups already existing within their districts. They also recruited new members and created new organizations in the surrounding countryside as well as in the cities themselves. (Two years later, in 1876, the Belfast organization claimed forty branches.) Also in 1875, the Sheffield Women's Christian Temperance Association was founded, and, in the same year in London, a short-lived Christian Workers Temperance Union was organized for women.[8]

In December, 1875, the Manchester and Salford Women's Christian Temperance Association was inaugurated to take care of the heavily populated area of Lancashire where the temperance reformation had always been strongly supported. By the 1890s it had twenty-six branches and a membership of 2,000.[9] This organization developed its own Police Court mission, and did other welfare work in the cities of Manchester and Salford and their environs. It was to continue well into the mid twentieth century.[10]

A few months later in early 1876, across the Pennines in Yorkshire, another stronghold of temperance, the British Temperance League, a northern-based national teetotal organization, working with widely scattered local women's temperance organizations helped found the Yorkshire Women's Christian Association. It was to become one of the largest county groups. That same year the Church of England Temperance Society organized a Women's Union which became very active in certain parishes, taking up mission work among the parish poor.[11]

At the same time, over the border in Scotland women were active in promoting the Gospel Temperance cause. In 1874 women of Dundee had successfully petitioned the authorities to reduce the number of licenses issued. This achievement stimulated women's temperance activity in other parts of Scotland, which had always been receptive to the temperance cause. Two years later, in 1876, the Scottish Women's Christian Union was organized in Edinburgh.[12]

On January 21, 1876, the National Temperance League gave a reception in London for a visiting American temperance woman, Mrs. Eliza Stewart. Two hundred and fifty men and women attended. Representing the Good Templars at this meeting was Margaret Bright Lucas, sister of John Bright. Although the main topic of discussion was women's work for temperance, Mrs. Lucas was the only woman on the official program, aside from the guest of honor, Mrs. Stewart.

Mrs. Lucas was a reformer in the Quaker tradition, exhibiting all the Friends' concern for social amelioration.[13] She was an early supporter of women's suffrage, as well as a member of the Women's Peace and Arbitration Society.[14] A widow, she waited until her children became adults before she entered public life. Then, in 1870, she became an active member of the Independent Order of the Good Templars, the same year that she was elected to the executive committee of Josephine Butler's Ladies National Association.[15]

Out of the January reception of the National Temperance League came a new attempt at forming a national women's temperance association. The national convention of Independent Order of the Good Templars to be held on April 21, 1876, in Newcastle-on-Tyne, appeared to be a good opportunity to bring together members from the dispersed and isolated women's temperance groups, to make some connection between the larger city and county unions already in action. A circular was printed inviting all interested women in the United Kingdom to meet in Central Hall, Newcastle-upon-Tyne, at 10 o'clock. Copies were sent around the United Kingdom to Good Templar branches and to local women's groups.

A NATIONAL WOMEN'S TEMPERANCE ORGANIZATION

On April 21, 1876, one hundred and fifty women gathered at Central Hall to create the first British national temperance association completely organized and run by women. Presided over by a Templar member, Mrs. Parker, the speakers were all women. The participants decided to set up a new organization which would be a federation of existing societies as well as a sponsor of new branches where no women's temperance group functioned. The purpose of the new organization was to promote temperance and work for the elimination of the drink trade.[16] It was to be called the British Women's Temperance Association and have its executive located in London.[17]

Meanwhile in London, that same year, the National Temperance League organized a three-day conference for women. Here Lady Jane Harriette Ellice presided. She had been converted to temperance by one of James B. Gough's addresses in the early 1840s and had immediately signed the total abstinence pledge.[18] Lady Ellice was president of a temperance organization called the Christian Workers' Temperance Union.[19] At the public meeting of this conference Mrs. Lucas presided and an American lady, a Mrs. Johnson, along with other English 'lady workers,' gave addresses. A report of its proceedings was published and circulated among all women's and temperance groups,[20] but no permanent organization was created by this meeting.

At the second meeting of the British Women's Temperance Association, held in December, 1876, a constitution was drawn up stating that 'the object of this association is to form a union or federation of the Women's Temperance Societies existing in the various districts within the United Kingdom,' so that 'much greater work can be effected in the extension of the cause of Temperance in the control and ultimate suppression of the Liquor Traffic . . . '[21] Mrs. Parker, of Dundee, was elected first president along with twenty-two vice presidents: four from Scotland, two from Ireland, two from London, five from the north of England, and the rest from around the west and south of England. Mrs. Margaret Lucas was appointed treasurer and Mrs. Mawson of Gateshead was the Hon. Secretary. An executive of ten, all from London, was appointed. The selection of officers from around the country was very important because there were fears that the Association would become monopolized by London and provincial members ignored. To balance the metropolitan influences with those of the provinces, there would be two national meetings a year: a spring one in London and an autumnal one in different towns around the country.

Most immediate was their need to get their message out to the public, and so their first project was to organize public meetings in London to explain their cause and what they were doing about it. Six such gatherings were successfully held in March, 1877, in different parts of London. Five were afternoon meetings and, though chaired by men, the speakers were all women. The one evening meeting was chaired by a popular reforming liberal MP, Samuel Morley, and the speeches were given by both men and women. Among the women were Mrs. Balfour, Miss Tod, Miss Weston, and Mrs. Macpherson – all popular, experienced platform speakers. These meetings were a great start for the new organization. Women had organized the proceedings, hired the halls, and arranged the publicity. They also had seen that the meetings were conducted properly and the audience did not get out of hand. The women had successfully carried out their first project and it was an achievement; few English women by themselves had previously done this kind of thing on such a scale.[22]

The first annual meeting of the British Women's Temperance Association was held in the Library of the Memorial Hall on May 22, 1877, where it was announced that Mrs. Parker had been elected president of the newly formed Women's International Christian Temperance Union, an honour the British organization applauded.[23] Mrs. Balfour was proposed as the president of the Association for the coming year and approved unanimously. A motto was also adopted: 'The harvest is truly great but the labourers are few.'[24] To expand their influence, the women decided to ask titled or other prominent ladies to become 'Lady Patrons' of the Association. The rest of the meeting was occupied with the reading of papers dealing with various aspects of women and temperance.

The annual meeting was a great success, and plans went ahead to expand the organization's work. Although the Association continued to grow, it also had great difficulties with some of its larger branches. In May 1877, at its first annual meeting, the British Women's Temperance Association had only eight affiliated societies, but one of these, Belfast, was a union with thirty-nine of its own branches. Some of these big unions saw no reason to come under the authority of any distant central office. Locally based and happy with their own independence, they saw little advantage in connecting themselves to a London-based association, especially when it would cost them some of their meagre funds. An annual affiliation fee of one pound was charged each society.[25] The Birmingham Ladies Temperance Association decided they would not affiliate with the London group: As one of the oldest women's societies and still active, they had done well on their own.[26] The United Working Women Teetotal League in London did not affiliate because it would have difficulty paying the fees,[27] and the Liverpool Ladies Temperance Association, for some unstated reason, also refused to join.[28]

The Scottish connection was an uneasy alliance.[29] The Scots wanted their own 'national' society that would not be run by an English executive. Headquarters in London, they realized, would not fully serve Scottish interests. They 'affiliated' with the Association, but no one specified just what such a connection meant. As *sister* societies they were happy – as *daughter* affiliates they were not. Conflict between London and Edinburgh soon arose over the affiliation of branches in border towns.[30]

The biggest affiliate was Belfast, which by 1880 had grown to be a union of 45 branches; Scotland was second with 21 branches, and the Yorkshire Union third with 12 branches. By 1880, a total of 136 women's temperance societies were 'connected' with the British Women, as the organization was popularly called, but many were only loosely tied to the central executive. Provincial societies often could not afford to send representatives to London to the annual meetings in May, where the main business was carried out. Neither could they send representatives to meetings at other provincial towns, so their connection was minimal. How large or small these societies were is unknown; accurate membership figures are difficult to get from any temperance organization in the nineteenth century.[31]

A PUBLIC VOICE

In its early years the association was fortunate to have the support of a handful of experienced women speakers, the nucleus of a group that was to help other women go on the public platform. Mrs. Woyka, of Glasgow, a veteran on the evangelical platform, was a dynamic speaker and always willing to talk anywhere in the country on behalf of temperance. Mrs. Parker, the first president of the Association, was an expert speaker as was Mrs. Hilton, the founder of the *Children's Creche* movement and a strong supporter, along with her advocate husband, John Hilton, of the temperance reformation. Mrs. Burns, wife of the Rev. Dawson Burns (who had done so much to further women's work for temperance) and her mother, the indefatigable and greatest female temperance veteran of them all, Mrs. C. L. Balfour, president of the Association from 1877–78, could be counted on to give good service. Mrs. Margaret Bright Lucas, who became the third president of the Association in 1878, was always willing to travel around publicly speaking for temperance and other causes. All these women were pressed into service for the first meetings where veterans paired with beginners in order to train them and produce more platform workers.[32]

But the biggest problem for the organizing women was the reluctance of many of their sex to take the first step. One branch reported some of their members 'were thinking of commencing speaking in meetings'.[33] Throughout the 1870s and 1880s a chronic shortage of women speakers resulted in grossly overworking those who were available. From the beginning, the Association received many requests for speakers to address meetings, from both religious and temperance groups, who particularly wanted a lady.[34] The committee had to turn down most of these requests for want of good public speakers. Consequently, the women lost many opportunities to publicize their work. A few professional women speakers asked the Association to sponsor their speaking engagements, but the Association generally refused. It was a dangerous practise to hire women about whom they had little knowledge and over whom they had little control. (One woman, for example, speaking at a public meeting and identified as a member of the BWTA, expressed the desire to have museums open on Sundays. This was reported in a temperance journal and generated great criticism. The executive committee had to stress in a letter to the journal that these were not 'the sentiments of the BWTA'.)[35]

It took courage for a woman to get up before a public audience in London and ask their support for a women's temperance group. Temperance itself was not respectable in many English eyes, and neither were women on a platform. But it was not just the women who were targets for disruption by men looking for some excitment. Any temperance meeting or Salvation Army gathering was vulnerable to rowdyism.[36] In order to reduce such problems and have better control over their gatherings, the women devised a new type of semipublic assembly which was a 'drawing room meeting in a public hall'. Here the audience was restricted to those with invitations, but it was a larger group, much bigger than the traditionally small private 'drawing room' gathering.[37]

In 1886, to get more women involved in temperance work, Miss Forsaith, a member of the Executive Committee, gave a speech on 'The Work done by our Association' which was later printed and circulated to the branches. Her speech told women:

> If we are to be successful workers . . . (as we all, I am sure, desire to be, not for our own sakes, but for the glory of God) we must be delivered from that miserable cowardice, born of unbelief which so often makes us shrink back from undertaking any offered work . . . with the words 'Oh I could not possibly do that'. We like to call this sort of thing by nice names, 'shyness', 'timidity' almost a feminine grace, and our gentlemen relatives take care to foster that delusion . . . . Let us say no more '*I am* so weak, *I am* so nervous, I am this or I am that' It is not what

> I am but what God is . . . . This courage of faith is a totally different thing to the mannishness which some women unfortunately adopt which deservedly excites the ridicule and contempt of sensible men and fills the hearts of good women with shame and sadness . . . Let us avoid equally self-confident and unwomanly boldness and self-conscious unbelieving cowardice.[38]

This speech indicates some of the conflicts that women in the temperance movement felt about going on the public platform; they wanted to take action but without bringing themselves and their movement into disrepute. Balancing the demands of society with those of the organization was something that women were going to have to do. Miss Forsaith herself would only accept a public role for women if it was done 'for the sake of God.' Her work and that of other members appears to have been effective because two years later it was reported to the executive committee that more women were available as public speakers.[39]

The nineteenth century was a period of great emphasis on the printed word, and the temperance reformation utilized it to the greatest possible degree. The leadership of the British Women wanted to have a journal, because such publications were useful in connecting the branches and reinforcing the ties forged at the annual meetings. But publications cost money and the Association lacked the funds. In January, 1883, it was decided to have a journal, but one owned by a male proprietor who would pay all expenses, take all risks, and get all profits. The proprietor would decide on editorial positions and the Association would merely insert a monthly letter in it. This journal, *The British Women's Temperance Journal*, would be sold to the branches as the official paper of the Association.[40] Mr Edward Bennett, a temperance man and owner of other temperance publications, became the proprietor.[41]

From the beginning of the Association finances had been difficult. The women got few bequests and had to keep affiliation fees low. All branches of the women's temperance movement appear to have had a great deal of difficulty financially and many programs were put off because of cost.[42] Few members in the early years of the Association had their own funds and so they mostly had to rely on male sympathisers for financial support.[43] For two years running they were fortunate to receive fifty pounds from a Mrs. Davies of Bury, which helped keep them solvent in 1887 and 1888.[44] (When the Manchester Women's Christian Temperance Union was given fifty pounds as bequest from a brewer, they rejected it.)[45] The handful of wealthy women temperance supporters in England at this time preferred to leave their money to other temperance organizations.[46]

The Association was particularly careful to avoid any religious controversy. Prayer meetings were sponsored by both the executive in London and the affiliates, but they appear to have been unsuccessful, especially in London where they received little support.[47] In the less sophisticated provinces, these gatherings helped draw in some very conservative women as well as mute some of the criticism against women coming together in a public fashion.[48] Though many Association members were nonconformists, others were staunch Anglicans, including some clergymen's wives. Particularly popular to chair meetings were the well-known evangelical leaders of both the established church and the non-conforming chapels. Prominent Anglican, Methodist, and other non-conforming ministers presiding over a gathering could attract people who otherwise saw the temperance reform as not quite respectable, or even as causing religious infidelity.[49] Women who came for the prayers often stayed to join the group and eventually became involved in other activities.[50]

THE WOMAN QUESTION AND THE BRITISH WOMEN'S TEMPERANCE ASSOCIATION

One of the problems that made some temperance branches and individuals careful about allying themselves to any women's organization was the position it might take towards the 'Woman Question'. This matter was raised by one of the prospective 'lady patrons' who asked about the Association's position on 'women's rights'. She received the following answer:

> that as an association we never commission speakers to say a word on the subject of women's rights, which we hold is entirely distinct from that of Temperance: that we do not wish it to be alluded to in our meetings, but cannot control our speakers.[51]

In March 1878 the executive decided to print pledge books, reports and membership cards with *Work for Women* as a heading on the title pages (with a religious text underneath). This caused much controversy as it could be interpreted as making the Association a part of the women's movement. So on March 22, 1878, bowing to the criticism, the Committee reported that they had 'rescinded printing of the text *Work for Women* as it is open to some objection'.[52]

The issue of women's suffrage and its relationship to the Association was particularly persistent and insistent. The Association's leadership under Mrs. Lucas believed there were other organizations to support this work.[53] Temperance was and should be the sole focus of the Association. In the early 1880s the Association published a small pamphlet written by an executive member that dealt with women's suffrage. This publication was ignored when it appeared, but in later debates over the issue of women's suffrage it was the subject of a bitter argument, especially at the 1892 annual meeting when the executive committee claimed that the Association had never officially supported women's suffrage.[54] In February, 1887, when the topic of 'Women's Suffrage in its relation to Temperance Work' was proposed for a conference the executive council decided it was 'premature'.[55] (Not until after the death of President Lucas, when a new president took over, was the issue revived.) Whatever its position on other women's issues, the Association was a female one; men held no official positions and their services were utilized only when those of women were unavailable. Even the printing was done by women printers, by the Women's Printing Society or the E. Faithful company that hired women.[56]

The British Women, as the temperance women were popularly called, had a unique position in England. In the late 1870s and early 1880s no other national movement in Britain had such potential for promoting women's causes as did this Association. Their network of branches encompassed women of all classes and from all areas. Such a broad spectrum of women under one tent could have been an important force in any reforming cause, but during Mrs. Lucas's presidency the Association was a leader neither in the temperance reform nor in the women's movement. This was in part because Mrs. Lucas lacked the charismatic presence of her American counterpart, Frances Willard, and also because she did not have the passion and drive of her own successor, Lady Henry Somerset. But primarily it was because the temperance movement in England was a conservative cause.[57] Everything the British Women's Temperance Association did during Mrs. Lucas's presidency was initiated by other reform organizations. No truly innovative programs, either for temperance or for women, were introduced by the Association in the 1880s. Prayer meetings, petitions, demonstrations, lecture meetings and public appeals were all standard activities of reforming groups.

A NEW ADMINISTRATION

At the end of 1889 Mrs. Lucas became ill and resigned, and Lady Henry Somerset was elected new president. This inaugurated a new era for the Association. Lady Henry Somerset, the daughter of an earl, wanted the

Association to embrace a 'wider sphere' – to become active in all issues connected to the woman question. A strong woman from a very privileged background, she developed close ties with the American, Frances Willard, who persuaded her to bring the British organization into the forefront of the women's movement, emulating the American role of the Women's Christian Temperance Union. Consequently, Lady Henry Somerset's presidency became surrounded by controversy.

For the first year everything went fairly smoothly. Membership continued to grow, and in the year 1891–92 it was reported that there were 577 branches, with a membership of about 50,000. But even with such large numbers, their income was still small – just over one thousand pounds for the year.[58] Membership was loosely defined in some of the local groups and, as in the past, some of the branches were the work of only one or two active women.

By the second year a split developed in the Association, with the president and her supporters wanting the American 'Do Everything' policy implemented. With this the Association would take up such women's issues as women's suffrage and 'social purity' (anti-contagious diseases work and allied concerns dealing with sex and the individual) along with their traditional temperance work. This would make the Association a feminist organization. Opponents to this change were led by a Miss Docwra, a Quaker woman from a temperance family, who was president of the Association's Executive Committee. She and her supporters wanted to 'concentrate' on temperance: Just as the Contagious Diseases Acts had been repealed with the 'single issue' work of the Ladies National Association for the Repeal of the Contagious Diseases Acts, so would the laws authorizing grocers' licenses, Sunday sales, and eventually all liquor licenses be repealed if the anti-drink reformers would focus on the single issue of drink.

The provincial branches were mostly unaware of the developing problems at their headquarters because they were too far removed from the capital, both physically and psychologically, to be involved. They did not understand, or in many cases care about, the issues of concern to the officers of the Association. They were wrapped up in local issues.

Throughout 1891 and 1892 the Association's administration was polarizing around two opposed policies and leaders. The majority of the executive, headed by Miss Docwra, supported concentration, staying with the traditional work of the Association. They were mostly the conservative wing, though a number of important adherents to their side were active in other parts of the women's movement. What united them was their belief that the Association was founded on the principle of women working for the anti-drink issues only. If a member wanted to support other causes she should join the organizations set up specifically for them. Miss Forsaith, for example, was part of the executive majority supporting the concentration policy, but also held membership in the Ladies National Association and in a women's suffrage society.

Lady Henry Somerset led the more radical minority group in the executive supporting the 'Do Everything' policy. They planned to introduce innovative methods and controversial issues into the Association as well as increase its ties to their American counterparts. Under the new leadership the British Women's Temperance Association was to become a 'woman's party'.

The concentrationists had the support of the more traditional temperance groups – the women's Yorkshire Union, for example – and most of the mixed organizations of the British temperance reformation. But though the concentration party was nearer in philosophy to the women most closely tied to the temperance cause, most of these women were more interested in their local anti-drink organizations than in an Association run by a distant and seemingly indifferent London Committee.

The president of the Association, on the other hand, had personal support in the provinces because she gave time and attention to visiting provincial branches, particularly the small ones who appreciated her personal help. Often isolated, these groups wanted to be part of the mainstream of English life, especially of the women's movement. A visit from an earl's daughter gave them a great deal of local prestige and validated the respectability of their cause. A woman of great energy as well as great financial resources, Lady Henry Somerset visited all corners of Britain and met all classes of men and women. She was a charming woman and no doubt her title helped her gain support (traditional British deference to a member of the aristocracy was still very strong, especially among the middle classes) but, most importantly, she personally reached out to the branch members and showed her concern for their successes, offering them practical help in running their organizations.

As earlier noted, while on one of her visits to the United States, the president had attended the Rev. Moody's Training School for Christian Workers, a school of 'Methods',[59] where she learned much about the way to run an organization and gained important practical suggestions on public platform presentations. When she returned home she put her new knowledge into practise and, more importantly, she passed it on to others through her 'workshops' – one-day methods schools for women in the provinces.[60] For many women in the provinces these lessons were vital to a successful transition from domestic seclusion to public life; it was the only training they would ever receive. These workshops brought Lady Henry Somerset into immediate contact with the women and made her many staunch supporters within the movement.

THE BATTLE OF 'THE TWO PRESIDENTS'

The conflict between 'the two presidents' of the British Women's Temperance Association became public at the annual council meeting of 1891, when the Association's titular president told the members to take up the work of 'Social Purity'; following the inspiring model of Josephine Butler, they 'must not shirk' from it. Lady Somerset also raised the matter of greater provincial participation in the work of the Association, as she wanted to have a more organized national body. The opposition managed to prevent any immediate changes by invoking the rule that at least one month's notice must be given before any resolution could be considered by the delegates. This meeting then adjourned, thus postponing controversial decisions until the next year. In October 1891, Lady Henry Somerset went to the United States to attend two women's temperance conventions and stayed on until April, 1892, returning less than a month before the next annual meeting.

At the 1892 annual meeting, two hundred and forty seven delegates attended and conflict between the two sides erupted immediately, first over the credentials of delegates. The conservatives accused Lady Somerset of introducing women as voting delegates who were not the legitimate representatives of the branches they purported had sent them.[61] There followed a discussion of the changes that were to be introduced: The American departmental system with seven departments was to be immediately established, including one to deal with politics. An argument ensued: It was feared that if the Association went into political work, there would be increased controversy within the organization.[62] No clear decision was made.

The Association then took up the report of the Journal Committee set up by the executive to investigate ways for the Association to take full control of the *Journal*. Earlier it had been suggested that a limited liability company be formed to issue shares for sale only to members of the Association. The executive committee was convinced that in 1892, unlike the 1870s and early 1880s when a journal was first proposed, there were members who had the money to invest in the project. They were right, it was now reported: Immediately shares were offered more than half had been bought by the conservative members of the executive. It was further reported that because the branches had been asking to have a woman editor, Miss Forsaith (a concentrationist) had agreed to take over this position. All this had happened while the president was in the United States. By the time Lady Somerset returned the journal had already come under the control of her opponents.[63]

A resolution proposed by the president was then presented to the meeting. It stated that the Association would support women's suffrage and that 'responsible women should participate in framing laws by which they are governed. We hold that the spiritual and moral forces of women must be brought to bear directly on the ballot box . . . . We ask that the Parliamentary vote should be extended to them.' Lady Henry Somerset also proposed that the Association set up a Department of Suffrage work.

This resolution elicited strong and vocal opposition. Lady Elizabeth Biddulph led the conservative forces and battled it out with Lady Henry Somerset – they were both earls' daughters and thus equal in social rank. Lady Elizabeth said she had come to temperance through the Blue Ribbon movement and had been assured that the British Women's Temperance Association was 'unsectarian and unpolitical'. She pointed out there was a society for women's suffrage and those who would support it should join it. It was a passionate speech, and the minutes reported that 'hisses, cheers and cries' erupted from the delegates at the end of it. Lady Henry Somerset replied: 'Those who hold deep convictions cannot remain silent.'

Both sides of the issue were heard. Mrs. Servante, a member of the executive committee and a fourteen-year veteran of the Association, told the council that if the resolution supporting women's suffrage were passed, 'I should not be allowed to stand upon your platform tomorrow night . . . . ' She was the wife of a clergyman.[64] Mrs. Sutteridge pointed out that they had followed the traditional methods, presenting petitions, but 'where did they get us?' Sister Lily of the West London Mission was in favour of women's suffrage because temperance was a political matter and women's votes would support protemperance candidates. A Miss Beck of Brighton felt there were different views 'but we need to preserve the union' at all costs. Mrs. Thomson of Clapham must have echoed the sentiments of many when she said such a resolution would split her branch. The debate was punctuated throughout by emotional outbursts of support along with expressions of rejection.

The president then claimed that the delegates were not being asked to support women's suffrage on a public platform, but only 'to say whether you think Women's Suffrage will help our work . . . . ' Eventually the resolution was passed 63 to 36, but fewer than half of the delegates voted. Over 240 delegates had come to the meeting, it was late when a vote was taken and many of the delegates had already left. Clearly support by only 63 delegates was a minority vote and could not be seen as a vote of confidence in any new policies. There were other questions as to the constitutionality of the vote, and the day's meeting ended with a lot of confusion. The next day the meeting took another contentious turn when a resolution to change the constitution was proposed. Its proponents wanted to remove the requirement of a month's notice for resolutions to be presented, but it was agreed that such a move would need additional study and should be sent to the branches for their comment. The meeting ended with both sides more apart than ever.

1892–1893: AN UNHAPPY YEAR

The annual council meeting of 1892 had ended in a postponed fight with nothing settled. Many provincial members hoped a reconciliation between the two parties could be affected, and meetings between them were twice proposed. But there remained a great deal of distrust between the contending parties and nothing came of these attempts.

During the following year the two sides continued their civil war, battling for the support of the provincial branches. Circular letters presenting the different positions on various issues were sent to the branches by both sides. The opening shot of the new campaign was a letter published in the *Temperance Record* in May signed 'A Lover of Peace'; it proposed that 'those who prefer to work under the system and leadership of Lady Henry Somerset leave the Association with her' and that those who would continue along the 'old lines' remain. 'Lady Henry Somerset cannot expect a large and old established Association to give up its traditions and adopt her 40 departments and what practically amounts to a new constitution . . . .'[65]

The following month the executive committee sent another letter to all the branches, explaining what they saw as the main differences between the warring sides. The president sent out a letter outlining her policy for the Association. Other letters to the branches were sent by both sides. One of the major branches, the Manchester Christian Temperance Union, a strong supporter of Lady Henry Somerset, declined to be drawn into the feud and so sent a rather innocuous reply to the concentrationists expressing 'our pleasure that matters seem to be more harmonious amongst them'. They also informed Miss Docwra that a unanimous vote of confidence for Lady Henry Somerset had been passed by their Association.[66]

In September 1892, the executive took control of the *Journal* and changed its name to *Wings*. This paper became the most important weapon for the conservatives in their fight for the support of the branches. (Its new owners claimed that circulation doubled in the first three months of their tenure.)[67] In the new year articles started to appear that had a strong conservative bias. Accusations of unconstitutional behavior and of acting in bad faith were made against the president and her supporters. A leaflet against the influence of Frances Willard was circulated, and the executive suspended the Association's affiliation with the World's Women's Christian Temperance Union.

Meanwhile Lady Henry Somerset had once again gone to the United States to attend various conferences and renew her friendship with Frances Willard and others in the WCTU. This time she was gone two months and when she returned Frances Willard came with her. Along with other Americans who came over, they worked out the strategy for the forthcoming showdown at the next annual meeting, scheduled for May 3–5, 1893. The alliance between the president and the Americans was flaunted, and exacerbated a situation already extremely tense. The American women felt they were giving their 'sister' 'moral support,' but in fact they were giving credence to a growing belief that Lady Henry Somerset was a puppet in the hands of the brilliant but autocratic reformer Frances Willard and her compatriots.[68] Accusations made on this theme were answered by counter-accusations of anti-Americanism on the part of the progressives. Lady Henry Somerset moved her office from the building of the executive and set up in another she had ostensibly hired for her work with the World's Women's Christian Temperance Union.[69] Other parts of the temperance movement were drawn into the fight and took sides according to their own views on the suffrage and strategy issues.

The two sides came to the annual Council Meeting in 1893 prepared for a battle, knowing this was to be a turning point for the British Women's Temperance Association. The issues were too deep and feelings too bitter for reconciliation. Only a fight to the finish would resolve the dispute. Either way, a large part of the membership would be unhappy. It was a crowded meeting. Over four hundred voting delegates from all over Britain, double the number of the previous year, along with many visitors, packed themselves into Memorial Hall. All members entering the hall were checked to see if they were proper delegates, and visitors were sent to the gallery. Only women were admitted: Men were 'vigorously excluded' from all the proceedings except for two male guards patrolling the corridors.[70] The meeting was chaired by a Mrs. Lloyd Jones of Rhyle, wife of a Wesleyan minister, a teetotaler who belonged to no organization and knew nothing of the BWTA controversy.[71]

Lady Henry Somerset had become a veteran of the the public platform and was therefore adept at manipulating an audience. The leaders of the opposition having little experience in working with crowds had their ineptitude revealed at this meeting.[72] No reporters were present, but some of those present gave a description of the proceedings to interested newspapers. Some newspapers were sympathetic to the women but others were not. The *Christian World* condescendingly wrote, 'the distinctly logical mind in women is however of such comparatively modern development that some allowance must be made for the passionate disputation of those . . . in the older school.'[73]

The full day was taken up with speeches. In the morning the two sides presented their respective positions, and the afternoon was given to the delegates. Throughout the proceedings many of these normally staid women rose in their seats and cheered or jeered, according to the views expressed. Some waved handkerchiefs and others their umbrellas.[74] Two main issues emerged from the long day of debate. One concerned the personality of the president herself: She was too autocratic, said her opponents. The other dealt with the work of the Association: Should it adopt the 'Do Everything' program – leading it into the battle for women's suffrage, the purity work, and other women's issues along with temperance – or should it concentrate on its traditional anti-drink work?

At 8 p.m. the balloting commenced and more than 450 women cast votes. It took until 10:20 p.m., almost two and a half tense hours, to complete the voting. The description of the scene in one journal told of exhausted women waiting around the lobby, along the corridors, even lining the steps of a wide stone staircase, some lucky enough to have chairs, while others sat on tables. It was more than twelve hours since the meeting had started. Some enterprising soul managed to bring in fresh milk and sold it at a penny a glass.

> Finally at 24 minutes passed ten a woman came in and said 'Ladies I can tell you the result'. In that second the place was transformed. Everyone stood up and waited breathlessly with eyes fixed on the pale woman in black . . . the words came clear and slow. The total number of votes given for the minority [Lady Henry Somerset's party] was 262 and for the majority [Miss Docwra's group] 192. In another second the long pent up enthusiasm found expression in wild whoops of hurrahs . . . . (and other expressions of rejoicing.)[75]

A SPLIT MOVEMENT

Almost as quickly as the result was known the losing conservative leaders decided to quit the Association, leaving the Association president and her supporters to carry out the changes they had fought for. The National British Women's Temperance Association, as it was renamed after the split, developed an extensive program of activities based on the 'Do Everything' policy. It drew closer to the World's Women's Christian Temperance Union, which Lady Henry Somerset eventually headed. Because the dissidents kept control of *Wings*, a new journal was started by Lady Henry Somerset, *The Woman's Herald*, which she personally edited.

Though the Association retained the loyalty of the Manchester Union, it lost the Yorkshire and Scottish unions, which decided to become completely independent. The Belfast and Dublin unions, among the first to be members of the British Women's Temperance Association, withdrew. They soon declined and then disappeared, but their leaders formed a new group, the Irish Women's Temperance Union, with headquarters in Belfast. This union eventually claimed 64 branches but did not affiliate with any national association. (Miss Isabella Tod, who had fought the changes in the BWTA, was the leader in this new group and was also a leading woman in the Women's National Unionist Association – a group opposing Gladstone's Irish policy. She did not want her temperance mixed with politics dominated by the Liberal Women's dogmas, which had Home Rule for Ireland as one of its main planks.)[76]

The dissidents organized a new association devoted to anti-drink work called the Women's Total Abstinence Union, At its first conference, on November 2, 1894, a man presided – a situation that its leader, Miss Docwra, said she hoped would not happen again.[77] After a slow start, this union grew until by 1900 it claimed to have 310 federated societies.[78] It did not manage to win over any of the larger county unions, but it did set up branches in towns where the Association also had affiliates. Many major temperance towns came to have two women's groups, one affiliated with each national body. (Bradford, for example, had a branch of the Women's Total Abstinence Union, called the Bradford Women's Society for the Suppression of Intemperance, organized by the well known Quaker Mrs. Edward Priestman, and also an affiliate of the National British Women's Temperance Association.)[79] But the role of the Women's Total Abstinence Union was overshadowed by Lady Henry Somerset and the National British Women's Temperance Association. The Union was not a part of the women's movement but only of the temperance reform where it acted as an adjunct to other temperance groups and, consequently, was always a supporting player, never a leader.

One of the major problems facing temperance women at this time stemmed from political developments outside their control. In the first half of the 1890s all branches of the anti-drink movement throughout Britain were scenting success in their long-time efforts against the drink trade. The National Liberal Federation had adopted temperance as part of the official Liberal Party platform in 1891, and the whole temperance movement was focused on the coming election fight of 1895. At the same time the women's suffrage movement was also anticipating some success at this election. The suffrage bill of a Conservative backbencher, Sir Albert Rollits, in 1892 had embroiled the country in a debate over women's suffrage, many of whose supporters thought the tide was turning and some women might finally get the vote.[80] Women's suffrage supporters, like their counterparts in the anti-drink movement, felt there was a good chance of success if they could only exert enough pressure on sitting Members of Parliament. Women in different organizations found themselves having to decide their priorities. But none achieved their goals, because the Liberal Party lost the election. It was widely believed that the temperance issue had brought down the party.

Lady Henry Somerset continued her high-profile campaign to 'agitate, educate, and organise' for the women's movement.[81] She found herself in trouble in 1897 for supporting a new version of the old Contagious Diseases Acts – this time for the British army in India. Her position caused a great outcry. Josephine Butler was upset at her position as was Frances Willard. Under a barrage of criticism, like any good politician, she quickly retracted her support, claiming she had been misunderstood.[82]

Despite the anger and hostility directed against Lady Henry Somerset, the publicity she and her supporters gained during and after the split encouraged many women to join and participate in the movement's activities. For every woman who left the Association because of disagreement with Lady Henry Somerset's policies, many others joined. By 1900 the Association claimed 1,111 branches with over 100,000 members. (It did admit, however, that a precise count of the individuals belonging to the branches was difficult.)[83] The president continued to work for the women's movement. However, the importance of the National British Women's Temperance Association to the greater women's movement was not in its leadership, but in its ability to activate large numbers of women to take part in public demonstrations and public rallies throughout the country. Whether these women would have been involved without the Association no one can say, but this temperance organization had branches reaching into the smallest villages as well as the largest towns, linking British women together in a way no other organization could.

Though the British Women's Temperance Association was the largest women's organization in the country in the 1870s and 1880s, it did not become the leader of the women's movement as did its counterpart in the United States. It failed to take control of the women's movement when the opportunity presented itself. By the late 1880s, political organizations of conservative and liberal women began and by the 1890s the temperance women's moment had passed. During subsequent decades the National British Women's Temperance Association helped bring out large numbers of women to demonstrate for women's suffrage, adding invaluable resources of publicity and organization to this cause.[84] Without such efforts women's voices would not have been so loud.

The British Women's Temperance Association trained large numbers of women to speak on the public platform, to mount public campaigns, and to organize petitions, but many of their most talented women by the late 1880s were leading other women's groups and using their knowlege to aid other goals. Women needed the franchise: They had only a limited local franchise and no vote at all for Parliament. But in order to get it they had to pressure the political parties. Thus we find in the late 1880s and early 1890s the baton of women's leadership picked up by new groups of politically active women. Women's voices were now heard on the political platform and in political circles where they came to focus their energies.

12 For Church, Crown and Empire

A CHANGING FRANCHISE

When property became the basis for political representation in nineteenth-century Britain, its role in the conferment of the franchise was already being challenged by a new concept of citizenship originated in the 'enlightenment' of the eighteenth century: that all people born and residing within the boundaries of a state are citizens of that state, with citizenship rights and duties. The scope, privileges and obligations of citizenship were endlessly debated. In particular, were women citizens[1] and should the franchise be considered a right of citizenship? Philosophically, it was difficult (though not impossible) not to answer both questions affirmatively.

Thus such debates served to increase the pressures for female suffrage, and sharpened awareness among women of their second-class status when their demands were continually rejected, as in the Reform Bills of 1867 and 1884. Not all public women sought the vote. As late as 1889, in 'An Appeal Against Female Suffrage', published in *The Nineteenth Century*, women against women's suffrage argued that 'citizenship does not require the franchise'.[2] But the majority of women involved in public life supported the view expressed by such leaders as Lady Carlisle, a leading female radical, that the vote was indeed part of citizenship.[3]

As the franchise expanded through the adult male population of English society, politics ceased to be the preserve of a small politically conscious minority operating through their individual families. New political organizations now had to be created out of the old alliances. Expediency created new types of associations as well as new ways of politicking, and laws had to be passed to control these innovations. These laws, in turn, led to further alterations in the political world. Changes begat more changes, in a way, and of a kind, that were unanticipated. Both Liberals and Conservatives in the mid-nineteenth century found themselves reaching out into the electorate to draw into the party as many voters as possible. Modern political parties, their organizations and their campaigns, were being born – out of the necessity of the times.

Party motives enfranchised new groups, just as party motives kept others out.[4] Prominent among the excluded were the women, regarded by party chiefs as an unknown quantity in politics.[5] To be sure, individual women of the upper classes continued their traditional involvement in national politics, especially if the men in their families were in office.[6] Both Lady Palmerston and Mrs. Gladstone were the 'intimate political confidants' of their husbands,[7] and Mrs. Gladstone spent so much time in the House of Commons that she had her own seat in the Visitors' Gallery.[8] During election time wives, daughters, and mothers, often wearing the colours of their party, canvassed the districts for brothers, sons, fathers, and husbands. Lady Carlisle's mother did it, and so did she.[9] Lady Milbank, wife of Sir Frederick Milbank, a well-known Member of Parliament from Yorkshire, was another active worker in her husband's campaigns.[10] Women belonging to a political family often were expected to help their men get elected. There being no mass media to dispense political messages, wives and daughters worked the district, handing out leaflets and talking to the electorate, possibly the only personal contact the voter had with the candidate.

LOCAL GOVERNMENT

The first small success for the women suffragists came in the late 1860s when women were given the municipal franchise on the same basis as men. During the 1870s, women expanded their role on the local political scene. They not only voted in municipal elections but stood for office, were elected, and served on borough councils and the new school boards, set up by the 1870 Education Act.[11]

But the work of the local government was of a different category from that of the national government. In nineteenth-century England there was a wide class difference between men who stood and served in national office and those in local positions, just as there was a great difference in the relationship of the elected to the electorate in local and national government. Members of Parliament seldom had prior connections to the areas they came to represent – they were Liberals or Conservatives in search of a seat.[12] And they were often of the upper classes, separated from their constituencies by class differences as well.

In contrast, candidates for local office were usually well-known citizens in their constituencies, supported because of their individual worth rather than party affiliation or social class. Many ran as 'independents', and much of their political work was done by local organizations; the national parties were unconcerned with these parochial contests, there being little national influence to be gained in serving on provincial boards. Although the work the women did on the School Boards, Boards of Guardians, and other local bodies was highly commended, even by some against Parliamentary suffrage for women, it was often regarded as an extension of their domestic role.[13] National government, on the other hand, was the province of men:[14] Parliament meant power, imperialism, and force – 'masculine' attributes, according to many public men and women of the time. Parliament made laws while local government implemented them.[15]

Consequently, women in local government soon learned that they had minimal effect on national policy towards women, and that the supporters of women's issues would only bring about substantial change by working on the national level.

NATIONAL CONSERVATIVE POLITICS: THE PRIMROSE LEAGUE

In the 1850s and 1860s societies had been organized by the political parties to register voters and bring non-resident voters to the polls. These Registration Societies quickly branched out into other political work, coming to represent party interests on a local level.[16] Their work expanded greatly in 1867 when Disraeli doubled the electorate by giving the urban working man the vote; for the first time in English history, borough votes outnumbered those of the counties.[17] Unfortunately for the Conservatives, it was in urban areas where they were weakest in organization and influence. In rural areas they had the support of the landlords and parish officials, including the clergy. Traditional control over the villages and small towns was still effective, so the Conservatives had few problems in winning the rural vote. It was in towns and industrial cities where they faced problems.

Although Gladstone and his Liberals were first to go to the people in their successful 1879–80 political campaign, Conservatives set up the first national organization to educate the ordinary voter in party ideas and to create party loyalty – important for political parties during the late nineteenth and early twentieth centuries. The Primrose League came into being in 1883, partly as a result of the recently enacted Corrupt Practises Act, but also because the Conservative defeat at the polls in 1880 made the Tories realize that they needed the support of the ordinary man to get the borough vote – now essential in gaining control of government. Throughout the country large numbers of new uncommitted voters had little political knowledge and no political affiliation.[18] Now, in 1883, when the 'fortunes of the party were at their lowest ebb',[19] four leading Tory politicians – Lord Randolph Churchill, Sir Henry Drummond Wolff, Sir Algernon Borthwick, and John Eldon Gorst – met at the Carleton Club to discuss broadening support for their party.[20] These young politicians wanted to educate the ordinary voter in 'Tory principles' and to attach him to their party so his loyalty could be counted on at election time.

The four men decided to take advantage of current fads by combining popular crazes for rituals, badges, pledges and social activities with an equally popular fashion for all things medieval that had been stimulated by the romances of recent writers and poets. They proposed to set up a new organization based on a sentimental mythical past, in a spirit kindled by such writers as Sir Walter Scott, Tennyson, and others. This pseudo-historical past appealed to the inhabitants of the ugly, dingy workaday world of nineteenth-century Britain. Dreaming of lords and ladies, of castles and chivalry, many Britons temporarily forgot their real lives, which were the complete opposite of this new fantasy. The new League, purporting to be based on old English traditions, had 'a Creed, a Prophet, and a Symbol'.[21] Named for what was said to be Disraeli's favourite flower, the primrose became its symbol, its prophet was, of course, the late Disraeli, and its creed 'the maintenance of religion, of the Constitution of the realm, and of the Imperial ascendency of Great Britain'.[22]

Because a major function of the League, according to one of its founders, was 'to help the newly enfranchised voter understand the issues of politics – to educate the masses and to organise them, so that they shall voluntarily vote for the cause of order',[23] the League originally enrolled only men. These men, particularly the young ones, it was thought, would be enthusiastic about a League based on the 'old' orders of knighthood.[24] When the Primrose League was judged a success, Lord Salisbury and Sir Stafford Northcote, the country's leading Conservatives, allowed themselves to be elected 'Grand Masters'.[25]

DAMES OF THE PRIMROSE LEAGUE

The 'men only' rule was soon disregarded under pressure from the many women who were eager to join the League. Within weeks of its inauguration, the League accepted women as full members on equal terms with men.[26] Women not only joined the League but became its most enthusiastic supporters. They set up a few branches (habitations) for women only, but the majority were connected to mixed groups where they could often without discrimination be elected leaders. The Dames could receive similar, if not the same, awards as the Knights. Only one body, the London-based governing Grand Council, specifically excluded women, and this was changed when it was told, first, that no women would apply to join, and, second, that a stated prohibition of women was bad publicity for the League as a whole.[27]

A separate Ladies Grand Council was set up in 1887 with membership open to any Dame proposed and seconded by two members who was willing to pay one guinea annually. This ladies' Council had an executive committee comprised of a president and four vice presidents who were to hold the position indefinitely unless they resigned.[28] The only joint central committee was the Literature Committee where five men and four women sat together. It was a rule of the League that 'No member of the Ladies Grand Council shall issue any circular, leaflet or other publication with the imprint of the League which has not been submitted and approved by the said Joint Committee.' This committee also worked to reconcile differences between the men and the women of their respective Grand Councils. A special Consultative Committee of gentlemen was formed to advise the women, important work because women raised large sums of money for the League.[29] Upper-class women often controlled – and spent – their own money.

The numbers of women who joined the Primrose League grew very rapidly, encouraged no doubt by the large number of titled ladies on the Ladies Grand Council. All the members of the executive committee were from aristocratic families: the Marchioness of Salisbury, the Duchess of Marlborough, and the Countess of Iddesleigh were all officers at the same time.[30]

In each branch there was a Ruling Councillor, an Honorary Treasurer, an Honorary Secretary, and several Wardens – the number depending on the size of the habitation. The Secretary did most of the work and, if the habitation were a large one, would have a great deal of power. All the property, except for the funds, was in the charge of this official, who also saw that all official vacancies were filled and that a program of meetings, work and entertainment was organized. Many of these Secretaries were women.

Each habitation was allotted and responsible for a clearly defined district in its own electoral division. This, in turn, was divided into segments put in the care of Wardens, who reported back to the habitation. Wardens were 'the backbone of the Habitation', according to an official publication,[31] and kept lists of members and took charge of seeing that those in their areas eligible to vote were registered. They distributed leaflets and were responsible for educating members in Conservative principles: 'to instruct working men and women how to answer the arguments of the Radicals and the socialists and the atheists in the workshops and in the public houses and at the street corners.' [32] Wardens also organized the social side of the Primrose League, which was to 'help break down class barriers'.[33] Many League wardens were women and they proved to be effective in their work, especially in canvassing homes in their areas. As pointed out by one of the leading Dames of the League, Lady Llangattock:

> Who is a better canvasser than a woman? and how many of our legislators owe the position of which they are so proud to efforts put forth by us, and to careful arguments which lost nothing of their irresistibility by coming from the lips of one of our sex. There are, of course, but comparatively few men who are able to devote any considerable amount of time to canvassing in its proper sense. By this I do not mean the hurried visit with the canvass-book during the few weeks that elapse immediately before an election: but rather that systematic, continuous, friendly visiting, with the kindly chat for the believer, the cogent reason for the objector, and the ready information for the inquirer. It is in such a work as this that the Primrose League offers the greatest field for women's labour . . . . [34]

Lady Llangattock went on to point out that through League work women have received 'a most excellent training in business system' as well as a great sense of responsibility in public matters.[35]

Local women were sometimes given the honorary title of Dame President in appreciation of their important work 'in helping to draw all classes together without distinction'.[36] According to the League's official manual:

> A few unaffected kind words, and a consistent effort to show that all sorts and conditions of men are united in the League for common objects and interests have done more to defeat the tactics of ignorant Socialists and revolutionaries than all the theories of politicians. Herein lay the real duty of a Dame President, and the scope of her work is practically unlimited in this direction.[37]

The Primrose League quickly proved to be a very popular organization and enrolled many middle- and upper-class members. The working class was attracted to it but the membership fee was prohibitive. The League then developed an 'associate' category of membership, one which paid nothing at all to the central committee and only the dues that the local habitation agreed on. But all classes of members had equal rights and privileges, an aspect that appealed to working-class members. Although these associate members were a small financial loss to the League – they got their brooches and 'diplomas' free – the League valued them as a validation of their claim that it was an organization for all, no matter the class.[38]

From the beginning members of the association were 'intended as a substitute for the paid canvassers about to be abolished by Mr. Gladstone's Reform Bill',[39] and in the early years, at least, the League was careful about its role in Conservative politics. Originally the habitations were dissolved on the approach of an election, to keep them officially apart from the contest.[40] There was much uncertainty as to how recently enacted laws dealing with parties and elections were to be applied. Eventually, there was some relaxation; the League not only stayed in existence but its members were asked to place themselves entirely at the disposal of the 'election agent of the party which the League supports . . . '[41] The Conservative victory in the general election of 1885 showed both political parties the importance of organizing the public, and the effectiveness of such organizations as the Primrose League in reaching the urban workers and young voters in particular.[42]

As the official object of the Primrose League was to 'maintain Religion, the Estates of the Realm and the unity and ascendency of the Empire',[43] no one thought the League anything other than a part of the Tories.[44] '*Imperium et Libertas*' (Power and Freedom) was its motto, which sat well with the supporters of British imperialism in the late nineteenth century. The League was firmly committed to maintaining the union with Ireland and could activate thousands, and sometimes tens of thousands, to demonstrate throughout the land against Irish Home Rule. Despite its avoidance of direct affiliation with the Conservative Party all knew its political role.

At one point a dispute occurred as to who should be in charge of the women's groups. Randolph Churchill, a founder, said that new habitations of women should be under the mixed or male habitations in the localities.[45] But much depended on the membership of the local organizations and their social rank. No ordinary gentlemen would try to control titled or socially prominent women if the latter had their own habitation. However, this was not a common problem, and more often than not the women and their husbands jointly ran the local habitations.[46] All-women habitations were only a minority in the League: In 1886 there were 57 of them against 400 mixed or all-male habitations.[47]

No doubt much of the success of the Primrose League was due to the socially advantageous positions of the members. In the country areas where the nobility and gentry were mostly Conservative supporters, landowning families had tremendous prestige, and if any members of such a family sponsored a Primrose League habitation, it would certainly get local support. For women of these families, the work of running a habitation was similar to community work they had traditionally done: organizing garden parties, local bazaars, and other county events. Furthermore, the links between church and manor house, vicar and squire, always strong in rural areas where they had customarily run the local society, could be reactivated to support a League dedicated to the established church and order.

For lower-class inhabitants in many English agricultural villages and rural areas, the League served a different purpose. While the upper and middle levels of that society had dances, private parties, visiting, and other forms of relaxation, for the poorer men and women there existed few entertainments and little broke the monotony of their every-day labours. Women in particular, often isolated in a farmhouse or hamlet, found the regular meetings of the Primrose League a welcome break. Teas and lantern slides were a treat for these women with little or no other social connections.[48] It is not surprising that more than half the membership of Primrose habitations was drawn from rural areas or small towns – many from families of agricultural labourers – and that women were the most active members.[49]

Women members played a particularly important role in taking the League into rural and other areas where aristocratic landlords still had much authority. Here the bicycle proved an important tool in increasing women's mobility. Taking advantage of the popular craze for this machine, a special Primrose League Cycling Corps was set up and became a popular branch of the League in the 1890s. Besides sponsoring recreational excursions, the Cycling Corps utilized the bicycle for other needs of the League, such as visiting homes and distributing literature.[50] Women also organized vans equipped with magic lanterns to give anti-Home Rule messages, and sponsored free concerts in poorer areas.[51] Women were employed by the Primrose League as speakers and organizers in all districts, some of them extremely successful, and some individual women were credited with the creation of numerous habitations.[52]

The Primrose League was a social club that took advantage of the snobbishness of English social life. To join an organization with so many titled members, even if far away, was considered by many English men and women to be the height of respectability and affirmed one's acceptance in local society at all levels. (The Liberals also exploited deference when they appointed many titled members to their boards, though they found most of the titled women were Conservatives.) The Liberal ladies, with understandable envy, complained that the Primrose Dames were recruited from society drawing rooms,[53] and have an 'illegitimate love of power and dictation'.[54]

From the first the League played an active role in so-called patriotic causes. On April 19, 1885, it held a 'monster meeting' at St. James Hall in London where 900 members came to support their party against Bradlaugh and the Secularists. Its extreme language appealed to the Primrose Leaguers' sentimental mode of thought. They saw the demand by the secularist Bradlaugh to be seated in the House of Commons without any religious oath as 'an insult to all Christendom' and believed that the 'inviolability of sacred religion was not assailed with impunity by this sinister homethrust . . . ' The meeting was also against Home Rule for Ireland.[55]

It is difficult to find accurate membership figures for the League. The official numbers published by the League and its adherents were somewhat inaccurate, since they reflected new memberships without subtracting resignations.[56] However, by looking at the figures we get some idea as to the League's scale and growth. In its first year, 1884, 747 Knights and 153 Dames were said to be enrolled.[57] By the next year, 1885, an election year, 8071 Knights, 1381 Dames and 1914 associates had reportedly joined. Then there was an explosion of enrollments: From 1885, when it had 11,366 members, it rose in twelve months to more than a quarter of a million members. By 1891, the League claimed over a million members – 63,251 Knights, 50,973 Dames and 887,068 associates – and by 1899 one and a half million, mostly associates.[58]

THE LEAGUE AND THE WOMAN QUESTION

Among all the members of the Primrose League the Dames became especially noted for their activities, as one of the four founders acknowledged.[59] Important in keeping the women happy and loyal was the League's avoidance of partisanship on the many issues that made up the Woman Question. Women's suffrage, the most important of these issues for women involved in politics in the 1890s, was divisive within many organizations, especially those with a large female membership; but not in the Primrose League.

Some of the most prominent of Conservative leaders supported women's suffrage, or at least publicly supported it, but those who did not usually abstained from openly taking sides. Thus, Lord Salisbury was believed by many Conservative women to support the view that women deserved the vote but their time had not yet come. Many Conservative women accepted that they would be enfranchised soon but had to wait for the best political time for their Party's official support.[60] In 1891, when the National Union of Conservatives held their annual conference, Mrs. Fawcett was invited to speak on the topic of women's enfranchisement, after which they voted 'to support Women's Suffrage when the next suffrage Bill comes up'. Lord Salisbury reportedly favoured this resolution as did Mrs. Balfour, wife of the Conservative politician.[61] It is also worth noting here that the two main bills for the enfranchisement of women in the 1890s came from Conservative backbenchers and some of the Conservative leaders, and that many of their backbenchers voted for these bills, while the Liberal leadership (and most Liberal backbenchers) did not.[62]

Recognizing the potential of the women's suffrage issue to create discord within the Primrose League, a 'precept' (order) was issued in 1889 forbidding all habitations from officially taking part in women suffrage meetings or passing resolutions supporting or opposing it. There was no rule against members attending in their nonLeague capacity, because the Primrose League officially held 'no position on Women's Suffrage'.[63]

Though rank-and-file women of the League were conservative and generally anti-women's suffrage, their women leaders were not. But these leaders were unwilling to challenge party leadership on this issue. Mostly of aristocratic background, and more politically free than their middle-class sisters, they usually valued class loyalty over gender rights in any conflict between them. Even if a Lady Palmerston or a Lady Nevill did not have all the opportunities or the privileges, or the influence of the men of her family, she certainly had more than middle- or lower-class males. Nevertheless, as we have seen, many upper-class women did work for women's causes, and the feminist paper, *Women's Penny Paper*, in the late 1880s, had regular columns devoted to the events of interest to feminists taking place in Primrose League habitations throughout England.

THE DAMES' SUCCESS

The *Women's Penny Paper* also reported that the 'great success' of the Primrose League had led to its imitation in France by the 'League of the Rose'.[64] One historian of the Primrose League in trying to explain the Dames'success has summarized its advantages:

> A larger proportion of Conservative leisured women free for party hack work and the day to day social contacts so valuable to local party organization; the unique position of women in rural community life where the Conservative party had its deepest roots; and lastly the

> more vivid appeal to women of the very issues, slogans and general propaganda of the Conservative Party during these years – all these factors together may account for the greater success of the Conservatives in mobilizing their women.[65]

The women of the upper classes were used to canvassing for family members, often having worked the districts for their husbands in the past. There was nothing new for them in this and, more importantly, such activities ran into none of the family opposition that sometimes occurred in many middle- and lower-class English families. A letter in the March 12, 1887, edition of the Liberal *Kent Times* criticizing the Primrose Dames indicates their effectiveness even in such early days. The author, A. W. Marks, claimed the Dames were taught how to 'secretly bribe and intimidate poor voters' and evade the provisions of the Corrupt Practises Act; and that they had learned to parrot a few empty phrases, but were actually politically ignorant, believing that the 'Church-going Conservatives are the cream of society'. He went on to complain of the 'Primrose League follies – tinsel badges, bragging mottos, sham titles and secret illegal doings'. However, in tacit acknowledgement of the great support of these ladies to their party at election time, the writer called on the Liberal women of Kent to organize and help the Liberal party capture the seats of Kent.[66] But Conservative women remained far more effective in their political work than their Liberal sisters.

13 Raised Voices for Justice

THE LIBERAL ASSOCIATIONS

The Liberals did not have the same resources as the Conservatives, and had to work with local volunteer help in organizing and fighting political campaigns. After the Reform Bill of 1867 there developed spontaneously, at election times, local volunteer associations to help the Liberal candidates fight their contests. In 1877 the National Liberal Federation was organized to coordinate the efforts of these individual associations. The Federation and its associations created a political organization that reached down into the homes of supporters, or potential supporters.[1]

Quickly Britain was blanketed by a network of these associations, as the Liberals sought to have one in every electoral division. At first most of them were active only at election time, as they were aids to an election campaign, not a permanent feature of political life. But soon they became a regular organization, doing party work between campaigns in addition to their original election work. The Federation met annually and became a powerful pressure group on the Liberal Parliamentary leadership as well as an important conduit of popular attitudes from the voters to the Parliament's leaders.[2]

Each independent association set its own terms of membership. Although some of them allowed women members, they were basically male organizations. Some of the local associations supported the women's suffrage movement, but, as each association individually set its own program, this did not affect the policies of the others.[3] Because many associations found that women were effective workers in door-to-door canvassing, they were recruited for this work.

THE WOMEN'S LIBERAL ASSOCIATIONS

In 1879 Gladstone's Midlothian Campaign took him around Scotland, making public speeches in support of his program and party. As part of this campaign, on November 26, 1879 he gave a speech at Dalkeith, in which he publicly invited women to help in the coming election:

> I think that in appealing to you ungrudgingly to open your own feelings and bear your own part in a political crisis like this, we are making no

> inappropriate demand, but are beseeching you to fulfil a duty which belongs to you, which, so far from involving any departure from your character as women, is associated with the fulfilment of that character, and the performance of its duties; . . . and to warrant you in hoping that, each in your own place and sphere, you have raised your voice for justice . . . .[4]

This speech was the go-ahead signal for Liberal women to organize locally.[5] As early as 1874, a Women's Liberal Association had been formed in Birmingham, but it does not appear to have had much connection with other groups around the country, nor did it later join the Women's National Federation when it was organized.[6] In 1880, the first 'official' Women's Liberal Association was organized in Bristol, where ladies from well-known local Quaker families were the leaders.[7] These ladies were not only dedicated Liberals but also ardent supporters of 'the cause of Women's Suffrage, and kindred questions'.[8] In 1884, the women of Plymouth asked the Bristol Association for help in forming a Women's Liberal Association in their town.[9]

A second Women's Liberal Association was organized by Sophia Pease Fry, wife of the Liberal Member of Parliament for Darlington, Theodore Fry. From a prominent Yorkshire Quaker family noted for its Liberal Party support, Mrs. Fry had always worked for her husband at election times; in 1880 she and some local women organized a Women's Liberal Association with the twofold aim of helping her husband at election time, and disseminating Liberal propaganda to the Darlington voters.[10] Another Yorkshire group formed the third association, at York, in 1881, where Lady Milbank worked in her husband's election campaigns.[11] The first London Women's Liberal Association was started in South Kensington soon after and continued to be active to the end of the nineteenth century.[12]

These new organizations played an important role in local Parliamentary elections, but their value to the party increased greatly when Gladstone, to eliminate the financial advantages of the Conservatives, introduced the Corrupt Practises Act, which became law in 1883. This act severely limited the amount of money a candidate and his party could dispense in an election; thus it became necessary for both parties to use unpaid volunteer help at election time. Such help was needed because, although by law it was the voter's responsibility to see that he was registered to vote, the candidates and their parties had taken on this work.[13]

Soon it was discovered that while entering the names on the register, the canvasser was in an excellent position to talk to the householders and their families about political issues. This became a very important way of spreading political information in a time when there were few ways of reaching large numbers of electors and their families. The candidates with the most canvassers would be able to reach, and they hoped influence, the most voters. Women were particularly good at door-to-door canvassing; middle-class women at home became a great potential source of volunteer help, and one of the primary aims of the new Women's Liberal Associations was to educate them in party matters to enhance their effectiveness even more. If it cannot be said that the few women active in the election of 1879 made any great difference in the outcome, the victory of the Liberals at that time encouraged many other women to take up the fight so that by 1886 fifteen Women's Liberal Associations had been created.[14]

THE WOMEN'S LIBERAL FEDERATION

The Conservative victory in the 1885 elections gave a great boost to the activities of the Primrose League. At the same time the defeat of their party led the Liberal ladies to reassess their organizations. Sarah A. Tooley, a later spokesperson for the Women's Federations wrote:

> When the Home Rule agitation of 1885–6 agitated the Liberal Party to its foundation, it aroused Liberal women to a more public interest in politics, and was in a measure the factor which brought into existence the Women's Liberal Federation.[15]

On May 27, 1886, a meeting was held at Mrs. Fry's London home to which came representatives of the various Women's Liberal Associations.[16] Lady Milbank, presiding over this meeting, was not enthusiastic about a new national Federation. Though she had helped organize a Women's Liberal Association at York to aid her husband's election campaigns, she worried that a more permanent national organization would encourage women 'to enter into the excitement of political struggles' and take them away from their home duties.[17]

Reports from seventeen Associations scattered around the country, with about 6,000 members, were given.[18] Four Members of Parliament addressed the meeting – Prof. Stuart, Messrs. H. G. Reid, Theodore Fry and H. J. Wilson – and proposed a resolution that the Women's Liberal Associations should be supported on the grounds that 'they have the special object of promoting more extensive knowledge of Liberal principles amongst women of all classes such as shall enable them to form sound opinions upon public questions'.[19] Mrs. Fry warned that though well-educated women were needed in this work 'they must not allow their superiority to be so felt as to mar the harmony of the society to which they belong'.[20] Seeking to get the support of all classes, Mrs. Fry said, 'It is the workingman's vote that turns our elections' and 'the views of this class should be studied.'[21] It was agreed to set up a new national women's organization; and with this aim a general meeting was convened on February 25, 1887.[22]

By the time of this first general meeting of the Women's Liberal Federation there were already 40 Women's Liberal Associations with over 10,000 members.[23] It was decided to draw up a list of the 'Objects' of the Federation. The first three were as follows: 'to promote the adoption of Liberal members in the government of the country'; 'to promote just legislation for women and protect the interests of children'; and 'to advance political education by meetings, lectures and the distribution of literature'.[24]

There was concern over the role the Central Committee should play in the Federation, since the provincial associations would not want to be controlled by a London body.[25] It was agreed that the Central Committee 'would assist but in no way supersede the work of the Local Association'.[26] Consequently, unlike the habitations of the Primrose League, the Women's Liberal Associations were to be independent of the London central office; the women who organized each Association remained responsible for its program and projects. Neither were the local Associations controlled by the Liberal Party or any other organization: The Federation's only power was to be that of persuasion.[27] It would send speakers and give other aid, but only if asked. Furthermore, although the Executive of the new Federation would be fixed in London, annual meetings would be held in different parts of the country.

To show official support for the new organization, Mrs. W. E. Gladstone, never publicly active in political work, agreed to be the president of the new Federation. In her inaugural address, her first public speech, she said she was 'old fashioned' in her views on women's role in politics, 'but do not think when I admit that my views are old fashioned that I think they are out of date. I stick to my guns about that'.[28] Having the leader's wife as president gave the Liberal Party some control over program and activities. In her annual address of 1888, Mrs. Gladstone reported that the Women's Liberal Federation had over sixty branches, 'all doing quiet, steady, but excellent work in the country. We have only to work on bravely, patiently, hopefully towards a triumph of right and justice . . . for Ireland . . . Listen to prudence to courage and to honour . . . . '[29]

Mrs. Gladstone herself did little in the organization, treating her position as a ceremonial one. She chaired the annual meeting of the Women's Liberal Federation and the special women's meetings that were becoming regular events at the annual gatherings of the National Liberal Federation. The actual leadership of the Federation, however, was exercised by two very loyal Liberals, both wives of leading Liberal politicians. One, the vice-president, was the Countess of Aberdeen, daughter of a leading Liberal family;[30] the other was Mrs. Fry of Darlington, who preferred to keep a low public profile.[31]

The new Federation quickly took hold and by 1888 the number of affiliated associations had grown to 63 with a membership of 16,500.[32] Some existing Women's Liberal Associations refused to join the Federation, believing their local affiliations were sufficient.[33] The most powerful Liberal constituencies often did not have a Women's Association, Liberal politics being dominated there by an all-male or a mixed association. Frequently Women's Liberal Associations were formed in Conservative districts where the males were uninterested in a Liberal organization.[34] By the time of the 2nd Annual Report, in 1889, a total of 96 Associations, with a total membership of 33,500, had affiliated with the Federation. Weak in London, their greatest strength was in the north of England. Individuals could affiliate directly with the Federation if there were no Association in their area, but few did.

Any Liberal association admitting women was made eligible for membership, with the result that many local Liberal Associations composed largely of men joined the Women's Liberal Federation. This showed up on the membership rolls in a sizable male minority. Although men could attend the annual meeting and even speak on motions, it was an association organized by women, run by women, with a program selected by women. Most of their speakers were women, though men were frequently invited onto their platforms (necessary, of course, if they wanted a Member of Parliament to address them.

By 1890 the Federation claimed 133 affiliated associations with a membership of over 51,300, of which 45,350 were women. The greatest increase was in the north of England, the least in London. Many of the groups became active only at election time, either during a general election or when the area had a by-election; then a 'band of trained workers' were ready to 'spring into action' for the Liberal cause.[35] The Federation now had a large list of vice-presidents mostly made up of women from prominent Liberal families.

Connections between local groups were formed by setting up regional and local unions. Some of these held their own annual meetings.[36] The first, the East London Liberal and Radical Union, had been organized by the Countess Schack. In the capital there was also the North London Liberal and Radical Union of Women's Liberal Associations as well as the Metropolitan Counties Liberal and Radical Women's Associations. In the provinces there was the Union of Midland Associations. Another large and active union, founded in 1888, was the North of England Women's Liberal Association, which held its own annual conferences. The Women's Liberal Federation determined that these unions would be treated not as rivals but as allies in the Liberal cause, fully supported whenever aid was requested.[37]

Local organizations were the real centers of activity of the Liberal women. Sometimes as in the Primrose League a prominent lady was the moving force. The Countess of Carlisle organized and paid the expenses of a Women's Liberal Association in Carlisle.[38] In the local associations there was a much broader representation of the social classes than was to be found in the national Federation. Some of the local groups were made up of working-class women who could not afford the full affiliation fee of the Federation.[39] Even if they had the money, some associations would not have joined because it would bring them little advantage. They could not afford to send representatives to annual meetings nor could they come up to London for consultation with the executive. They were strictly parochial organizations working for Liberal candidates for practical reasons – not because of support for abstract Liberal principles.[40] Often the candidate was someone who had promised to support legislation of local importance. Many of the working women were self-supporting; unlike their wealthier sisters, they had little surplus time or money to devote to favourite causes.[41]

Once the effectiveness of women in political work was recognized by candidates and their supporters,[42] women were admitted into many Liberal Associations – sometimes as regular members but often as 'affiliates'. Not infrequently, men voted to admit the women into their associations after a separate women's association had already been set up and was functioning well. The opening of formerly all-male groups to female members led many women to declare the women's organization 'superfluous'.[43] Like the Dames of the Primrose League, they wanted to have an equal voice in local party organizations, not a separate place in the party. However, other women for various reasons wanted to keep the women's organizations. Lady Carlisle, for example, believed that women without a vote could never be equal to men in a political organization, and also that women did not yet have the political experience of the men and were 'overmatched' in a mixed society:[44] Experience could only be gained in an all-female organization.[45]

The major role of the members of the Women's Liberal Associations was to help Liberal candidates at election time. They canvassed their areas much as the Primrose Dames did, going house to house with pamphlets and talking to householders. They made a special point of working with women – educating them politically and encouraging them to participate in the elections for which they were eligible. They were active in local contests – for instance for school board candidates and poor-law guardians – paying particular attention to contests where women were involved.[46]

Almost from the beginning, a close affinity existed between the women of the Federation and those of the British Women's Temperance Association, reflecting a broader alliance at this time – in the late 1880s – between the Liberal Party and the anti-drink movement; it continued until the defeat of the Liberals in 1895.[47] A number of women were leaders of both. The Countess of Carlisle headed the North of England Temperance League and was also a prominent Liberal supporter. Lady Henry Somerset, the head of the British Women's Temperance Association, was a member of the executive of the Women's Liberal Federation. Lady Battersea, an active worker for the children's temperance movement, the Band of Hope, was a member of both women's groups. However, not all the Liberal Federation members were protemperance – some were very much against it.[48]

In May, 1889, the Women's Liberal Federation bought a weekly journal *Woman's Gazette*, and Miss Orme, a member of the executive committee of the Federation, was made editor and manager of the paper.[49] All the local Associations were asked to support the paper by sending in their news and buying copies.

Like other women's groups, the Federation suffered from a great shortage of women speakers in its early days, felt particularly keenly in a political organization. If women were to provide political leadership, they would have to mount the public platform where most public discussion of political issues occurred. Fortunately a few trained or naturally talented women knowledgeable in political issues were available, some seasoned in other activities such as the anti-Contagious Diseases Acts movement or the temperance reform. At the Federation's annual meeting in May, 1890, it was proposed and passed that the Federation provide 'lady lecturers whose work should be the organizing of local Associations and the visiting of existing affiliated ones'.[50] In addition local Associations were to be asked for names of women willing to speak on behalf of the Federation.

WOMEN'S SUFFRAGE: 'A BURNING QUESTION'

The Federation was deeply involved in women's issues. It published pamphlets and material of particular interest to women;[51] and activist women in the Federation set up Parliamentary Committees to monitor all legislation affecting women. Acting as unofficial advocates for all the country's women they went to Westminster and lobbied for the benefit of their sisters. These committees issued reports on current legislation which were discussed at the annual meeting of the Women's Liberal Federation and published in relevant journals. One special project of these committees was to persuade the government to appoint women as official inspectors in factories and other workplaces. Under their guidance the Federation's executive committee in 1892 sent a letter to the Liberal Home Secretary expressing satisfaction at his appointment of two women as factory inspectors and requesting the appointment of more women, particularly for workplaces where women were employed. They also asked that any women thus employed be recompensed 'at an equal salary with male inspectors for equal work'.[52]

The Parliamentary Committees watched for bills that regulated women's labour and petitioned the government to let the opinion of the women themselves be ascertained before legislating on their behalf, not trusting male legislators who passed laws for the benefit of women.[53] These committees also examined the legal treatment of men who had committed violent acts against women. At the annual Federation meeting in 1892 a resolution was passed condemning government policies on sentencing men for assaulting women and children. The penalties, the women claimed, were 'inadequate' for such violence, and they asked Parliament to see that the laws on such matters were more strictly enforced.[54]

By now the foremost women's issue was suffrage. As we have seen, Conservatives navigated the stormy seas of women's rights by leadership support of women's suffrage in theory, but not in practice: The claim was that its time had not yet come. Officially women's suffrage and allied women's issues were not matters for the Primrose League; a member who wanted to take a stand on them, would have to do so elsewhere.[55] The Liberals could not take such a stance: As a party of reform, they needed the support of radicals and more moderate advocates of change. Disagreements over the various issues that made up the Woman Question eventually caused splits within Liberal ranks. At first many leading Liberal politicians, including W. E. Gladstone and Herbert Asquith, who were not supporters of women's suffrage or other women's causes, chose not to alienate advocates of women's rights, by avoiding the issues. They claimed, for instance, that only a small militant minority of women wanted women's suffrage. Instead of 'wasting time' on matters of little interest to the party, the Liberal women were directed by the party leaders to focus on 'Liberal' issues, particularly the controversial 'Home Rule of Ireland'.[56]

Granting suffrage to any group was not so much a matter of justice as a move of party strategy.[57] By 1884 women were the last adult citizens completely excluded from the Parliamentary franchise. Paradoxically the party that should logically have supported their franchise claim was the one most distrustful of women's political behavior. Liberal leaders believed that if women got the vote, they would support Conservatives – voting for the established church, for the throne, for Empire, and for other Tory icons.[58] The Conservatives, on the other hand, were not eager to enfranchise women because the most active women in the movement tended towards radicalism and Liberalism in their politics. They feared that only if voting were made compulsory would they gain by it.[59] To avoid Party divisiveness over women's suffrage, the leaders of both parties made it a non-party issue. This allowed both Conservatives and Liberals to 'vote their conscience' without any party discipline.

The Women's Liberal Federation tried to keep to the strict party line, supporting Home Rule for Ireland, Welsh Disestablishment of Church, and the temperance reform: the program as approved by the National Liberal Federation and the Liberal Party. In the late 1880s and early 1890s when a number of issues divided members of the Liberal Party they also caused divisions in the women's Federation. Prominent among these was the matter of Home Rule for Ireland; a separate Women's Liberal Unionist Association was created in 1888.[60] Lady Carlisle, for example, was a Liberal, as were her mother and husband. But her family was split over Home Rule; her husband and mother joined the Liberal Unionists, while Lady Carlisle herself remained loyal to Gladstone. She was a great admirer of the Liberal leader, her loyalty sometimes strained over the suffrage question.[61]

The Women's Liberal Federation was a Liberal party organization, and so its first *Object* was 'to promote the adoption of Liberal members in the government of the country'. As a second *Object* the Federation was committed 'to promote just legislation for women and to protect the interests of children'. Soon it became evident that not all the members approved of the order of these priorities. Increasingly women active in politics were unwilling to promote Liberal principles at the expense of women's rights; pressure was growing from the rank and file to take up these matters – particularly women's suffrage. Despite what the Liberal party leaders said about women's indifference to the franchise,[62] support for women's suffrage was growing rapidly, especially in the 1890s when more and more women's organizations were throwing their support to it. As the British Women's Temperance Association had to deal with bitter disputes within its ranks over its relationship to the women's movement, so did the Women's Liberal Federation face the same conflicts.

From the beginning of the Federation the issue of women's suffrage was a thorny one, but it had been kept suppressed by the leadership. They had managed to exclude it from the explicit formulation of the official 'Objects of the Federation', because they did not want to support a stand that the Liberal Party leadership opposed. Many of the Federation leaders were wives of Liberal MP's and committed to a strict party line. Their political role was as auxilaries of their husbands, not as leaders of the women's movement. When Gladstone told them that Ireland must take precedence over any other issue, including women's suffrage, the leadership of the Women's Liberal Federation agreed.[63]

Mrs. Gladstone, president of the Federation, was very much against taking up the women's suffrage issue. She supported her husband in the view that the Irish cause and other Liberal issues were more important. Two other leaders of the Federation divided on this issue. The Countess of Aberdeen, a vice president and soon-to-be president, was a strong supporter of women's suffrage but would have preferred the issue to be pursued elsewhere, allowing the Federation to follow more orthodox Liberal concerns. Her husband was a luminary in the Liberal Party galaxy, given prominent party posts when the Liberals were in power, and so she preferred not to offend the leadership if it could be avoided. Mrs. Fry, on the other hand, was a vigorous opponent of women's suffrage and led the Federation opposition to it.[64] She accepted the official line: that the time was not ripe for such a move, that most of the women did not want the vote, and though women would ultimately get it, right now they must be patient. Meanwhile, she believed, the Federation should accept party priorities, educate women in Liberal principles, and avoid controversial issues that would 'cut off members who do not agree'.[65]

While the Executive for five years was succeeding in fending off any move to make the Federation active in the suffrage movement, many affiliated local groups were giving women's issues, particularly women's suffrage, top priority in their programs.[66] Many women joined their local Women's Liberal Association in order to promote women's role in the political life of the country, and this usually meant getting the franchise. The rank and file of the provincial Associations were less concerned with party strategies than with their personal conditions. Nor did the issue of Ireland press on the lower-class Liberal supporters in the same way as did their own economic and social situations.

However, in the early days of the Federation only a minority of members of the executive committee belonged in the prosuffrage camp. These worked hard to increase their numbers and influence within the committee.[67] There was an ever-deepening split, with the prosuffrage supporters becoming known as 'Progressives', while their opponents were called 'Moderates'.[68] The Progressives made the stated *Objects* of the organization the focus of their fight. No one disputed having 'the promotion of Liberal principles' as the primary goal of the Federation, although there was trouble in interpreting what this actually meant. To some women, suffrage for all citizens was a true Liberal principle.[69]

It was the second *Object* of the Federation that became the center of the suffrage controversy from the beginning of the Federation. At the first organizational meeting in February 1887, it was agreed that 'to promote just legislation for all' would have to do until the first Council meeting, scheduled for the following May, took up the issue and decided what this really meant. At the May meeting, *Object 2* was discussed and altered to read: 'To promote just legislation for women and to protect the interests of children.' The Progressives were displeased with this new wording which seemed to avoid the issue of the Federation's commitment to women's suffrage. At the second Council Meeting, May 8, 1888, they asked for a change. Miss Priestman of Bristol and Mrs. Josephine Butler, of anti-Contagious Diseases movement fame, proposed to have *Object 2* read: 'To obtain the Parliamentary Franchise for women, and to promote just legislation for all.' With only thirty-one voting for this amendment and a 'large majority against', it failed.[70]

At the third annual Council meeting, held May 22, 1889, the same amendment was proposed. Speaking for it again were the 'Bristol ladies', Mrs. Bright Clark[71] and Miss Priestman, along with such other well-known suffragists as Miss F. Balgarnie, Mrs. Ormiston Chant, and Miss Jane Cobden – now a member of the London County Council and soon to be Mrs. Fisher Unwin. Mr. Walter S. McLaren, Liberal MP and a dedicated member of the Women's Liberal Federation, also spoke for it. The motion was opposed by such luminaries as Lady Hayter, Lady Sandhurst, and Mrs. Oscar Wilde as well as the Countess of Aberdeen who chaired the meeting. The motion again failed, this time with 90 votes for and 173 against.[72]

In May 1890, the Progressives came to the annual meeting with increased help from new executive members and a tremendous growth in the number of voting delegates supporting the prosuffrage side. Joining the Progressive leadership was the new executive member, the Countess of Carlisle, a lifelong Liberal but also a suffragist. The Countess had earlier refused to join the Federation because it would not support women's suffrage, but she had changed her mind, now believing she could be more effective working within the organization.[73] Using her considerable social and political prestige, and aided by the Bristol ladies and other dedicated supporters, she led a renewed effort to reformulate *Object 2*:

> This Council is of the opinion that the Franchise should be extended to women on the same terms as to men, and that the earliest suitable opportunity should be taken of including the enfranchisement of women in the Liberal programme.[74]

At this enlarged meeting, swollen by the addition of representatives of new prosuffrage associations actively recruited by Lady Carlisle and her party,[75] 400 delegates voted for it and only 10 against. It was a great and overwhelming victory for the Progressives. Not only had they officially changed *Object 2*, they had done it with such a great majority that it could not be questioned. The Women's Liberal Federation was now committed to supporting the enfranchisement of women. The move was controversial and could have serious consequences for the Federation. If pursued actively its support would bring the Federation into conflict with the party's official program. Mrs. Gladstone recognized that they were in for a stormy time and asked for careful thought before they moved further along the path they had chosen. After the vote, in her address to the Council she said:

> Questions no doubt will arise in the future requiring great thought and time. May I respectfully advise you, my friends . . . that our duty should be to forbear with one another. In Parliamentary life, and in life outside Parliament, differences of opinion must arise now and then. We must meet these differences of opinion with patience and forbearance. Questions so large and so serious will require thought and time; and I would end by saying, emphatically, let us not be precipitate.[76]

Those opposing the adoption of women's suffrage managed to reorganize their forces at the next (1891) annual meeting. Though they could not change the motion passed at the previous council meeting, they hoped to prevent its implementation: It was still only a theoretical statement of principle. The Progressives, however, were able to get another resolution passed that stated, 'it is the duty of the Executive and it be an instruction to them accordingly, to keep the Associations during the ensuing year carefully and immediately informed of every opportunity that may arise of promoting the political enfranchisement of women . . . . '[77]

Many delegates were unhappy at this 1891 annual meeting. The rank and file of the Associations were mostly in support of women's suffrage, an issue growing in importance throughout the country, but the majority of the London executive members, many not representing any local group, were not. The Moderates knew it was only a matter of time before the Federation would adopt a full women's suffrage policy.

A YEAR OF STRIFE

The period 1891–92 was an important time for supporters of women's suffrage. There was great excitement among the suffragists in all classes and parts of the country, and in many different organizations, when a Conservative backbencher, Sir Albert Rollits, introduced a bill that proposed to give Parliamentary suffrage to certain single women. The limitation was intended to avoid the allegedly much feared family split of husband and wife voting for different political parties.[78] A large public meeting was held in St. James Hall, London in April 1892 with the stated purpose of supporting the Rollits Bill. The meeting was an emotional and controversial one, and some women suffragists expressed anger at the proposed exclusion of married women. In the end they won the day: A resolution was passed denouncing the bill.[79]

With the excitement over the Rollits bill the issue of women's suffrage took on a new importance among politically active women. The majority of women working in the local Associations were supporters of the bill and believed their Federation should support it. It was a sad fact for many Liberal women that it was the 'enemy', the Tories, who had introduced this bill.[80] But it had much support among the rank and file Liberals both within and without Parliament, and some of the Associations of the male Liberal Federation came out in favor of it. Although the bill lost in the House division, it was by only 23 votes – 152 votes for the bill and 175 against.[81] There was a feeling among many suffragists that with a bit more effort victory would be theirs.

Within the Women's Liberal Federation the Rollits Bill intensified the efforts of the Progressives to get the Federation fully committed to women's suffrage. A war of circulars developed between the Moderates and the Progressives, with each side sending out their own information on the suffrage issue to branches in London and the provinces. The official journal of the Federation, the *Woman's Gazette*, was edited by the Moderate leader Eliza Orme and so became the voice of that faction. *The Woman's Herald*, an independent women's journal,[82] was pro-women's suffrage and published the views of the Federation's Progressives.

Suddenly, with great drama, the five-year fight between the Progressives and the Moderates was ended when the *Herald* on April 30, 1892, just before the annual Council meeting, printed an *open letter* signed by seventeen members of the executive of the Women's Liberal Federation who opposed the adoption of women's suffrage as an official *Object*. This letter 'to the Members of the Women's Liberal Federation' claimed that a circular issued in the name of Lady Carlisle and others makes 'it apparent that there is an organized scheme on foot to change the basis on which the Women's Liberal Federation was originally formed, viz., to promote the accepted principles of the Liberal Party'. The seventeen then wrote that they had 'judged it best to withdraw our names from the Federation' for reelection to the executive. Among the names listed were Sophia T. Fry, Henrietta Hayter, and Eliza Orme.[83]

The announcement of a Federation split came at a time when a general election was imminent. The Conservatives had been in power since August 1886, and in 1892 were preparing to resign. The Liberals felt they had a very good chance of taking control of the government. With Home Rule for Ireland at stake, many Liberal diehards believed that this was not a time to split their party over such a side issue as women's suffrage.[84] But, at the same time, many party workers and leaders realized that women played an important role in the election campaigns and should not be alienated. The Primrose Dames were giving invaluable service to Conservative candidates during electoral campaigns and the Liberals wanted to be able to call on their women to play a similar role in the upcoming general election.

The Moderate party leaders in the Women's Liberal Federation would not delay their resignations from the executive, and fifteen resigned. Because this was done before the annual meeting of the Council in May, few Moderates were present at that meeting.[85] For the first time in Federation history, there was little fighting at the Annual Meeting when adoption of women's suffrage was proposed. Twelve of the withdrawing members took their local Associations with them out of the Federation, but this loss was more than offset by the increase in the number of Associations joining the Federation because it now pledged support for women's suffrage.[86]

Contrary to the expectations of those that resigned, Mrs. Gladstone continued officially as Federation president. In this important period she did not want to draw any more attention to the organization's split than it had already received. At the same time, however, she wanted to distance herself from the open fight that was inevitable. When the annual meeting of the Council of the Women's Liberal Federation met in May, 1892, Mrs. Gladstone was absent; in her place, chairing the meeting, was Lady Aberdeen, the vice-president. Lady Aberdeen opened the proceedings with the information that Mrs. Gladstone 'is not equal to coming to meetings such as this, but she bids me welcome you in her name, and she wishes us God speed in our work today'. Lady Aberdeen acknowledged the difficulties facing those present: 'We are on the eve of a national crisis, and we are, at this moment going through an internal crisis in our own Federation.'[87] Mrs. Fry had sent a letter explaining that she and her fellow Moderates thought that the Federation which was formed for 'the Promotion of all Liberal measures' was being 'subordinated to the desire to make Women's Suffrage the most important item in the program.' Mrs. Fry added that those who had resigned had done so 'with the full belief that Mrs. Gladstone would also retire'.[88]

Lady Carlisle, the candidate to replace Mrs. Fry as honorary secretary, gave a long, impassioned speech defending herself and her Progressive party against the attacks of the Moderates. After lunch she moved the following resolution:

> That in pursuance of the resolution passed in May, 1890, this Council now instructs the Executive Committee that they shall promote the Parliamentary enfranchisement of women among the Liberal reforms now before the country whilst not making it a test case.[89]

Only one voice was raised in protest against the resolution, a Mrs. Thompson's, who spoke her disapproval of the changes proposed. But she had no allies present to support her.[90] The rest of the speakers gave support to the resolution.

The meeting then adjourned with the Progressive party in charge. On October 27, 1892, Mrs. Gladstone resigned as president of the Federation, stating in explanation that she had too much work.[91] Lady Aberdeen was elected to replace her but served only one year.[92] (The Countess of Carlisle, leader of the Progressives, was elected president of the Federation in 1894 – a position she held for the rest of the decade.) In 1893, at the next annual meeting of the Council of the Federation, *Object 2* of the Federation was formally amended to read:

> to promote just legislation for women (including the Local and Parliamentary franchise for all women, married, single or widowed, who possess any of the legal qualifications which entitle men to vote) and the removal of all their legal disabilities as citizens.[93]

After the Progressive victory at the 1892 annual meeting, a small dedicated band of suffragists organized a *Society of Practical Suffragists* within the Women's Liberal Federation to persuade their less committed sisters to continue the struggle for the franchise.[94] They argued that the vote was essential to all reforms; women once enfranchised could support all other issues. The Federation continued to move closer to the women's suffrage movement and eventually it was made a condition of affiliation: All branches had to state in their 'official purpose of association' that they supported women's suffrage.

For a time the Federation continued to flourish after the departure of the Moderates. In 1893 it claimed to have 369 affiliated associations with a membership of 75,000. The peak was reached in 1895. In that year the Federation claimed a membership of 82,000 individuals, a number that after 1896 it did not reach again until 1907.[95] 1895 was the year when there was great excitement over the election throughout the country, and the Liberals went to the country with a program including almost everything: Home Rule for Ireland, restraint for the Lords, support for temperance, religious equality, and so on – everything but enfranchisement for women. The defeat was shattering.

The years 1898 to 1905 were not good ones for the Federation, or Liberalism generally.[96] Membership in the Women's Liberal Federation dropped in 1902 to a bottom figure of 49,000. (Compare the numbers with the Primrose League which in 1891 claimed 50,973 Dames and many women among its associate ranks and, in 1901, 64,906 Dames – almost as many Dames as Knights.)[97] But the Liberal faithful hung on, and eventually, in 1905, the Liberal Party came back into power.

No matter how close it became to other women's groups, the Women's Liberal Federation continued to be a part of the Liberal Party. Its leaders were always conscious of their unique role as a bridge between their Party and the women's movement. In 1911, when the Liberal Prime Minister invited five members of the Women's Liberal Federation to join a women's suffrage deputation meeting with him and the Chancellor of the Exchequer, the Liberal ladies asked the Prime Minister to 'receive their deputation on its own before the deputation of the Suffrage Societies are received, inasmuch as the Women's Liberal Federation is an integral part of the Liberal Party and they have always refused to associate themselves in any way with the anti-government militant suffragists'.[98]

Members of the Federation had special access to their party leaders and to government members when Liberals were in office. Wives of prominent Liberal politicians continued to join the Federation and many served on its executive committee. They were sometimes asked to use their influence with their husbands on the Federation's behalf.[99] Mrs. Lloyd George and Mrs. Winston Churchill were just two of these wives on the executive. Such connections gave the Federation a special *entree* to the inner circle of politics. (On July 17, 1910, it was recommended to the executive committee that Mr. Lloyd George be 'asked to receive a friendly call should his wife, Mrs. Lloyd George, undertake to arrange the interview and be present.')[100]

In the last decade of the nineteenth century and the first of the twentieth, the women's suffrage issue continued to dominate the woman's question, and the Women's Liberal Federation had to juggle its roles carefully as a part of the political establishment as well as of the women's movement. Throughout this period the Federation did not neglect its other work. The publication and distribution of literature of special interest to women was continued as was the business of the old parliamentary committees, established in the early years of the Federation. They still kept track of legislation affecting women, and issued reports on such subjects as 'the Royal Commission on Sweating', 'Protection of Child Life' and 'The Midwives Registration Bill'.[101]

The Federation also continued working for the political education of women, giving special support to training women speakers for the public platform. The Liberal Women's Speakers Club was organized to encourage young speakers, with classes coached by such well-known female speakers as Lady Bamford-Slack, Mrs. Eva McLaren, Miss Balgarnie, and Miss Somerville. As an aid to this work a Dramatic Section was started which sponsored playreading.[102] Like all reformers in the late nineteenth and early twentieth century, Federation members knew that the best way to contact the masses was through the public platform.

A SPLINTER: THE WOMEN'S NATIONAL LIBERAL ASSOCIATION

The defeated Minority, after they resigned over the suffrage issue, quickly assembled, on July 20, 1892, to set up a new organization. Under the leadership of Lady Hayter, the fifteen executive members called a public meeting which met on December 1, 1892. It was chaired by a man, Sir Arthur Hayter, and dominated by men. Sir Arthur apologised for his role but said he had been invited by the ladies committee as an officer of the 'men's National Liberal Federation' which welcomed them. Mrs. Gladstone, who wished them well, but did not join them, had sent a letter to be read. The second speaker, a Mr. Woodings, was quite critical of the women and told them that 'women should work among women' and not try to influence men, because a 'working man does not want to think he is influenced by the wife of the man next door'.

The new organization was to be called the Women's National Liberal Association, a name suggested by Sir Arthur Hayter. He also suggested they stay close to the men's Federation by locating their offices close to them and using the men's literature. Mrs. Byles (wife of a Member of Parliament, later to become Lady Byles) suggested that men should be invited to join their executive. She also wanted any Women's Liberal Association not in sympathy with the Women's Liberal Federation to be invited to join them. Another speaker, a Miss Biggs of Liverpool, talked of the hostility among Liberal women in her city where there were now five Women's Liberal Associations: one Moderate (anti-suffrage) and four Progressive. If support were not given soon, she said, the Moderate association would disappear.[103]

The Women's National Liberal union was not a successful one, failing to get much support from women around the country. Isolated by choice from the women's movement, their sole focus was the Liberal Party, a male organization. They were without any commitment to the women's issues and so had no special purpose or function: Their affiliates could do the same work as women's auxiliaries of the male National Liberal Associations, and this is what they in effect became. Like the auxiliaries the Women's National Liberal Association was controlled by men.

Furthermore, the new group suffered from a lack of women speakers: The majority of the women activists had stayed with the Federation, while those who were attracted to the new Association were often women who saw their role as one of support for a male-dominated Party. Lady Byles in commenting on this problem pointed out that the major difficulty for their women was that public speaking was not part of that 'side field in which women could exercise those household virtues whereon rests their unconquerable state'.[104] The few women speakers they had were 'overtaxed by the number of invitations they receive',[105] and the Association found it necessary to ask male Liberals to speak on its official platforms – reinforcing the belief among women that the organization was merely a handmaiden to male Liberals. Years later, at the 1912 annual meeting another discussion on holding speakers' classes took place; it was reported that a Miss Mellon was giving them. The Association never developed the great women speakers that were to be found in many other women's organizations and the platform at their annual meetings was always dominated by men, a fact that *The Woman's Signal* was quick to publicize in its columns.[106]

THE WOMEN'S LIBERAL UNIONIST ASSOCIATION

In 1888, two years after the Liberal Party split over home rule, the Women's Liberal Federation had suffered from the loss of some of its most active leaders when Lady Stanley of Alderley (mother of the Countess of Carlisle) organized and presided over a new group – the Women's Liberal

Unionist Association. Active among the small but extremely talented group of women comprising the Association were Miss Isabella Tod, Lady Frances Balfour, and Mrs. Millicent Fawcett, all to become ardent suffragists. In contrast, Lady Stanley's name had headed an anti-suffrage petition published in a popular journal.[107] This difference in positions on the subject of suffrage did not affect their cooperation in the Association because it was a loosely joined group without much structure. They came together to fight the Home Rule Bill of 1886 and continued their struggle against the Bill of 1893.[108]

Headquartered in London, the Women's Liberal Unionist Association supplied women speakers for the Unionist cause. They were fortunate to have within their ranks some of the finest women political speakers to be found in England in the 1890s: Lady Frances Balfour, Mrs. Millicent Fawcett, and Miss Tod were all noted platform speakers.[109]

Miss Isabella Tod of Belfast got her start on the public platform in 1867 when she read a paper on the Higher Education of Girls to the Social Science Association. A worker in the movement supporting the Married Women's Property Bill, she had remained active in reform causes throughout her life. In an interview with the *Women's Penny Paper*,[110] she said, 'My mother trained me to work for women'. Secure financially, she never married and led a life of great independence. She was on the executive of the Ladies National Association and was one of the English women who accompanied Josephine Butler to the Geneva Conference.[111] A prolific writer and contributor of pieces to a number of journals on a variety of subjects, she believed her writing contributed to her success on the public platform.[112] Miss Tod was a Presbyterian and a life-long temperance supporter, a founder and leader of the Irish Women's Temperance Union. She also started a Belfast branch of the National Society for Women's Suffrage.

Although Mrs. Millicent Fawcett was active in the Liberal Unionist cause, her name was mainly connected with the women's suffrage movement. She made her first public speech in 1868 at one of the early meetings in support of women's suffrage. Her husband was a Member of Parliament, and through his influence she became a political leader.[113]

The third woman in this trio of great women speakers was Lady Frances Balfour. Daughter of the Duke and Dutchess of Argyll, a Whig family, she married into a prominent Conservative one, but was a Liberal all her life. Like Mrs. Fawcett and Miss Tod, she was an active feminist and completely committed to equal rights for women. Her high political connections – her husband was a nephew of Lord Salisbury and brother of Arthur Balfour – gave her access to circles useful in her political work and she became one of the best known women political orators on the English platform.[114]

Besides organizing and speaking at public meetings, members of the Women's Liberal Unionist Association wrote and published political articles and pamphlets. Their major work was to fight against the Home Rule policies of Gladstone. In all other ways they were traditional Liberals, supporting most of the traditional policies of the Liberal Party, including free trade. Although this association was not a large one (it does appear to have published membership figures), it had an executive committee that met in London and held regular council meetings in the metropolitan area. As a political force this Association had little impact on the political life of the country, outside of London and Ireland. Its greatest effect was on the women's movement. Through the activities of the Association many of its members made contact with other parts of the women's movement, particularly the women's suffrage cause.[115]

By the end of the Victorian age, the situation of English women was vastly different from that of their mothers and grandmothers at the beginning of the Queen's reign. Between the 1830s and the first decade of the 1900s, many English women had come to realize that they had different concerns and perspectives than their menfolk and so needed to have a separate voice. The experience they gained in creating and sustaining national movements gave them a confidence that enabled them to challenge the notion that they were physically and psychologically unfit to participate in national affairs. First in the anti-Contagious Diseases movement, then in the temperance reform and now, finally, in the political world women were having an effect on the destinies of Britain. The most active women at the turn of the century were members of political organizations; they became the leaders of the women's movement, organizing and directing the campaigns to give women a greater control over their own destinies.

Conclusion:
With Overwhelming Voices

> 'Mr. Gladstone has told us that if the women of England care for the franchise, we must show him that it is so. Well, we must do so with overwhelming voices.' [1]

When the early evangelical women preached they knew they were breaking the social taboos of their time. Despite overt hostility they persisted, secure in the conviction that they were doing the Lord's work.[2] But eventually women preachers were banished from mainstream Methodism and most of their voices were stilled. Others were soon heard, this time mostly Quaker women speaking out for social reform in the anti-slavery movement, temperance reform and other causes of the 1820s, 1830s and 1840s. Though their efforts met with some success these women were in the end relegated to the gallery, figuratively and sometimes literally. They were consigned to auxiliaries and non-decision-making positions, even in such organizations as the Band of Hope, a children's group cofounded by a woman. But it was out of such reforming movements, particularly temperance in the 1850s and early 1860s, that individual women emerge into positions of public leadership, their message often muffled however by a chorus of Victorian opposition, unchallenged by any national women's organizations.

It was the British government that activated a true feminist movement among British women by passing new laws discriminating against the civil rights of women. The anti-Contagious Diseases Acts movement of the 1870s and 1880s spawned the first truly national women's organization in nineteenth century Britain. Ultimately successful in repealing the Acts, the Ladies National Association stimulated greater activity on other issues constituting the 'Woman Question'. The leaders it trained went into other organizations and in turn trained other women in other reforms. In addition it focused women's attention on the political process and gave impetus to a small but growing sentiment already planted among a few women that the most important women's issue, the way to power and protection in nineteenth century England, was the suffrage.

From 1867 when the first women's suffrage societies were formed the cause of suffrage steadily gained support throughout Britain which eventually coalesced in a nationally organized movement. During the 1870s women expanded their role in local government as candidates as well as electors in local elections. But many came to believe that the key to all reform was the parliamentary vote.[3] Laws were made in Westminster, not on local boards.

From the beginning of attempts to form a national women's movement, women were handicapped by their class as well as their sex. Led primarily by middle-class women, deeply committed to the Victorian value of respectability, the women's organizations had frequently to face the paradoxical charge that confronting women's issues was itself unwomanly.[4] For instance, in 1871 there was disagreement over the suitability of the Contagious Diseases Acts as a topic for action by women: To many traditional women, Josephine Butler and her Ladies National Association forfeited respectability by association with such work. An early setback for the suffrage movement was a dispute over the official relationship between a suffrage society and the anti-Contagious Diseases Acts movement. Some of the suffragists in the London National Society for Women's Suffrage who could not support Josephine Butler's campaign withdrew in 1872 to organize the competing Central Committee for Women's Suffrage.[5]

Other issues split the movement from time to time. In 1888 discord arose over the admission to Central Committee membership of political organizations such as the Women's Liberal Associations: Some of the members believed the Committee should stay non-party. A division in committee ranks ensued, and a breakaway Central National Society for Women's Suffrage was founded.[6]

But in the years after 1889 such disagreements were of diminishing importance in the wave of new suffrage support. Many women's groups were persuaded to take up suffrage reform and in so doing became increasingly identified with the greater women's movement.[7] Some, like the Women's Liberal Federation and the British Women's Temperance Association, adopted women's suffrage as an official object of their organization, while others such as the Primrose Dames encouraged individual member support. By the end of the century Conservative and Liberal Unionist women who wanted a full commitment to the movement could join the Conservative and Unionist Women's Franchise Association, led by Lady Selborne and Lady Frances Balfour. At the same time within the Women's Liberal Federation a group of dedicated suffragists were working to get the National Liberal Federation to adopt women's suffrage as part of the Liberal programme.[8] The leaders of many women's organizations were also leaders in the women's suffrage movement. Lady Carlisle, Lady Henry Somerset, Miss Tod and Mrs. Millicent Fawcett, to name a few, had widespread influence among British women, and used it to promote the suffrage cause.

British women were making their voices heard internationally as well. Together with women from the United States in 1888 they created the International Council of Women, joining together women of the temperance, political and suffrage movements. An English woman, Mrs. Millicent Fawcett, was its first president and others were active on its executive and in its membership ranks. Other countries joined the Council until affiliates existed in many European countries as well as the English-speaking ones.[9] The Council 'has not specially identified itself with any one movement', but had the object of providing 'a means of communication between women's organisations in all countries . . . '[10]

'EDUCATE, ORGANISE AND AGITATE'

'*Educate, Organise* and *Agitate*, must be the watchwords for all women', wired Lady Henry Somerset to a Prohibition conference.[11] Women were becoming educated on the 'woman question', they were organizing their movement, and they were agitating for their rights. Leaders had come forward, and 'the troops', those ordinary women who wanted to do their bit for the cause, were going into battle – a battle for social justice. The women demanded to be heard and Parliament had become the primary target for their voices.

Some remarks of Gladstone served as a goad. In 1892, the Liberal leader wrote a widely circulated letter to a Mr. Samuel Smith, a Liberal Member of Parliament, discussing his views on women's suffrage. In this letter Gladstone wrote that 'there has never within my knowledge been a case in which the franchise has been extended to a large body of persons generally indifferent about receiving it';[12] and he cited 'a widespread indifference' on women's suffrage as a reason for delaying it. Mr. Gladstone elsewhere told the women of Britain that if they cared for the franchise they must show him that it was so.[13] Mrs. Bateson, at the annual meeting of the Women's Liberal Federation in 1892, replied to the Prime Minister that they would indeed do so, 'with overwhelming voices'.[14] This they sought to do in large demonstrations and public meetings through this decade and later.

One of the largest was held in 1894. When Parliament was considering a Registration Bill that did not include women, a 'mass meeting' was organized in London with the Women's Liberal Federation, the British Women's

Temperance Association, the Central Society for Women's Suffrage, the National Women's Suffrage Society, and the Women's Trades Union all cooperating. Advertised under the heading 'Shall Women have the Vote', this meeting had eleven women speakers, among whom were some of the most famous women orators of the times: Lady Henry Somerset, Mrs. Millicent Fawcett, Mrs. Eva McLaren, and Mrs. Wynford Phillips.[15] The speakers were, as advertised, representative of every political party. The occasion for this great gathering was the enfranchisement of women in New Zealand.[16] The crowd was such that an overflow meeting had to be set up nearby with the same speakers as the main meeting.[17]

English society was finally accepting women on the platform, and an increasing number of women were able and willing to use it for forceful advocacy of their rights as citizens. 'Monster Public Meetings' were the order of the day, held by women in London and the provinces for temperance and the various political issues that made up the Woman Question, with and without men's help. Always present was the goal of the franchise, which would make them full participants in the country.

It took the English women another two decades to get the vote; that is a story that has been told elsewhere. And the vote turned out to be only one more step in a struggle for full equality by no means completed seventy years later. But what we have seen is how some women broke away from their allotted domestic sphere and dared to take an unconventional stand first just by the act of speaking out, as preachers and reformers, later by speaking out on behalf of full equality for women. John Wesley had bidden women to preach only with an extraordinary call to do so, and indeed this is what was required, then and later in a more secular age. The extraordinary leadership of a few was needed to open public life to other women with more ordinary gifts.

These women, according to Lord Asquith,

> gradually trained the stolid masculine audience at political meetings to regard the spectacle of women sitting on the platform – sometimes in the chair – moving resolutions and even amendments, not with a silent conventional curtsy and smile, but with flights of rhetoric and flashes of humour, as part of the normal machinery of a 'demonstration' or a 'rally'.[18]

It was a triumph, albeit an 'unwomanly triumph'. As Florence Fenwick Miller wrote: 'The walls of Jericho have fallen before the voices and the confidence in their cause of a handful of women in a manner that is as remarkable as any miracle.'[19]

Notes

Introduction

1. Lady Dorothy Nevill, *Under Five Reigns* (London, 1910) pp. 146–47. Note the role bankers played in late Victorian society. The Prince of Wales, later King Edward VII, was a close personal friend of Ernest Cassel the banker.
2. Palmerston was the first major politician to make election speeches around the country and Gladstone developed and refined this type of election activity in his Midlothian Campaigns. R. K. Ensor, *England 1870–1914*, Oxford History, pp. 63–64.
3. H. Asquith, *Memories and Reflections 1852–1927* (Boston, 1929) vol. I, p. 264.
4. Well into the twentieth century do we find strong kinship ties that give support to the working class families. See Michael Young and Peter Willmott, *Family and Kinship in East London* (New York, 1957).
5. See below, chap. 2.
6. So wrote Lady Henry Somerset in a telegram read to a prohibition convention in 1897 in Newcastle. See below, Conclusion, note 15.

Part One 1750–1850: The Voice of the Lord

1. For a variety of roles of women in the Old Testament, see the *Song of Deborah*, Judges 5.
2. See Nina Coombs Pykare, 'The Sin of Eve and the Christian Conduct Book', *Ohio Journal of Religious Studies*, v. 4, 1976, pp. 34–43, and Derwood C. Smith, 'Paul and the Non-Eschatological Woman', *Ohio Journal of Religious Studies*, vol. 4, 1976, p. 12.
3. Galatians 3:28. Recently, however, at least one theologian believes that Paul was really a misunderstood supporter of women. G. B. Caird, 'Paul and Women's Liberty', *The John Rylands Library*, vol. 54, 1971–72, pp. 268–81. See also Jessie Penn-Lewis, *The Magna Charta of Woman* (Minneapolis, 1975).
4. 1 Timothy 2:11–15.
5. Acts 21:9.

1 They Sat Not Still

1. According to one theologian, when Christian churches emphasize the role of the individual – that man (and woman) is made in God's image, and that God is in each of us – there appears to be little gender discrimination. When the organization of the church is emphasized then divisions appear. Paul Wesley Chilcote, 'John Wesley and the Women Preachers of Early Methodism', unpublished dissertation, Duke University, 1984.
2. Convents were under the authority of the local bishop and only a male priest could conduct mass.
3. Frank Stenton, *Anglo Saxon England*, 3rd edn, Oxford History, pp. 161–62. See also Edith Picton-Tuberville, 'The Coming Order in the Church of Christ', ed. Rev. B. H. Streeter, *Women and the Church* (London, 1917) p. 54.
4. A. Maude Royden, *The Church and Women* (London, 1924) p. 85.
5. Richard L. Greaves, 'The Role of Women in Early English Nonconformity', *Church History*, vol. 52, 1983, pp. 299–311.
6. Greaves, pp. 302–3.
7. Greaves, p. 301.
8. Greaves, p. 306.
9. Harry Leon McBeth, 'The Changing Role of Women in Baptist History', *Southwestern Journal of Theology*, vol. 18, Fall 1979, p. 86. Also Rosemary Reuther and Eleanor McLaughlin, *Women of the Spirit, Female Leadership in the Jewish and Christian Tradition* (New York, 1979) p. 20. Elizabeth Isichei, *Victorian Quakers* (London 1970) pp. 94–5.
10. Greaves, p. 304.
11. McBeth, pp. 86–87.
12. See story of Dorothy Hazzard, McBeth, p. 87; and Greaves, p. 302.
13. McBeth, p. 87.
14. Chilcote, p. 14.
15. Royden, pp. 81–2.
16. Arnold Lloyd, *Quaker Social History 1669–1738* (London, 1950), p. 107.
17. Lloyd, pp. 114–15.
18. Wm. Crouch, quoted Lloyd pp. 109–10.
19. Richard T. Vann, *The Social Development of Quakerism, 1655–1753*, (Cambridge, Mass., 1969), p. 112.
20. Jennie Kitteringham, 'Country work girls in nineteenth-century England', *Village Life and Labour*, ed. Raphael Samuel (London, 1975) pp. 98–112.
21. Lloyd, p. 107.
22. *Ibid.*, p. 107.
23. Joyce L. Irwin, *Womanhood in Radical Protestantism* (New York, 1979) p. xxvi

24. Lloyd, p. 118.
25. Lloyd, p. 118.
26. McBeth, p. 89.
27. McBeth, p. 94.
28. *The Woman's Herald*, August 20, 1892.
29. Lloyd, p. 130

2 The Call to Preach

1. Dale A. Johnson, *Women in English Religion 1700–1925* (New York, 1983) p. 62.
2. *Ibid.*
3. Brown, p. 26.
4. Johnson, p. 63.
5. *Ibid.*
6. Sarah Crosby, Letter Book, 1760–1774, unpublished manuscript, p. 56.
7 Crosby, p. 58.
8. Crosby, p. 38.
9. Crosby, p. 38.
10. Letter of March 18, 1769, Johnson, p. 68.
11. Crosby, p. 56.
12. Crosby, p. 56.
13. Crosby, p. 56.
14. Crosby Letter Book, p. 57.
15. 2 Samuel 20:14–22.
16. Crosby, p. 61.
17. Brown, p. 25.
18. Brown, p. 28.
19. Chilcote, p. 276.
20. Robert Currie, *Methodism Divided* (London, 1956), pp. 52–53.
21. Chilcote, p. 269.
22. Currie, p. 91.
23. Chilcote, p. 281.
24. Chilcote, p. 291.
25. Chilcote, p. 301.
26. Chilcote, p. 239.
27. Wesley F. Swift, 'Women Itinerant Preachers of Early Methodism', Part I, *Proceedings of the Wesleyan Historical Society*, vol. XXVIII, March 1952, p. 92.
28. Chilcote, p. 302.
29. Wesley F. Swift, 'Women Itinerant Preachers of Early Methodism', Part II, *Proceedings of the Wesleyan Historical Society*, vol. XXIX, p. 81.
30. Rupert E. Davies, *Methodism*, Penguin Books, 1963, p. 138.
31. Swift, II, p. 78.

32. Davies, p. 139.
33. Swift, Part II, p. 78, Deborah M. Valenze, *Prophetic Sons and Daughters: Female Preaching and Popular Religion in Industrial England* (Princeton, 1985) p. 128.
34. Julia Stewart Werner, *The Primitive Methodist Connection: Its Background and Early History* (Madison, 1984) p. 142.
35. Davies, p. 199.
36. Valenze, p. 23.
37. Werner, p. 211, n. 28.
38. *Ibid.*, p. 143.
39. Mollie C. Davis, 'The Countess of Huntingdon: A Leader in Missions for Social and Religious Reform', *Women in New Worlds*, vol. II, ed. Keller, Queen and Thomas (Nashville, 1982) pp. 164–65.
40. Dale A. Johnson, p. 167.
41. Johnson, p. 95.
42. Johnson, p. 65.
43. Johnson p. 167.
44. Davis, p. 175.
45. Davis, p. 173.
46. D. Colin Dews, 'Ann Carr and the Female Revivalists of Leeds', *Religion in the Lives of English Women, 1760–190*, ed. Gail Malmgreen (London, 1986). This essay gives an excellent description of this woman and her work. See also Valenze, pp. 191–204.
47. Greaves p. 302. This was not true at other levels of society. Families of the upper ranks often had the right to appoint clergy to 'livings' within their domains, while in the towns the merchants and other middle groups exercised control over the churches and chapels of their denominations. The poorer classes could only control their own religious practises at home.
48. Valenze, pp. 103–4.
49. Valenze, p. 137.
50. Valenze, p. 70.
51. Valenze, pp. 236–37.
52. See below, Chapters 4 and 7.

3 Class and Politics

1. G. E. Mingay, *English Landed Society in the 18th Century* (London 1963) p. 124.
2. Kenneth Mackenzie, *The English Parliament* (Pelican Books, 1951) p. 99.
3. Robert Blake, *Disraeli* (New York, 1967) p. 89.
4. Mingay, p. 114. See Mingay for a full discussion of eighteenth-century political life.
5. Carolly Erickson, *Our Tempestuous Day* (New York, 1986) p. 189.

6. Countess of Anacaster, 'Ladies and the Primrose League', *Lady's Realm*, vol. VI, May 1899, pp. 87–88. Also, Jane Rendall, *The Origins of Modern Feminism, Women in Britain, France and U. S., 1790–1860* (London, 1985) pp. 243–44.
7. Charles Roberts, *The Radical Countess* (Carlisle, 1962) p. 2.
8. Countess of Anacaster, p. 89.
9. Charles Roberts, p. 2.
10. *Ibid.*, p. 3.
11. Matilda Sturge, *Memorials and Letters of Ann Hunt* (London, 1898) p. 2.
12. Sarah Stickney, Ellis *The Women of England: Their Social Duties and Domestic Habits* (London, 1839) p. 13.
13. Male owners or lessees of property worth ten pounds or more a year were given the vote. Limitation to the male gender was specifically stated in this bill.
14. J. H. Plumb, *England in the Eighteenth Century (1714–1815)*, the Pelican History of England, 1965 edition, p. 86.
15. Blake, p. 78.
16. *Extracts from Priscilla Johnson's Journal and Letters*, privately printed and circulated, p. 58. Dinner clubs were quite common in London in the eighteenth century; and they were usually for men but occasionally women were members. See also Compton-Rickett, p. 324.
17. Arthur Compton-Rickett, *The London Life of Yesterday* (New York, 1901) p. 337.
18. For a discussion of the various borough franchises see Colin Rhys Lovell, *English Constitutional and Legal History* (New York, 1962) p. 428.
19. Dorothy George, *England In Transition* (Pelican edition, 1964) pp. 98–99.
20. Quoted in George, p. 49.
21. J. Steven Watson, *The Reign of George III*, Oxford History, 1960, pp. 236–39.
22. Robert F. Wearmouth, *Methodism and the Common People* (London, 1945) p. 25.
23. Dorothy Thompson, 'Women and Nineteenth Century Radical Politics', *Rights and Wrongs of Women*, ed. Juliet Mitchell and Ann Oakley (Pelican, 1976) p. 117.
24. Olwen Hufton lecture, Harvard, October 19, 1988.
25. Pat Hollis, *Ladies Elect* (New York, 1987) p. 31.
26. Samuel Bamford, *Passages in the Life of a Radical* (Oxford, 1984) p. 161.
27. Bamford, p. 150.
28. This is somewhat reminiscent of the complaints by the Quaker women concerning their mixed meetings: of men pushing and bumping the females in quite an aggressive fashion. See above, chap. 1.
29. Bamford, p. 181.

30. Joyce Bellamy and John Saville (eds), *Dictionary of Labour Biography*, vol. VII (London 1972) p. 1.
31. Thomas p. 93. For a discussion of working-class women activities at this time see Gail Malmgreen, *Women's Suffrage in England, Origins and Alternatives, 1792–1851* (London) p. 70.
32. William Lechmere, 'Commonplace Book, 1832–1835' ms. journal, London, England (Wm B. Hamilton Collection, Duke University). Entry for January 22, 1834.
33. Malcolm I. Thomas and Jennifer Grimmett, *Women in Protest, 1800–1850* (London, 1982) pp. 111–13.
34. David Jones, 'Women and Chartism', *History*, February 1983, p. 9.
35. Sheila Herstein, *A Mid-Victorian Feminist, Barbara Leigh Smith Bodichon* (New Haven, 1985) p. 80.
36. Llewelly Woodward, *The Age of Reform 1815–1870*, 2nd edn, Oxford History, 1962, p. 134; Jones, p. 2.
37. Dorothy Thompson, p. 134.
38. Jones, p. 14.

4 The Call to Social and Political Action

1. Geoffrey Best, 'The Evangelicals and the Established Church in the Early Nineteenth Century', *Journal of Theological Studies*, N.S. X (1959), p. 78.
2. Harold Perkin, *Origins of Modern English Society*, Ark Paperbacks (London, 1985) p. 281.
3. Lewis G. Pray, *The History of Sunday Schools and of Religion from the Earliest Times* (Boston, 1847) p. 137.
4. Kathleen Heasman, *Evangelicals in Action* (London, 1962) p. 69.
5. Rendall, pp. 89–90.
6. For a full discussion of the relationship between Anglican evangelicalism and women writers see Robin Reed Davis, 'Anglican Evangelicalism and the Feminine Literary Tradition from Hannah More to Charlotte Bronte', unpublished Ph.D. thesis, Duke University, 1982.
7. Carolly Erickson, p. 195.
8. Davis, p. 28.
9. *Extracts From Priscilla Johnston's, Journal and Letters*, p. 57.
10. Rendall, p. 246.
11. Alex Tyrrell, '"Woman's Mission" and Pressure Group Politics in Britain (1825–60)', *The John Rylands University Library Manchester*, vol. 63, no. 1, p. 224.
12. *Friendly Monthly Mag.*, April 1830; Alex Tyrrell, '"Woman's Mission" . . . ', p. 211.
13. 1st Report of Birmingham Female Society for the Relief of British Negro Slaves, 1826.

14. Report, p. 16.
15. *Annual Report*, p. 11.
16. *Annual Report*, p. 17.
17. These Quaker women of Birmingham were also pioneers in the women's rights movement in the 1870s and one of them, Elizabeth Mary Sturges, was the first woman to be elected to the Birmingham School Board.
18. Tyrrell, p. 211.
19. Rendall, p. 246.
20. *Ibid.*, p. 246.
21. Tyrrell, p. 50.
22. Tyrrell, p. 212; Erickson, p. 190.
23. Patricia Hollis, *Pressure From Without* (New York, 1974) p. 49.
24. *Birmingham Post*, December 2, 1931 'Women Workers Against Slavery'.
25. Tyrrell, p. 108.
26. *Wings*, vol. XII, no. 1, January 1894, 'Profile of Mrs. Stewart'.
27. E. R. Conder, *Josiah Conder: A Memoir* (London, 1857) p. 318.
28. *Wings*, 'Profile of Mrs. Stewart'; *Harriet Martineau on Women*, ed. Gayle Graham Yates (New Brunswick, 1984) p. 5.
29. Tyrrell, p. 198.
30. *The Nonconformist*, March 23, 1842.
31. Flexner Eleanor, *Century of Struggle*, Atheneum (New York, 1970) p. 71; Garrison supported the women's rights movement in the United States, Karlyn K. Campbell, *Man Cannot Speak For Her* (New York, 1989) vol. I, p. 82.
32. *Wings*, January, 1894. Louisa Stewart was on the Ladies Committee of the Anti-Corn Law League London Bazaar in 1845 and also helped organize and canvass for the first women's petition for the Suffrage in Parliament in 1866. She also organized a school for women.
33. *Birmingham Post*, December 2, 1931.
34. Rendall, p. 245. For a more complete description of this movement see Norman McCord, *Anti-Corn Law League, 1838–1846* (London, 1958).
35. Letter from George Wilson to Richard Cobden, September 18, 1841, Cobden Papers, vol. XVII, British Museum Add. Mss.
36. Wm Lechmere, entry August 14, 1834. For an excellent discussion on charity bazaars and women's roles in them see F. K. Prochaska, *Women and Philanthropy in Nineteenth Century England* (Oxford, 1980).
37. John Bright was one of the leaders and his female family members were active in its work.
38. Ruth Colodin letter, November, 1841, Wilson files, Manchester Public Library Archives.
39. See replies in Wilson files, Manchester Archives.
40. Letter October 28, 1841, Manchester Archives.
41. Prochaska, p. 63.

42. Prochaska, pp. 63–64.
43. Prochaska, p. 63, Rendall, p. 244.
44. *Wings*, January 1894, vol. XII, no. 1, 'Profile of Mrs. Stewart'.
45. Samuel Couling, *History of the Temperance Movement* (London, 1862) p. 35; and Dawson Burns, *Temperance in the Victorian Age* (London, 1897) p. 119.
46. Couling, p. 45.
47. For a discussion of women's work in the early English temperance reform see Lilian Lewis Shiman '"Changes Are Dangerous": Women and Temperance in Victorian England', *Religion in the Lives of English Women, 1760–1930* ed. Gail Malmgreen, pp. 193–216
48. See Lilian Lewis Shiman, *Crusade Against Drink In Victorian England* (London/New York, 1988) for a full discussion of temperance in nineteenth-century England.
49. Stockport Librarian communication. Just a brief notice of the group appears to be extant.
50. M. E. Docwra, 'A Glimpse at Woman's Work for Temperance during the Victorian Era', paper read Bristol, October 1897, published by Women's Total Abstinence Union, p. ll.
51. Out of the almost 150 Memorials of the Departed published by Sam Couling in his *History of the Temperance Movement In Great Britain and Ireland* (1862) only five are of women. Brian Harrison in his *Dictionary of British Temperance Biography* (1973) also lists very few women for the period before 1872. See also Shiman, 'Changes Are Dangerous', p. 195.
52. *Gospel Temperance Herald*, July 12, 1882, p. l.

Part Two 1850–1875: The Sound of the Horn

1. See above, chap. 2.
2. William Sturge, *Some Recollections of a Long Life*, Bristol, 1893, p. 41.
3. Matilda Sturge, *Memorials & Letters of Ann Hunt* (London, 1898) p. 9.
4. See above, chap. 3; and Dorothy Thompson, p. 134.
5. Men, who in former times wore colorful silks and satins, and were perfumed and carried muffs, now wore worsteds and linens and carried simple canes. Powdered hair, knee breeches and padded tight jackets were replaced by natural hair and three piece suits with trousers. See Arthur Compton-Rickett, *The London Life of Yesterday* (New York, 1909) for a description of this change in male dress. He notes that when umbrellas were first introduced in 1706 they were considered as 'desperately effeminate' while muffs were 'quite manly', p. 336.
6. Walter Besant, *Fifty Years Ago* (New York, 1888) pp. 1–2.

7. A good example of this was the founder of the British IOGT. Joseph Malins was a worker who, when he experienced bad times left England and went to the United States where he worked for a few years. While in the United States he became a member of the American temperance benefit and social organization, the Independent Order of the Good Templars. When he returned to England he organized and led the Order in Britain. See chap. 11 below. See also the story of Emma Paterson, trade unionist, in Elizabeth Roberts, *Women's Work 1840–1940*, Studies in Economic and Social History (London, 1988) pp. 60–61.
8. See Richard Carawadine *Trans-atlantic Revivalism* (Westport, 1978); and also L. L. Shiman, '"The Blue Ribbon Army": Gospel Temperance in England', *The Historical Magazine of the Protestant Episcopal Church*, vol. l, no. 4, (December, 1981).
9. Billy Graham and other American revivalists are in the same tradition. See W. G. McLoughlin, *Modern Revivalism* (New York, 1959). Also Richard Carawadine, *op. cit.*
10. Brian Heeney, *The Women's Movement In the Church of England, 1850–1930*, (Oxford, 1988), pp. 11–12. For a full discussion of this nineteenth century female ideal see Barbara Welter, 'The Cult of True Womanhood' *American Quarterly*, 1966, 18 (2 pt 1), pp. 151–74.

5 The Two Spheres

1. Valenze, p. 247.
2. For example, temperance societies were more than associations for furtherance of abstinence. They often sponsored other 'improving' institutions – schools, thrift clubs, etc. See Lilian Lewis Shiman, 'The Birstall Temperance Society,' *The Yorkshire Archaeological Journal*, vol. 46, 1974, and 'Temperance and Class in Bradford: 1830–60', *The Yorkshire Archaeological Journal*, January, 1986.
3. Matilda Sturge, *Memorials & Letters of Ann Hunt*, p. 2.
4. See Jacques Donzelot, *The Policing of Families* (New York, 1979) chap. 3.
5 Often cited were the biblical texts 1 Corinthians 11:3–9 and Ephesians 5:22–29.
6. Sarah Stickney Ellis, *The Women of England: Their Social Duties and Domestic Habits* (London) p. 13.
7. Ellis, pp. 21–22.
8. Priscilla Johnson, p. 60.
9. For a complete discussion of the Jockey Club see Tim Fitzgeorge-Parker, *Roscoe: the bright shiner* (London, 1987).
10. See Lenore Davidoff, *The Best Circles: society etiquette and the season* (London, 1986), for a full discussion of this domestic world.
11. This remained a standing grievance among women throughout the

nineteenth century and was part of the reason why women were so hostile towards the C. D. Acts – see below chap. 10.

12. Although there was much violence at home. In the 1850s there was much concern over wife beating. *Harriet Martineau on Women* ed., Gayle Graham Yates (Brunswick, 1985) p. 17. By law husbands could beat wives.
13. A similar argument was recently made on a television program discussing the position of women in Saudi Arabia. A woman schoolteacher declared that the seclusion of women from the public domain was an indication of the desire of the males to protect their female relatives; it was done in the interests of the female.
14. See replies to Anti-Corn Law invitations in the Joseph Wilson papers. The largest number of women declined to serve on a committee using 'ill health' as the reason (Manchester Archives).
15. Eliza Orme, *Lady Fry of Darlington* (London, 1898) pp. 20–21.
16. Francis Power Cobbe, 'Life in an English Boarding School', *Victorian Women*, ed. Erna O. Hellerstein *et al.*, p. 72.
17. Lee Holcombe, *Victorian Ladies At Work* (Newton Abbot, 1973) p. 25.
18. W. E. Moss, *Book of Memories* (Blackburn, 1951) p. 151. The British Women's Temperance Association also accepted the belief that women were particularly susceptible to drink. B.W.T.A., *Annual Report*, 1879.
19. See below, chap. 9, for her father's role in Florence Fenwick Miller's first public speech. In the biographies of nineteenth-century women who have personally achieved success, fathers often played an important part in encouraging their daughters to venture into public life. This role of fathers was the subject of an informal discussion at the Seventh Berkshire Conference on the History of Women (Wellesley, June 1987).

6 Economic Disabilities

1. A typical story of the mid-nineteenth century was that of Beatrice Potter's father who had a 'life of leisure' when he enjoyed inherited wealth but had to get a job when he lost it. Beatrice Potter, *My Apprenticeship* (Pelican Books, 1938) p. 19.
2. Dorothy George, *England in Transition* (Pelican Books, England) 1953, pp. 21–22.
3. Lloyd, p. 9.
4. George, p. 24.
5. Sally Alexander, 'Women's Work in Nineteenth Century London: A Study of the Years 1820–50', *The Changing Experience of Women*, ed. Elizabeth Whitelegg, Maud Arnot etc. (Open University, Oxford, 1982) p. 32.

6. Richard D. Altick, *Victorian People and Ideas* (New York, 1973) pp. 167–69.
7. Johnson, pp.195–96.
8. 'The Work We Have To Do', *The English Woman's Review*, October 1866.
9. Marian Ramelson, *Petticoat Rebellion* (London, 1967) p. 127.
10. Ramelson, p. 128. See also 'Public Opinion on Questions concerning Women', *Englishwoman's Review*, vol. V, no. V, October 1867, pp. 292–93.
11. There were large numbers of prostitutes in all cities but especially in London. One figure given for London was 30,000 above the age of 16 years in the early part of the nineteenth century. Erickson, p. 252.
12. See Eric J. Hobsbawn, *Labouring Men*, 1967, chap. 4, for a discussion of the tramping artisan.
13. John R. Gillis, *For Better, For Worse* (Oxford, 1985) p. 249.
14. Malcom I. Thomas and Jennifer Grimmett, p. 70. After the collapse of Owen's Consolidated Union, in which women were officially admitted on an equal basis with men, women were rarely admitted into trade organizations run by men.
15. Johnson, p. 162. See also Sally Alexander, 'Women's Work in Nineteenth Century London: A Study of the Years 1820–50', *Rights and Wrongs of Women*, ed. Juliet Mitchell and Ann Oakley (New York, 1976) p. 99.
16. E. Roberts, p. 17.
17. Originally women produced beer at home and then sold some to neighbours. Beer houses were the beermakers' houses where rooms were set aside for sale of beer which wives still produced in the traditional way. Not until 1830 when the Beer Act was passed were beer sellers required to be licensed.
18. Josephine Butler, *The Education and Employment of Women* (London, 1868) p. 196.
19. Sheila Herstein, p. 138.
20. Holcombe, p. 103.
21. Eileen Yeo and E. P. Thompson, *The Unknown Mayhew* (Schocken Edition, 1972) p. 121.
22 *Annual Report*, Women's Liberal Federation, 1892. This organization maintained a 'parliamentary committee' to watch and lobby for legislation affecting women's working conditions, particularly in the sweated trades.
23 Edward Cadbury, M. Cecile Matheson and George Shann, *Women's Work and Wages* (London, 1906) p. 50.
24. Holcombe, pp. 36–37.
25. Many of the upper-class women were volunteer teachers at the local Sunday School, but here they were doing 'charity work' and could leave at any time; their livelihood did not depend on it.

26. Holcombe, p. 16.
27. Sonya Rose, 'Gender Antagonisms and Class Conflict: exclusionary strategies of male trade unionists in nineteenth-century Britain', *Social History*, vol. 13, no. 2, May, 1988, pp. 198–99.
28. Cadbury, p. 190.
29. Rose, pp. 198–99.
30. Cadbury, p. 25.
31. E. Roberts, pp. 60–61.
32. Jennie Kitteringham, 'Country work girls in nineteenth-century England', *Village Life and Labour*, ed. Raphael Samuel (London, 1975) p. 85.
33. The Countess of Carlisle employed female instead of male servants as an expression of her support for women. C. Roberts, pp. 151–52.
34. Lady Dorothy Nevill, *Life and Letters of Lady Dorothy Nevill*, edited by Ralph Nevill (London 1906) p. 104.
35. The Women's Union of the Church of England Temperance Society, among other women's temperance organizations, made female laundry workers their special project. D. Burns, *Temperance in the Victorian Age*, p. 122.
36. Mayhew, quoted in Yeo, p. 428.
37. *The English Woman's Review*, vol. V, October 1867, p. 314.
38. Josephine Butler, *The Education and Employment of Women*, p. 195.
39. See above, chap. 4.
40. Monica C. Fryckstedt, 'The Hidden Rill: The Life and Career of Marie Jane Jewsbury', *The John Rylands University Library*, Manchester, vol. 39, 1956–57, p. 180.
41. See her *The Education and Employment of Women. The English Woman's Review* devoted many pages to this issue.
42. When women received the training, they had great difficulty in getting licenses to practise. The case of university graduate Florence Fenwick Miller, who qualified as a doctor but was not allowed to practise, is a good example of this. *The Woman's Signal*, September 26, 1895.
43. 'We shall have to educate our masters', said Forster in 1870 when proposing the setting up of state-run board schools. Beatrice Potter writes that her father also said this many times after the workingman got the vote. Potter, *My Apprenticeship*, p. 26.
44. Male teachers, especially in upper class private/public schools had some professional training.
45. F. Cobbe, 'Life in an English Boarding School', *Victorian Women*, ed. Hellerstein *et al.*, p. 72.
46. This was run by James Kay Shuttleworth. S. J. Curtis and M. E. A. Boultwood, *English Education Since 1800* (London, 1960) pp. 59–60.
47. Johnson, p. 212.
48. Holcombe, pp. 25–27
49. Johnson, p. 213.

50. Johnson, p. 213.
51. Woodward, pp. 480–82.
52. Testimony of Mary Frances Buss, given in *Victorian Women*, ed. Hellerstein *et al.*, p. 80.
53. *Ibid.*, pp. 78–79.
54. For a discussion on education and women in Victorian England see Joan N. Burstyn, *Victorian Education and the Ideal of Womanhood* (London, 1980).
55. This college was to become, Girton College in 1872, with a dedicated feminist, Emily Davies, as its head.
56. Newman Hall was opened in Cambridge in 1875. Lady Margaret Hall and Somerville Hall, two Oxford women's colleges, were both founded in 1879.
57. Margaret Hunt, 'Wife Abuse in Early Eighteenth Century London', paper given at American Historical Association Conference, Cincinnati, Ohio, December 1988.
58. Herstein, pp. 78–79.
59. Herstein, p. 140.
60. Named in honor of the Queen, it became Printer and Publisher in Ordinary to Her Majesty. Holcombe, p. 16.
61. The BWTA used it to print their annual reports and other material.
62. Herstein, p. 143.
63. Minutes of the Executive Committee, British Women's Temperance Association, January 4, 1888.
64. Herstein, pp. 40–41.
65. 'Interview', Amy E. Bell, *Women's Penny Paper*, December 22, 1888, p. 1.
66. Herstein, p. 80.
67. For a discussion of this issue see Philippa Levine, '"So Few Prizes and So Many Blanks": Marriage and Feminism in Later Nineteenth-Century England', *Journal of British Studies*, vol. 28, no. 2, April 1989.
68. See below, chap. 8.

7 Religious Revival

1. William Sturge, *Some Recollections of a Long Life* (Bristol, 1893) p. 41; also David Swift, *John Joseph Gurney, Banker, Reformer and Quaker*, (Middletown, 1962), p. 210.
2. Brian Heeney, *The Women's Movement in the Church of England, 1850–1930* (Oxford, 1988) pp. 77–78.
3. See above, chap. 1.
4. Carawadine p. 152.
5. Asa Briggs, *The Making of Modern England, 1783–1867* (New York, 1965) p. 466.
6. Heeney, p. 79.

7. Shiman, *Crusade Against Drink*, pp. 99–109.
8. *The Woman's Herald*, January 16, 1892.
9. Heeney, p. 95.
10. Heeney, p. 22.
11. *Ibid.*, p. 24.
12. Johnson, p. 201.
13. See below, chap. 8.
14 Johnson, p. 173. Margaret Asquith, Laura Chant, and Lady Battersea are three examples of well-to-do women teaching Sunday School.
15. Constance Battersea, *Reminiscences* (London, 1923) pp. 26–77.
16. Heeney, p. 33.
17. Johnson, p. 176.
18. Heeney, p. 67.
19. A revival of this female institution had already occurred in Germany in 1833. A good discussion of the deaconesses in England is to be found in the article by Catherine M. Prelinger, 'The Female Diaconate in the Anglican Church', in *Religion in the Lives of English Women, 1760–1930*, ed. Gail Malmgreen (London, 1986) pp. 161–92.
20. A. V. L., *Ministering Women and the London Poor*, edited by Mrs. Bayly, 1870, p. 10.
21. *Ibid.*, p. 25.
22. Heeney, p. 48.
23. Heeney, pp. 49–50.
24. Ann R. Higginbotham, 'Respectable Sinners: Salvation Army Rescue Work with Unmarried Mothers, 1884–1914', in Malmgreen, p. 219.
25. *Ibid.*
26. For a discussion of the work of this Society see Shiman, 'The Church of England Temperance Society in the Nineteenth Century', *The Historical Magazine of the Protestant Episcopal Church*, vol. XLI, no. 2, June 1972.
27. Heeney, p. 38.
28. See below, chap. 8.
29. By the end of the nineteenth century almost half a million women were in local rescue work. Heeney, p. 19.
30. See below, chap. 11.
31. Oliver Anderson, 'Women Preachers in Mid-Victorian Britain', *The Historical Journal*, vol. XII, no. 3 (1969), pp. 467–84, p. 469.
32. Carwardine, p. 179. Later, when the church of England was organizing missions in competition with the other religions they too used school rooms and other nonchurch buildings. *Church of England Temperance Chronicle*, July 14, 1888.
33. Carwardine, p. 188.
34. Carwardine, pp. 183–84.
35. See above, chap. 1.
36. Anderson, p. 481, Carawadine, p. 187.
37. Anderson, p. 469.

38. Anderson, p. 473.
39. Some antifeminists complained that women on a platform were 'shrieking sisters'. See below, chap. 9.
40. Anderson, p. 470.
41. Anderson, p. 483; and Carwardine, p. 188.
42. John Newton, *W. S. Caine, M.P.* (London, 1907) pp. 127–28.
43. Newton, p. 128.
44. Kathleen Fitzpatrick, *Lady Henry Somerset* (Boston, 1923) p. 158.
45. Fitzpatrick, p. 158.
46. Asquith, vol. I, p. 256.
47. See her letter to her sister Lady Henry Somerset, Fitzpatrick, p. 145.
48. Fitzpatrick, p. 157.
49. For more on the general work of this movement see Shiman, 'The Blue Ribbon Army: Gospel Temperance in England', *The Historical Magazine of the Protestant Episcopal Church*, vol. L, no. 4, December 1981, pp. 391–408.
50. The popular Methodist leader, the Rev. C. Garrett organized a fund to help the Lewises pay the expenses of the trial. *Alliance News*, April 25, 1890.
51. W. H. Burnett, *Sunlight in the Slums* (Manchester, 1888).
52. These originated in the Methodist church but were picked up by working class temperance groups of the 1840s and were very popular. In Yorkshire in the 1860s, a Mrs. Petty, the wife of a nonconformist preacher, held Experience Meetings, one of which had an attendance of more than 1,400. Headquartered in the rural Yorkshire Dales in Otley, she travelled the countryside and developed a large local following, but was little known outside her own county. *Temperance Advocate*, March 29, 1862.
53. In the United States females would also recount their experiences in public.
54. For a full account see W. H. Burnett, *Sunlight in the Slums*, and W. E. Moss, *Book of Memories* (Blackburn, 1951).
55. *The Signal and Gospel Union Gazette*, April 29, 1903.
56. *Alliance News*, February 24, 1883.
57. Anderson, p. 482.
58. Anderson, p. 482.
59. T. W. P. Taylder, 'The History of the Rise and Progress of Teetotalism in Newcastle upon Tyne, pamphlet, Newcastle upon Tyne, 1886, p. 41.
60. *Alliance News*, February 28, 1890.
61. Robert Currie, *Methodism Divided* (London, 1968), pp. 139–40. 'Chapel folk' was an identification common throughout the industrial towns and villages, especially in the North.
62. The fights in Parliament were no longer over whether to seat Roman Catholics or Jews, but whether any religious affiliation was necessary in order to sit in Parliament. The secularists wanted all religious tests

removed from Parliament. The Bradlaugh Case, which stemmed from Bradlaugh's demand to be allowed to take his duly won seat in Parliament despite being a secularist, heralded this new era.
63. Heeney, p. 96.
64. October 15, 1892.
65. Johnson, p. 112.
66. Brian Heeney, 'The Beginnings of Church Feminism: Women and the Councils of the Church of England, 1897–1919', ed. Malmgreen, pp. 260–84, p. 260.

8 Reform Leadership

1. See above, chap. 2.
2. Jabez Burns, *A Restrospect of Forty-Five Years Christian Ministry*, London, 1875, p. 165.
3. Later called the National Temperance League.
4. Dawson Burns, *Temperance in the Victorian Age* (London, 1897), p. 119, and M. E. Docwra, 'A Glimpse At Woman's Work for Temperance during the Victorian Era', paper read at Women's Total Abstinence Union meeting in Bristol, October 1897, published by Union in London, p. 13.
5. Burns, *Temperance in the Victorian Age*, pp. 119–20, and Docwra pp. 13–14.
6. Most of the branches set up in 1853 probably never had more than a formal existence, sustained by one or two people who sent in periodic reports.
7. M. Sturge, paper published in *Women's Work in the Temperance Reform* (London, 1868) pp. 62–63.
8. Most temperance histories do not mention it. See Burns, *Temperance in the Victorian Age*, p. 120, and Docwra, p. 14. Local and national temperance groups were usually initiated with great publicity, so it is not difficult to find out when an organization was founded. However, it is less easy to find out when it died. Rarely is the demise of an organization publicized, and so one can only hazard a guess as to how long these local societies existed.
9. Shiman, *Crusade Against Drink*, p. 74.
10. Burns, *Temperance in the Victorian Age*, p. 120.
11. '"Why I Signed the Pledge" by Eminent Temperance Women', *Wings*, January 1895.
12. Julia Wightman, *Haste to the Rescue* (London, 1860), pp. 19–20.
13. Wightman, p. 29.
14. J. M. J. Fletcher, *Mrs. Wightman of Shrewsbury* (London, 1906) p. 142.
15. Fletcher, p. 120.
16. Fletcher, pp. 116–17.

17. This London-based temperance organization had received an anonymous gift of fifty pounds to pay for copies of the book for free distribution, Fletcher, pp. 289–90.
18. H. J. Ellison, *The Temperance Reformation Movement in the Church of England* (London, 1878) pp. 10–11. When the nonsectarian National Temperance League distributed those ten thousand copies of *Haste To the Rescue*, they sowed seeds that would have a great harvest. The book came out at a time when the Church of England was becoming aware that the nonconformist churches and chapels were gaining adherents through evangelical and temperance work. The Anglican hierarchy, responding to growing pressure among clergy and laity to show their concern for the common people, allowed, albeit reluctantly, a temperance society to be organized within the established church. It was cited over and over again as a manifestation of the Church's concern for the welfare of its people. For more about Julia Wightman and the founding of the Church of England Temperance Society see Julia Wightman, *Haste to the Rescue*; J. M. J. Fletcher, *Mrs. Wightman of Shrewsbury*; H. J. Ellison, *The Temperance Reformation in the Church of England.* Also Gerald Wayne Olsen, 'Pub and Parish. the Beginnings of Temperance Reform in the Church of England, 1835–1875' (Ph.D. thesis, University of Western Ontario, 1971); and Shiman, 'The Church of England Temperance Society in the Nineteenth Century'.
19. Wightman, pp. 257–58.
20. Wightman, p. 4.
21. Fletcher, p. 292.
22. *The Temperance Chronicle*, January 14, 1882.
23. Catherine Marsh, *English Hearts and English Hands*, and Mrs. Bayly, *Ragged Homes and How to Mend Them* were both very popular works and had tremendous influence when they were published. The latter, published in 1859, sold 8,000 copies – Docwra, *Women's Work For Temperance*, p. 40.
24. Fletcher, pp. 290–91.
25. She was an effective agent of the National Temperance League who had been charged with bringing the temperance message to the notice of many different groups, from those of high social position to a much lower class of Ragged and Sunday School workers. See William Gourlay, *National Temperance* (London, 1906) p. 333; and Docwra, p. 14.
26. *Temperance Advocate*, vol. I, July 27, 1861; Gourlay, pp. 332–33; Burns, pp. 120–21.
27. One temperance historian has claimed that more than twenty thousand men and women of all classes were brought into the temperance movement through her efforts. Gourlay, p. 333.
28. See above, chap. 4.
29. See *International Temperance and Prohibition Proceedings*, 1862., ed. Rev. J. C. Street, Dr. F. R. Lees, and Rev. D. Burns (London, 1862).

30. Charlotte H. Ferguson, 'Woman's Work in the Temperance Reformation', in J. C. Street, F. R. Lees, and D. Burns (eds) *op. cit.*, p. 132.
31. *Ibid.*
32. *Ibid.*
33. Gourlay, pp. 333–34.
34. Its chairman was Mr. Samuel Bowly, a member of an old Quaker family, a generous philanthropist, personally active in many reforming groups including temperance. He was a founder and president of the National Temperance League and had a great talent for working with the ladies. A very respectable leader of a movement that was often seen as not so respectable. Brian Harrison, *Dictionary of British Temperance Biography* (Coventry and Sheffield, 1973) p. 13.
35. See below, chap. 11.
36. *Alliance News*, August 26, 1892, p. 546.
37. As Catherine Marsh's book had earlier influenced Mrs. Wightman.
38. The ladies of Darlington, for example, set up a local Ladies Association in 1862 after reading her work. (Burns, *Temperance in the Victorian Age*, p. 121. Gourlay also reported that Mrs. Fison found this book was responsible for encouraging many ladies to take up religious and philanthropic work. Gourlay called it a 'celebrated book', p. 333.)
39. Hatford Battersby, *Woman's Work in the Temperance Reformation* (Wm. Tweedie publisher, London, 1868); Fletcher, p. 239.
40. Sarah Robinson's paper in *Women's Work in the Temperance Reformation*.
41. M. Sturge, *Women's Work in the Temperance Reformation* (London, 1868).
42. Jennie Chapell, *Noble Workers* (London, 1910) p. 83.
43. Sir Henry Havelock, reported in *The Temperance Record*, June 21, 1877.
44. Gourlay, *A Jubilee Biograph*, p. 224.
45. Winskill, *The Temperance Movement*, vol. III, London, 1892, p. 82.
46. E. M. Tomkinson, *Sarah Robinson, Agnes Weston, Mrs. Meredith: 'The World's Workers'* (London, 1887); Winskill, *ibid.*
47. These women and children were brought back to England at army expense but then left in Portsmouth. Mostly they were widows and children but not infrequently orphans with no parents.
48. Chappell, p. 96.
49. Quoted by Tomkinson, p. 17.
50. Winskill, vol. III, p. 81; Chappell, p. 70.
51. Stewart, p. 75.
52. Miss Wintz remained Miss Weston's associate in her naval work for many years. See Agnes Weston, *My Life Among the Bluejackets* (London, 1912).
53. *The Temperance Record*, April 1, 1886, p. 215.
54. 'Why I signed the Pledge', *Wings*, January 1895.
55. Gourlay, *National Temperance*, pp. 183–84.

56. Agnes Weston, p. 127. Robert Whitehead, the inventor of the torpedo, donated a thousand pounds and a 'Manchester lady' gave the same. *Ibid.*, p. 132.
57. One not so careful and thus subjected to publicans' accusations of financial malfeasance was Mrs. Lewis of Blackburn. (See above, chap. 7.)
58. Weston, *op. cit.*; and E. M. Tomkinson, *op. cit.*
59. In the 1830s and 40s, notoriety was always a problem for reformers trying to live down the widely publicized objectionable doings of self-proclaimed temperance advocates. See Shiman, *Crusade*, p. 38.
60. Its great coup came when Frederick Temple, bishop of Exeter and later archbishop of Canterbury, served as its president from 1884 to 1903; but even earlier Dr. Temple was closely identified with the League. In 1906 when the National Temperance League celebrated its jubilee there were still no females among its executive officers, though by then some were active on other temperance boards.

Part Three 1875–1900: The Great Shout

1. M. Fawcett, 'Female Suffrage: A Reply', *Nineteenth Century*, July 1889, CXLIX.
2. In about forty boroughs the franchise was given to any householder paying taxes. Lovell, p. 428. See also *Encyclopedia Britannica*, 11th Edition, vol. 24, New York, 1911, p. 411, for a brief discussion of this franchise.
3. Fawcett, 'Female Suffrage: A Reply', *op. cit.*
4. Llewellyn Woodward, *The Age of Reform*, Oxford History, 2nd edn, 1962, p. 92 footnote.
5. Nicola R. Mills, 'The Formation and Development of the Women's Liberal Federation and its Contribution to the Suffrage Movement, 1886–1918', thesis presented to Thames Polytechnic College, p. 1. Pat Hollis, *Ladies Elect, p. 30.*

9 Speaking Out

1. Lillian O'Connor, *Pioneer Women Orators* (New York, 1954) p. 19.
2. While in the United States Lady H. Somerset learned to edit journals from Frances Willard (Chappell, p. 49.) The *British Women's Temperance Journal* was owned and edited by a Mr. Edward Bennett, proprietor and editor of other temperance journals.
3. See remarks of Mrs. Leavitt regarding importance of the *British Women's Temperance Journal*, in the Minutes of the Executive Committee, October 30, 1889.

4. See below, chap. 11.
5. For more information about these journals see David Doughan and Denise Sanchez, *Feminist Periodicals, 1855–1984*, Brighton, 1987.
6. Asquith, vol. I, p. 264.
7. See above, chap. 5.
8. Two well-known temperance workers.
9. O'Connor, p. 25. In the United States the later renowned orator, Frances Willard, early in her career got a man to read speeches she had written. Ruth Bordin, *Frances Willard: a biography* (Chapel Hill, 1986) p. 76.
10. Jennie Chappell, *Four Noble Women*, p. 144.
11. *Ibid.*
12. Elizabeth Daniel Stewart, *The Crusader in Great Britain* (Springfield, 1893) p. 101.
13. *Ibid.*, p. 124.
14. Sheppard, p. 117.
15. Tooley, p. 19.
16. For a discussion of the interaction between speaker and audience in Britain in the late nineteenth century see *Before an Audience* by Nathan Sheppard (London, 1886) pp. 116–32.
17. *Ibid.*, p. 118.
18. *Women's Penny Paper*, March 16, 1889.
19. Executive Minutes, January 4, 1888.
20. Charles Roberts, *Radical Countess*, Carlisle, 1962, p. 184.
21. Janet P. Trevelyan, *The Life of Mrs. Humphrey Ward* (London, 1923) p. 86.
22. *Ibid.* Mr. Humphrey, her husband, it was elsewhere reported, does 'not himself indulge in public speaking'. 'Husbands of Distinguished Women', *Lady's Realm*, June 1898, p. 67.
23. *Wings*, May 1893, p. 194.
24. *The Woman's Signal*, January 4, 1894.
25. *Ibid.*
26. Annie Besant: *An Autobiography* (London 1893) pp. 115–16.
27. St. John Ervine quoted in Kitty Muggeridge and Ruth Adam, *Beatrice Webb, A Life 1858–1943* (London, 1967) p. 116.
28. *Women's Penny Paper*, November 3, 1888, p. 5.
29. *Ibid.*
30. See below, chap. 10.
31. E. Moberley Bell, *Josephine Butler, Flame of Fire* (London, 1962) p. 77.
32. *Women's Penny Paper*, January 5, 1889.
33. *The Woman's Herald*, February 20, 1892.
34. *Ibid.*
35. Sheppard, p. 140.
36. See above, chap. 8.
37. See below, chap. 11.

38. Interview Margaret Bright Lucas, *Women's Penny Paper*, April 6, 1889. See also David Fahey, *The Collected Writings of Jessie Forsyth 1847–1937* (New York, 1988) p. 8.
39. Johnson, p. 173.
40. Battersea, p. 25.
41. Lucas interview, *Women's Penny Paper*, April 6, 1889, p. 2.
42. Elizabeth Isichei, *Victorian Quakers*, London, 1970, p. 95.
43. Lucas interview, *Women's Penny Paper*, April 6, 1889, p. 2.
44. Pat Hollis, *Ladies Elect*, p. 158.
45. *Ibid.*, p. 176.
46. C. Roberts, p. 178.
47. *Ibid.*, p. 182.
48. Letter, James Whyte to the Countess of Carlisle dated November 16, 1891. Copy in Castle Howard archives. I should like to acknowledge Professor David M. Fahey's help in bringing this letter to my attention.
49. C. Roberts, p. 184.
50. Bordin, p. 200.
51. Fitzpatrick p. 192, *Letters of Sydney & Beatrice Webb*, vol. 1, p. 341, Jennie Chappell, p. 49.
52. 'Portrait of Lady Henry Somerset', *Review of Reviews*, June 1893.
53. Bordin, p. 200.
54. Fizpatrick, p. 192.
55. Anderson, 'Women Preachers in Mid-Victorian Britain', p. 471.
56. Sheppard, p. 91.
57. *Noble Workers*, p. 60.
58. Frances Willard, 'Portrait of Lady Henry Somerset', *Review of Reviews*, June 1893.
59. Fitzpatrick, p. 192.
60. Tooley, p. 29.
61. *Ibid.*
62. Esther Simon Shkolnik, *Leading Ladies: A Study of Eight Late Victorian and Edwardian Political Wives* (New York, 1987) p. 174.
63. *Ibid.*, p. 249.
64. See above, chap. 8.
65. Elizabeth D. Stewart, p. 75.
66. Jennie Chappell, *Noble Workers*, p. 77.
67. Rosemary Van Arsdel, 'Florence Fenwick-Miller, Feminism and *The Woman's Signal*, 1895–1899', unpublished manuscript (Fawcett Library, London) p. 7.
68. Florence Fenwick Miller, *The Woman's Signal*, January 4, 1894, p. 4.
69. *The Woman's Signal*, January 4, 1894.
70. See below, chap. 10.
71. See below, chap. 11.
72. Elizabeth Stewart, p. 104.
73. Mary White's letter published E. Stewart's book, p. xiii.
74. Muggeridge and Adam, p. 117.

75. *The Ladies Realm*, November 1897.
76. Asquith, vol. I, p. 258.
77. Annmarie Turnbull, '"So extremely like parliament": the work of the women members of the London School Board, 1870–1904. *The Sexual Dynamics of History*, ed. The London Feminist History Group (London, 1983) pp. 120–33, p. 121.
78. *Women's Penny Paper*, December 22, 1888.
79. Elizabeth Stewart, p. 354.
80. See above, chap. 8.
81. Brian Heeney, 'Women's Movement in the Church of England', p. 95.
82. *The Woman's Signal*, January 4, 1894.
83. British Women's Temperance Association, Executive Comm. *Minutes* October 4, 1883.
84. BWTA Ex. Comm. *Minutes*, December 5, 1883.
85. BWTA Ex. Comm. *Minutes*, September 7, 1887.
86. BWTA Ex. Comm. *Minutes*, November 15, 1889.
87. *The Prohibition Movement*, ed. G. Hayler, Newcastle upon Tyne, 1897, p. 288.
88. *Annual Report* of the Executive Committee of the Women's Liberal Federation, May 22, 1889, p. 10.
89. *Ibid.*
90. Women's National Liberal Association, Leaflet no. 1, December 1895.
91. *Ibid.*

Chapter 10 'This Revolt of the Women'

1. Said by a member of Parliament to Josephine Butler, reported in Josephine Butler, *Personal Reminiscences of a Great Crusade* (London, 1898) p. 11.
2. M. E. Bell, p. 71.
3. Judith Walkowitz, *Prostitution and Victorian Society: women, class and the state* (Cambridge, 1982) p. 80.
4. Myna Trustram, 'Distasteful and derogatory? Examining Victorian soldiers for venereal disease', *The Sexual Dynamics of History* (pp. 154–64), p. 161.
5. E. M. Bell, p. 74.
6. Gayle Graham Yates, *Harriet Martineau on Women* (New Brunswick, 1985) p. 242.
7. Glen Petrie, *A Single Iniquity* (New York, 1971) p. 109.
8. E. M. Bell, p. 73.
9. E. M. Bell, p. 74.
10. Walkowitz, p. 91.
11. *Ibid.*
12. Isabella Tod, *Women's Penny Paper*, October 12, 1889.

13. *Ibid.*
14. Priscilla Bright McLaren, sister of John Bright, entered public life after her sister-in-law, Mrs. Jacob Bright, 'opened her eyes' to the evils of the C. D. Acts. *Women's Penny Paper* vol. 1, no. 2, October 27, 1888, p. 5.
15. Petrie, p. 61.
16. E. M. Bell, p. 18.
17. E. M. Bell, p. 60.
18. Butler, *Reminiscences*, p. 8.
19. *Wings*, May 1893, p. 193.
20. Quoted E. M. Bell, p. 99.
21. Yates, p. 243.
22. Yates, p. 265–67.
23. Butler, *Reminiscences*, p. 54.
24. Walkowitz, p. 93.
25. E. M. Bell, p. 92.
26. E. M. Bell, p. 99.
27. E. M. Bell, p. 80.
28. Butler, *Reminiscences*, pp. 26–33.
29. E. M. Bell, p. 86.
30. Quoted Bell, p. 91.
31. *Reminiscences*, p. 45.
32. *Reminiscences*, p. 49.
33. *Ibid.*, pp. 45–54; Bell, pp. 105–7.
34. *Reminiscences*, p. 21.
35. *Ibid.*, p. 31.
36. E. M. Bell, p. 114.
37. *Reminiscences*, pp. 111–114; Bell, p. 131.
38. *Reminiscences* p. 162. Unlike the abolitionists in the London Anti-Slave Conference of 1840 who kept the women in the gallery, these later 'abolitionists' were true partners to the ladies of their movement.
39. *Reminiscences*, p. 175.
40. *Reminscences*, p. 175.
41. *Reminiscences*, p. 176.
42. Petrie, p. 254.
43. Fawcett, cited in E. M. Bell, p. 105.
44. With the repeal of the Contagious Diseases Acts the organization changed its name to the Ladies National Association for the Abolition of the State Regulation of Vice.
45. Walkowitz, p. 224.
46. Walkowitz, p. 119.
47. E. M. Bell, p. 166.
48. Petrie, p. 157.
49. *Women's Penny Paper*, vol. 1, no. 2, October 27, 1893, p. 4.
50. See below, chap. 13, note 7.
51. *Reminiscences*, p. 105.

52. *Ibid.* p. 108.
53. Walkowitz, p. 139.
54. E. M. Bell, p. 101.
55. Petrie, p. 53. Mrs. Bright Lucas when working for the Anti-C. D. campaign had her first contact with the Independent Order of the Good Templars, a temperance organization. She joined, and quickly climbed its hierarchy. 'Interview', *Women's Penny Paper*, April 6, 1889.
56 Julie L. Kitze 'Enter Every Open Door: The British Women's Temperance Association 1876–1900', unpublished thesis, Cambridge, 1986, p. 86.
57. *Minutes*, Executive Committee, October 13, 1910, Women's Liberal Federation.
58. Petrie, p. 63. However, as she got older she appears to have modified her position.
59. *Reminiscences*, p. 37.
60. See below, chap. 11.
61. Ramelson, p. 127.
62. See below, chaps 12 and 13.

Chapter 11 A National Temperance Movement

1. See above, chap. 8.
2. David M. Fahey, *The Collected Writings of Jessie Forsyth, 1847–1937* (New York, 1988) p. 15.
3. Josephine Butler was one of many women who signed the teetotal pledge at a Good Templars' meeting. Petrie, p. 53.
4. In the United States, the IOGT, as it was commonly called, had provided the training for the leaders of the Women's Christian Temperance Union. See Fahey, p. 56.
5. Chapter 8.
6. For more about the Gospel Temperance Movement see Shiman, 'The Blue Ribbon Army'.
7. Burns, *Temperance in the Victorian Age*, p. 121.
8. Docwra, 'A Glimpse at Women's Work . . . ', pp. 15–16; Burns, p. 122.
9. Docwra, p. 17.
10. The papers of this Association are in the archives of the Manchester Public Library where the author was given the opportunity to examine them.
11. Olsen, 'Pub and Parish, p. 365, Burns, *Temperance in the Victorian Age*, p. 126, See also Shiman, 'The Church of England Temperance Society in the Nineteenth Century'.
12. Docwra, p. 25.
13. She was sister to John Bright of Rochdale and wife of a radical journal editor. She had worked in the anti-corn law agitation in 1845, Louisa

Stewart, *Margaret Bright Lucas: A Memoir* (London, 1890), p. 11. See also above, chap. 4.

14. 'Interview', *Women's Penny Paper*, April 6, 1889. Also Louisa Stewart, *Margaret Bright Lucas: A Memoir* (London, 1890).
15. See above, chap. 10.
16. Docwra, p. 21. The elimination of the drink trade was to be controversial in the Association's later years when its president, Lady Henry Somerset, told a Royal Commission on Liquor Licensing in 1898 that she was not a prohibitionist. See Fitzpatrick, pp. 207–8.
17. Lucas, p. 25.
18. *Wings*, January, 1895.
19. Burns, p. 122.
20. William Gourlay, *National Temperance: A Jubilee Biograph* (London, 1906), p. 334.
21. Minutes, Executive Committee, December 4, 1876.
22. For details see Minutes of Executive Committee for February and March, 1877.
23. Report, lst Annual Meeting, May 22, 1877.
24. Report, lst Annual Meeting, May 22, 1877.
25. Minutes of Executive Committee, December 4, 1876.
26. Minutes of Executive Committee, November 24, 1877.
27. Minutes of Executive Committee, July 26, 1878.
28. Minutes of Executive Committee, May 24, 1878.
29. See Minutes, March 15, 1878, May 14, 1878, and January 14, 1879.
30. Berwick, for example, wanted to affiliate directly with Edinburgh not London; but London, not willing to lose a membership fee or set a precedent for this type of cross-border affiliation, rejected the request and told Berwick that it was undesirable to allow 'such a procedure in breaking through recognized boundaries of our counties' (Minutes, January 14, 1879, February 4, 1879). But Berwick went ahead and decided to affiliate with the Scots, and the London committee had to confess that they 'have to let them go' (Minutes, March 25, 1879).
31. There was much instability among the groups, and it was in the movement's interests to claim the largest number of members possible. Also there was a cross-membership within the temperance reformation, with members often being members of many societies – especially in the 1880s and 1890s when there was a great proliferation of temperance organizations, many at the local level. Shiman, *Crusade*, pp. 156–57.
32. Minutes, Executive Committee, March 5, 1877.
33. Minutes, Executive Committee, November, 1878.
34. Minutes, Executive Committee, March 26, 1877.
35. *Ibid.*, June 3, 1879.
36. There were many complaints to the police about this but little was done. Both were unpopular with the general public in the late nineteenth century (Petrie, p. 203); and the *Gospel Temperance Herald*, April 26, 1882. In 1866 two temperance workers were assaulted and fatally

wounded. Ethel J. Wood, 'Sixty Years of Temperance Effort', paper read at I.O.G.T. meeting and published as tract (n.p., n.d.).

37. *Wings*, May 1893, p. 194.
38. 'The Work done by our Association', by Miss Forsaith, printed as a leaflet (n.p., n.d.).
39. Minutes, Executive Committee, January 4, 1888.
40. Minutes, January 3, 1883.
41. He was editor of the *Crusade*, a monthly temperance paper which became the *British Women's Temperance Journal*. ('British Women's Temperance Association', by M. E. Docwra, published in *Temperance in All Nations*, ed. Stearns (New York, 1893)). His tenure (1883–1892) was a controversial one, as he ran the paper completely independently of the Association, sometimes taking stances that were at variance with those of the organization. Minutes, General Executive, January 4, 1888.
42. The Working Women's Teetotal League, founded in 1876, lasted until 1887 when it folded due to lack of funds. Dowcra, p. 26.
43. M. E. Docwra, 'The British Women's Temperance Association', speech published as tract. (n.n., n.d.).
44. Minutes of Executive Committee, October 23, 1888.
45. Minutes of Executive Committee, December 19, 1900, Manchester W.C.T.U. papers in Manchester archives. In 1888, when the male dominated National Temperance League were offered a legacy from a wine merchant they accepted it. *Alliance News*, November 24, 1888.
46. The British Temperance League reports show that women donated money to their male dominated organization. In 1884 a widow, Mrs. Jane Rickaloy of Middleton, left six hundred pounds to the League for temperance work in her area. *British Temperance League Annual*, 1885.
47. Minutes of Executive Committee, July 2, 1878, March 18, 1879.
48. 'The Work Done by Our Association', by Miss Forsaith, paper presented to the BWTA Annual Meeting, 1886.
49. Infidelity was a common accusation in the nineteenth century against the temperance movement (ref. Shiman, *Crusade*, p. 67).
50. Forsaith, paper, 1886.
51. Minutes, June 5, 1877.
52. Minutes, March 22, 1878.
53. Letter in *Alliance News*, May 31, 1884. Copy of letter also in Manchester Women's Christian Temperance Union in Manchester archives.
54. See President's address at the Council Meeting of the BWTA May, 1892.
55. Minutes, February 9, 1887.
56. Minutes, October 22, 1879, April 21, 1880, June 2, 1880.
57. Shiman, *Crusade*, pp. 208–9.
58. Docwra, 'British Women's Temperance Association', *Temperance In All Nations*, p. 256.

59. See above, chap. 9.
60. Fitzgerald, p. 192.
61. *Annual Report*, Council Meeting, British Women's Temperance Association, May 5 and 6, 1892.
62. *Ibid.*
63. *Annual Report*, Council Meeting, 1892.
64. *Ibid.*
65. Was reproduced in the *Annual Report* for 1893. Mrs. Atherton was accused of writing it but it was the work of another member, Kate Thornbury. *Annual Report, 1893.*
66. Minutes, Manchester Women's Christian Union, June 15, 1892.
67. Docwra, 'British Women's Temperance Association', p. 258.
68. Lady Battersea, *Reminiscences*, p. 432.
69. *Annual Report*, Council Meeting, 1893.
70. *The Woman's Herald*, June 1893.
71. *Ibid*, June 1893.
72. 'How the Women Fought', *Christian World*, May 11, 1893.
73. *Ibid.*
74. *Ibid.*
75. Reported in *Christian World*, May 11, 1893. Frances Willard wrote a report of the meeting which was printed in *The Woman's Herald.*
76. Minutes of Council Meeting 1892. See below, chap. 13.
77. M. E. Docwra, Minutes, Executive Committee, Women's Total Abstinence Union, November 2, 1894.
78. *Annual Report*, Women's Total Abstinence Unions, 1900.
79. P. Rastrick, 'The Bradford Temperance Movement' (unpublished paper, Margaret MacMillan Training College, Bradford, 1969) p. 52.
80. See below, chap. 13.
81. Lady Henry Somerset sent a telegram to the National Prohibition Convention in 1897 in which she stated: '"Educate, organise, agitate" must be the watchwords for women in these anxious days.' See below, Conclusion.
82. Letter to Lord George Hamilton, January 27, 1898 quoted Fitzpatrick, pp. 205–6.
83. As M. E. Dowcra, Executive chairman admitted. B.W.T.A., *Temperance in All Nations*, p. 256.
84. Jill Liddington and Jill Norris, *One Hand Tied Behind Us: The Rise of the Women's Suffrage Movement* (London 1978) p. 240.

Chapter 12 For Church, Crown and Empire

1. The question whether a woman was a citizen was also discussed in the ruling circles of the new United States. Lecture, Linda Kerber, Harvard, December 2, 1988.
2. *The Nineteenth Century*, 'Appeal Against Female Suffrage', no. 148,

vol. 25, June 1889, pp. 781–87.
3. C. Roberts, p. 169.
4. M. Fawcett, 'Female Suffrage: A Reply', *The Nineteenth Century*, July 1889.
5. *Ibid.*
6. See above, chap. 3.
7. Asquith, vol. 1, p. 256.
8. Battersea, p. 198.
9. C. Roberts, p. 56 .
10. Orme, *Lady Fry*, p. 115.
11. See Patricia Hollis *Ladies Elect: Women in English Local Government, 1865–1914, op. cit.* for an excellent account of women's work in local government.
12. When one became vacant, wherever it was, the local party office, often on the advice of the central party office, would invite a candidate to stand for office. Then the politician would move temporarily to the constituency to fight the election. If successful the Member went to London to deal with national issues, not local; the defeated candidate would seek another invitation to stand, from wherever there was a vacancy.
13. Louisa Twining, 'Women as Public Servants', *The Nineteenth Century*, December 1890, pp. 950–58.
14. Leader in *The Times*, January 5, 1889. Also, 'An Appeal Against Female Suffrage', p. 782.
15. Later, in the last decade of the century, when the political parties decided that local government was a good nursery for their politicians women were pushed out and replaced by men. See P. Hollis, *Ladies Elect*, p. 140.
16. Helen M. Lynd, *England in the 1880's: Toward a Social Basis for Freedom* (New York 1968) p. 198.
17. David Thomson, *England in the Nineteenth Century* (Pelican, Baltimore, 1966) pp. 128–29.
18. Many new urban working-class voters disliked Liberals, believing they represented the industrial masters – the enemy of the workingman. In Disraeli's time Conservatives had developed a 'Tory Democracy' to make theirs a party of the people.
19. Borthwick, 'The Primrose League', *The Nineteenth Century*, July, 1886, p. 33.
20. Lady Nevill has written that the first ideas for the organization were discussed at her London residence. *The Reminiscences of Lady Dorothy Nevill*, edited by Ralph Nevill (London, 1906) p. 287.
21. Borthwick, p. 33.
22. *Ibid.*, p. 34. On April 19, Disraeli's birthday, all members were expected to wear 'a bunch of primroses'. *Primrose League Manual*, p. 3.
23. Borthwick, p. 33.

24. Members were to be called 'knights', their clubs 'habitations', their membership dues 'annual tribute', and official notices 'precepts'. A habitation could be set up with a minimum of 13 members and a payment of 'four crowns' to the central office in London. The individual member paid an entrance fee of 2/6 and an annual tribute of 2/6 to the London headquarters. Other local fees were set by each habitation and had to be paid by their members. In London there was a Grand Council made up of a Grand Master, four Trustees (or Vice Grand Masters), a Treasurer *ex officio,* and 45 other members. Soon various degrees of membership with exotic titles were introduced: Knight Harbinger in the first year, Knight Companion later. Special badges and clasps were awarded to denote the grades of the wearer.
25. Henry Drummond Wolfe, 'The Primrose League', *Encyclopedia Britannica*, 13th edition, p. 341.
26. *The Primrose League: Its Rise, Progress and Constitution* (London, 1887) p. 4.
27. Janet L. Robb, *The Primrose League*, New York, 1968 (A.M.S. reprint) p. 116.
28. *Primrose League Manual*, p. 55.
29. Robb, p. 113.
30. At least one American visitor noted the English love of titles. Eliza D. Stewart wrote that if an organization can get titled people to be associated with it then the work not only gets prestige but 'consideration of the upper classes'. E. Stewart, p. 102.
31. *Primrose League Manual*, pp. 30–31.
32. Primrose League Pamphlet no. 237, quoted Janet L. Robb, *The Primrose League* (New York, 1968; reprint of 1942 edition) p. 49.
33. *Primrose League Manual*, p. 31.
34. 'The Primrose League, Why Women Should Support It', *Lady's Realm*, June 1898, p. 183.
35. *Ibid.*
36. *Manual*, p. 23.
37. *Manual*, pp. 23–24.
38. Eventually so many associates joined that the League had to institute a one-penny charge for their 'diploma'.
39. Wolfe.
40. Bothwick, p. 36.
41. Robb, p. 71.
42. Robb, p. 48.
43. *Primrose League Manual*, Statutes and Ordinances 1886–87.
44. However, when one habitation made all its members pledge support for the Conservative candidate at election time, the London office had to ask them to desist to avoid accusation of illegality. Robb, p. 78.
45. Robb, p. 113.
46. Robb, p. 115.
47. Robb, p. 116.

48. Other than the periodic, infrequent rural fairs, women found few opportunities to escape their isolation. Later Women's Institutes and Mother meetings were established in the villages.
49. Robb, p. 134.
50. Robb, p. 120.
51. Robb, p. 111.
52. Robb, p. 116.
53. Women's National Liberal Association, *Annual Report*, 1897.
54. C. Roberts, p. 177.
55. *The Primrose League: Its Rise* . . . , p. 17.
56. Robb, Appendix.
57. Junior males were first enrolled as *squires* but this was changed to associates.
58. *The Times*, May 10, 1899. The great support the public gave to the Conservative Party in the last decades of the century was reflected in the popularity of the Primrose League. The Conservative position on 'Church, Crown and Empire' was in tune with popular sentiments, and after such national events as the British defeat in Sudan and the Boer War, the League's membership rose. An attack on any of the established values of the British Empire, such as the Bradlaugh affair, also sent large numbers of Britons, male and female, into the associate ranks of the League.
59. Borthwick, p. 38.
60. Many Conservative women believed in women's suffrage but accepted that the time was not right for it.
61. *The Woman's Herald*, vol. IV, no. 161, November 28, 1891.
62. See below, chap. 13.
63. Robb, p. 126.
64. *Women's Penny Paper*, p. 4, October 27, 1888.
65. Robb, p. 131.
66. March 12, 1887, p. 2.

Chapter 13 Raised Voices for Justice

1. For a full description of the beginnings of the National Liberal Federation, see Robert Spence Watson, *National Liberal Federation* (London, 1907).
2. In 1891, at the annual meeting of the National Liberal Federation at Newcastle, when a Liberal programme was drawn up and presented to the Liberal Party leadership, 2,500 delegates were present. Watson, p. 130.
3. In 1897 the Special General Committee of the National Liberal Federation, a nationally elected body, passed a women's suffrage motion but it had little effect on the Liberal Party's program. Watson, pp. 218–19.
4. Quoted in Orme, *Lady Fry*, pp. 110–11.

5. Orme, p. 111.
6. Nicola R. Mills, 'The Formation and Development of the Women's Liberal Federation and its Contribution to the Suffrage Movement, 1886–1918', unpublished thesis, Thames Polytechnic.
7. Sarah A. Tooley, 'The Women's Liberal Federation', p. 19. The Priestmans, connected to John Bright by marriage, were the most active, with the wife as president, a daughter as treasurer and another daughter on the executive. Miss Helen M. Sturge, from another well-known Quaker family, was the honorary secretary. Names from other notable west country Friends' families were found among those of the executive committee. Bristol Women's Liberal Association, *Annual Report*, 1884.
8. Bristol Women's Liberal Association. *Annual Report*, 1884.
9. *Ibid.*
10. Orme, p. 113.
11. Orme, pp. 115–16.
12. It was the only 'representative body for Liberalism in that district'. Tooley, p. 19.
13. It had become a common practice for candidates in an election to send someone around his district to see that eligible men were registered to vote.
14. Tooley, p. 19.
15. *Ibid.*
16. Three women were responsible for the creation of the Federation, a Mrs. Stirling (sister of Marcus Stone), Mrs. Broadley-Reid and Mrs. Theodore Fry, all related to leading politicians of the day. Miss Orme, biographer of Lady Fry, gives credit for the creation of the Federation to that lady, who was the wife of a Member of Parliament. Orme, p. 114.
17. Long active in her husband's elections; she and her daughters had canvassed among the constituents encouraging the men to vote and the women to study the issues. Orme, p. 116.
18. *Ibid.*, p. 117.
19. *Ibid.*
20. *Ibid.*, p. 119.
21. *Ibid.*
22. Tooley, p. 20; Orme, p. 121.
23. Orme, p. 122.
24. There were also Object IV 'to promote a Women's Liberal Association in every constituency and also the admission of women to membership in any existing Liberal Association'; and Object V, 'to bring into union all Liberal Associations of which women are members and so encourage their cooperation in the promotion of reform.' *Annual Report*, WLF, 1889.
25. *Report of the Annual Council and General Meeting*, May 8, 1888, reprinted 1900.

26. Mrs. Gladstone's speech quoted by Orme, pp. 124–25.
27. Sarah Tooley called the basis of the new Federation a *republican* one, 'and may be fittingly compared to the constitution of the United States of America', Tooley, p. 20.
28. Orme, pp. 123–25. See also Tooley, p. 21.
29. *Report of the Annual Council and General Meeting*, May 8, 1888.
30. She was born a Marjoribanks, and married a Liberal Scottish peer. Her husband had been the Liberal Lord Lieutenant of Ireland for a brief period. Tooley, *The Women's Liberal Federation*, p. 23.
31. She did not like to make public speeches or go on public platforms but was a good organizer and worked effectively behind the scenes – an excellent parliamentary wife.
32. *Annual Report*, WLF, 1888.
33. The women of Birmingham had been active for many years and did not believe that a central Federation was of such importance. In that city there were three main Liberal groups that cooperated closely – the Liberal Association, its women's Auxiliary, and a Women's Liberal Association.
34. *Annual Report*, WLF, 1889.
35. *Annual Report*, WLF, 1890, pp. 12–13.
36. *Annual Report*, WLF, 1891.
37. *Ibid.*
38. Roberts p. 115.
39. The lack of money was always a problem as the Minutes of the Executive constantly reveal. 'How to secure an income for a Women's Liberal Association' was a topic at the second annual meeting of the Council. *Annual Report*, WLF, 1889.
40. *Annual Report*, WLF, 1890.
41. For the class difference between the WLF and the individual Associations see Nichola R. Mills, *op. cit.*
42. As it most certainly was by the election of 1892. See *Annual Report*, WLF, 1893, p. 8.
43. *Annual Report*, WLF, 1890.
44. Speech printed in C. Roberts, p. 184. Lady Carlisle was from a radical family. Her mother, Lady Stanley of Alderley, was a founder of the Women's Liberal Unionist Association – an anti-Home Rule organization. Lady Stanley was also the first name on the 'Appeal Against Women's Suffrage' published in *The Nineteenth Century*, see above, Part Three, Introduction.
45. In 1890 this prominent Liberal organized the Carlisle Women's Liberal Association and when her daughter married and went to live at Oxford, the newly-wed set up a Women's Liberal Association in her new hometown. Roberts, p. 176. Both mother and daughter eventually served together on the executive committee of the Federation.
46. *Annual Report*, WLF, 1891.
47. A defeat many blamed on the anti-drink measures the Party adopted in

its election program. See Shiman, *Crusade Against Drink in Victorian England*, p. 229.

48. The British Women's Temperance Association women were shocked when told that at a Women's Liberal Federation meeting there was a favourable reference to children getting beer from public houses. *Alliance News*, June 5, 1891.
49. Trained as a lawyer, with an LLB degree, Miss Orme was a close associate of Mrs. Fry. Shares of the journal were owned by the Federation and members of the Executive Committee were made its directors. *Annual Report*, WLF, 1890.
50. *Annual Report*, WLF, 1890.
51. Once they tried to set up a series of political readings for sewing groups making and repairing clothes 'for Irish evicted tenants', but this was unsuccessful and soon disbanded. *Annual Report*, WLF, 1890.
52. *Annual Report*, WLF, 1892.
53. See *Annual Report*, WLF, 1892. Women found that women's protection laws carried a very high price which women themselves had to pay because they often eliminated women from the segment of the labour market that was regulated.
54. *Annual Report*, WLF, 1892.
55. See Chap. 12.
56. At the 1888 Conference of the National Liberal Federation, women were given their own special meeting over which Mrs. Gladstone presided, and 2,000 women attended. Home Rule, not women's issues, was discussed and, not unexpectedly, they voted to support the party's Home Rule policy. In 1889 the only public meeting organized by the executive committee of the Women's Liberal Federation was one held in Manchester on December 4, 1889, during the time of the annual meeting of the National Liberal Federation. With Mrs. Fry presiding and Mrs. Gladstone attending, again only the Irish policy of the government was discussed. *Report of the Annual Council and General Meeting*, WLF, May 1888, p. 4.
57. The middle classes obtained the vote in 1832 because, after years of strenuous agitation, they could not be denied it. The excluded urban workers, becoming increasingly organized and a potential force in political circles, had received the franchise in 1867 from the Conservatives, who hoped to make Tory Democrats out of them. In 1884, the Liberal Party hoping to get the support of rural male householders, gave them the vote. Women, on the other hand, had only been given the consolation prize of the local government vote in 1867.
58. That was why, it was claimed, Gladstone and many leading Liberals refused to support women's suffrage, even though their political principles advocated it. See C. Roberts, p. 191.
59. *The Spectator*, February 28, 1891, p. 294.
60. See below. Some of the most active women went over to this group – Lady Stanley of Alderley, Lady Frances Balfour, Mrs. Henry

Fawcett, Miss Tod of Belfast, and Mrs. McLaren, the last four leading suffragists.

61. See her speech at the Annual Council Meeting of the WLF of 1892, published in the *Annual Report* of 1892.
62. See Gladstone's letter to Samuel Smith of April 11, 1892, reprinted in *Women in Public 1850–1900*, ed. Patricia Hollis, pp. 319–21.
63. *Annual Report*, WLF, 1891.
64. Mrs. Fry was a member of the Pease family, known for their opposition to women's suffrage. Nicole Mills, p. 16.
65. Speech at Women's Liberal Federation Conference, Newcastle, 1891, Orme, pp. 132–33.
66. Bristol and many others according to the delegates statements at the 1892 annual meeting.
67. When one parliamentary wife, Mrs. Wynford Phillips, president of the Westminster Women's Liberal Association and executive member of the Federation as well as an executive of the Central National Committee for Women's Suffrage, was asked what her husband thought of her suffrage activities, she answered, 'he is too true a Liberal to object to any work in the cause of Liberalism'. *The Woman's Herald*, February 20, 1892.
68. *Ibid.*
69. Eva McLaren, *The History of the Women's Suffrage Movement in the Women's Liberal Federation*, 2nd edn, 1903, p. 4.
70. McLaren, p. 8.
71. The women of the Bright family were all very active in politics: Sisters, wives, daughters could all be found engaged in Liberal politics, in many parts of the country. John Bright had originally supported women's suffrage, but he later changed his mind on the grounds that politics was too dirty for women.
72. *Annual Report*, WLF, 1889.
73. Roberts, p. 114.
74. *Annual Report*, WLF, 1890. But according to Eva McLaren Miss Cobden moved the motion and her husband, Mr. Walter McLaren, MP, seconded it (McLaren, p. 9).
75. C. Roberts, pp. 114–15.
76. Tooley, p. 22.
77. *Annual Report*, WLF, 1891, and McLaren p. 10.
78. The Bill not only brought the issue of women's suffrage to the front of public discussion but also caused dissension in suffragist ranks. Many reformers supported the view that single women property-owners with the same qualifications as men should have the vote: The growing number of women who had inherited property and money from their families deserved the rights and privileges men enjoyed when they had such economic advantages. But married women, according to one way of thinking, were part of a family group represented by the male householder; giving the wife a vote could introduce discord into the

family circle. Others saw the bill as discriminating against married women: Why should women with the vote be disenfranchised by marriage? Marriage itself would then entail a penalty for woman. A third position was supported by some suffragists who, though wanting the vote for all women, were willing to support any extension for women on the grounds that it was a gain, even if a piecemeal one: After each such increase, more women could cast a ballot for further extension. (Lady Carlisle could be placed in this category; see Lady Carlisle's speech to WLF, 1892).

79. David Rubenstein, *Before the Suffragettes*, New York, 1986, p. 144.
80. It was a great fight on both sides in the House with an 'energetic whipping up' of support for and against it. None of the Liberal leaders supported it, but some of the Conservative ones did. *The Woman's Herald*, April 30, 1892.
81. The next major suffrage bill was also introduced by a Conservative backbencher. In 1897 Ferdinald Faithful Begg sponsored a bill that also won a second reading but lost in the division. Rubenstein, p. 146. For an excellent discussion of those hostile to the enfranchisement of women see Brian Harrison, *Separate Spheres: The Opposition to Women's Suffrage* (London, 1978).
82. Edited and owned at this time by Florence Fenwick Miller, who took it over from Lady Henry Somerset in January 1894.
83. An editorial leader in the same issue of *The Woman's Herald* disputed what the letter claimed, asserting that there was no organized scheme and that it had always been the intention of those Federation members who supported women's suffrage to have women's parliamentary enfranchisement included in the second Object.
84. Mr. Gladstone asked Lady Carlisle to 'defer the question of Women's Suffrage in the interest of Home Rule. She refused . . . ', Roberts, pp. 116–17.
85. Unlike the experience of the British Women's Temperance Association the following year. See above, chap. 11.
86. *The Woman's Herald*, May 21, 1892, Eva McLaren, p. 5.
87. Report in *The Woman's Herald*, May 21, 1892.
88. *Ibid.*
89. *Ibid.* In a test case all candidates in order to get support from the Federation would have to agree to support the Parliamentary enfranchisement of women.
90. On a show of hands the resolution had only 12 dissidents.
91. Tooley, p. 22.
92. She left England when her husband was appointed governor general of Canada.
93. *Annual Report*, WLF, 1893. See also McLaren, p. 11.
94. McLaren, p. 6.
95. All these membership figures come from the Annual Reports of the WLF.

96. The election campaign and subsequent defeat of the Liberal Party in the general election caused many former supporters to leave the party and join the Conservatives. The Tories were on the popular side of the anti-drink campaign of 1895 and the imperialist issue of the Boer War of 1902.
97. Robb, Appendix III.
98. November 16, 1911, Minutes of Special Meeting.
99. Minutes of Executive Committee, May, 1912.
100. Minutes of Executive Committee, July 17, 1910.
101. Set up at the 1890 Annual Meeting, the Parliamentary subcommittee on Current Legislation issued reports at every Annual Meeting dealing with all legislation affecting women, particularly working women. See 1891 *Annual Report* of the Women's Liberal Federation.
102. Minutes of the Executive Committee, February 11, 1911.
103. Miss Biggs, Report of the Preliminary Conference of the Women's National Liberal Association, Held at the National Liberal Club, Thursday, December 1, 1892. Organizational Meeting.
104. Annual Meeting, 1912 Women's National Liberal Association.
105. Letter from Lady Fry printed *Quarterly Report*, December, 1895.
106. *Annual Report*, WNLA 1897. These three-day meetings, held in London, with 'lectures and social gatherings', were reported in the Annual Report to be a welcome 'break from household routines.' *Annual Report*, of the WNLA, 1897.
107. See above, chap. 12. Lady Stanley was particularly well known for her work in education.
108. Leaflet published by Association in 1903.
109. Asquith, vol. I, p. 258.
110. October 12, 1889.
111. See above, chap. 10.
112. 'Interview', *Women's Penny Paper*, October 12, 1889, p. 1.
113. See above, chap. 9.
114. Olive Banks, *Biographical Dictionary of British Feminists; vol. 1: 1800–1930* (New York, 1985) pp. 9–12. Asquith, vol. I, p 259.
115. Lady Frances Balfour's work with the Women's Liberal Unionist Association brought her into contact with the women's suffrage movement, which she joined in 1887; soon after, it assigned her a leadership role. Banks, pp. 10–11.

Conclusion

1. Said Mrs Bateson at the 1892 Annual Conference of the Women's Liberal Federation.
2. See above, chap. 1.
3. Said Eva McLaren during debate over Women's Suffrage at the Annual Meeting in 1898. *Annual Report*, WLF, 1898.

4. Martin Pugh, *Women's Suffrage in Britain, 1867–1928*, The Historical Assn. General Series 97 (London, 1980) p. 6.
5. *Ibid.*
6. In 1897, the original Committee reorganized, changed its name to The National Union of Women's Suffrage Societies, and brought under one banner all societies that organized exclusively for women's suffrage, and took up the movement's leadership.
7. Even the Liberal breakaway group, the Women's National Liberal Association, recognized the importance of the suffrage and supported its adoption 'in the future' (when it would not conflict with official Liberal policies).
8. McLaren, p. 17.
9. See Sarah A. Tooley, 'The Woman's International Conference', *Lady's Realm*, vol. 6, May–October 1899, pp. 90–95.
10. *Ibid.*, pp. 91.
11. Read to Section VIII, 'Women's Help For Prohibition,' of the National Prohibition Convention in Newcastle, 1897. See Guy Hayler (ed.), *The Prohibition Movement*, Newcastle-upon-Tyne, 1897, p. 287.
12. Letter to Samuel Smith, April 11, 1892, reprinted in *Women in Public 1850–1900*, ed. Patricia Hollis, pp. 319–21.
13. Annual Meeting, Women's Liberal Federation 1892, reported in *The Woman's Herald*, May 21, 1892, p. 12
14. *Ibid.*
15. Miss Frances Willard and Mrs. Pearsall Smith, two Americans prominent in the temperance and suffrage movements, were also invited to be speakers.
16. Like their counterpart in the United States, the Women's Christian Temperance Union of New Zealand was in the forefront of the struggle for the franchise for women: hence the presence of Willard and Smith, both officials of the WCTU in the U.S.
17. *The Woman's Signal*, June 1894.
18. Vol. I, pp. 258–59.
19. *The Woman's Signal*, January 4, 1894.

Bibliography

Unpublished Manuscripts

Paul Wesley Chilcote, 'John Wesley and the Women Preachers of Early Methodism', Ph.D. thesis, Duke University, 1984.
Sarah Crosby, Letter Book, 1760–1774, Special Collections Dept, Duke University, N.C.
Robin Reed Davis, 'Anglican Evangelicalism and the Feminine Literary Tradition from Hannah More to Charlotte Bronte,' Ph.D. thesis, Duke University, 1982.
Julie L. Kitze 'Enter Every Open Door: The British Women's Temperance Association 1876–1900', thesis, Cambridge University, 1986.
William Lechmere, 'Commonplace Book, 1832–1835'. London, England (Wm B. Hamilton Collection, Duke University).
Nicola R. Mills, 'The Formation and Development of the Women's Liberal Federation and its Contribution to the Suffrage Movement, 1886–1918', M.A. thesis, Thames Polytechnic College.
Gerald Wayne Olsen, 'Pub and Parish. The Beginnings of Temperance Reform in the Church of England, 1835–1875', Ph.D. thesis, University of Western Ontario, 1971.
Joanne Cooper Scott, 'Bradford Women in Organization 1867–1914', 1970, thesis, Archives, Bradford Public Library.
Rosemary Van Arsdel, 'Florence Fenwick-Miller, Feminism and *The Woman's Signal*, 1895–1899', Fawcett Library, London.

Letters and Archive Collections

George Wilson Collection, Archives, Manchester Public Library.
Cobden Papers, Manuscript Department, British Library.
Manchester Women's Christian Temperance Association, Minute books, letters and papers, Archives, Manchester Public Library.
William B. Hamilton Collection, Duke University.
Lady Rosalind Howard, Countess of Carlisle, letters, Howard Castle archives.

Minutes

British Woman's Temperance Association, Minute Books of Executive Committee for 1876–1878, 1879–1880, 1882–1884, 1885–1892, Annual Council meetings, 1894–96.

Manchester Women's Christian Temperance Association, Minute Books Minutes of the Executive Committee, January 1880–January 1889, January 1889–January 1892, January 1892–January 1900.
Minute Books of Women's Total Abstinence Union, Executive Committee 1896–1898, 1898–1900, 1901–1904, 1904–1906, General Committee 1900–1904, 1905–1910.
National British Women's Temperance Association, Subcommittee Minute books 1920–24, 1924–28.
Women's Liberal Federation, Minute Books of Executive Committee 1910–1912

Reports

Birmingham Female Society for the Relief of British Negro Slaves, *Annual Report* 1826.
Bristol Women's Liberal Association, *Annual Report* 1884.
British Women's Temperance Association, *Annual Reports* 1880–1900. 1893 special report.
Manchester Women's Christian Temperance Union, *Annual Reports* 1885–1900.
National Women's Liberal Association, *Report of the Preliminary Conference*, December 1, 1892.
National Women's Liberal Association, *Quarterly Reports*, Dec. 1895–Oct. 1901, Dec. 1902–Oct. 1906, Jan. 1907–Oct. 1912.
Women's Liberal Federation, *Annual Report of the Executive Committee and Report of the Annual Council Meetings* 1888–1918, Summary Federation News, no. 1, vol. ix, no. 4, July 1893–Dec. 1918.
Women's Liberal Unionist Association, assorted leaflets.
Women's National Liberal Federation, *Annual Reports*, 1923–1928.
Women's Total Abstinence Union, *Annual Reports*, 1893–98.
World's Women's Christian Temperance Union, *Report* of 1st conference in England, May 6, 1892.
Yorkshire Women's Christian Temperance Union, *Annual Report*, 1899.

Periodicals

Alliance News.
British Women's Temperance Journal.
The Church of England Temperance Chronicle.
The Englishwoman's Review.
Gospel Temperance Herald.
Ladies Realm.
The Nation.

The Nineteenth Century.
Review of Reviews.
The Signal and Gospel Union Gazette.
The Spectator.
Temperance Advocate.
The Temperance Record.
The Times
United Temperance Gazette.
The Woman's Herald.
The Woman's Signal.
Women's Penny Paper.

Articles

'A Reply to Mr. Gladstone's Letter on Woman Suffrage', by a Member of the Women's Liberal Federation, London.

Sally Alexander, 'Women's Work in Nineteenth Century London: A Study of the Years 1820–50', *The Changing Experience of Women*, ed. Elizabeth Whitelegg, Maud Arnot *et. al.*, Oxford, 1982.

Countess of Anacaster, 'Ladies and the Primrose League', *Lady's Realm*, vol. VI, May 1899.

Olive Anderson, 'Women Preachers in Mid Victorian Britain – some Reflexions', *The Historical Journal*, 12, 1969, pp. 467–84.

'An Appeal Against Female Suffrage', *The Nineteenth Century*, June, 1889, no. 148.

Hatford Battersby, *Woman's Work in the Temperance Reformation*, Wm. Tweedie publisher, London, 1868.

Carol Bauer, Lawrence Ritt, 'Wife-Abuse, Late-Victorian English Feminists and the Legacy of Frances Power Cobb', *International Journal of Women's Studies (Canada)*, 1983, vol. 6, no. 3.

Amy E. Bell, 'Interview', *Women's Penny Paper*, December 22, 1888.

Geoffrey Best, 'The Evangelicals and the Established Church in the Early Nineteenth Century', *Journal of Theological Studies*, N.S. X, 1959.

Lady Elizabeth Biddulph, 'What Women have done for Prohibition', Paper read at National Prohibition Convention, 1897, printed in *The Prohibition Movement*, ed. Guy Hayler, Newcastle-upon-Tyne, 1897.

'Women Workers Against Slavery', *Birmingham Post*, December 2, 1931.

Mrs. Blaikie, 'Women's Help for Prohibition', National Prohibition Conv. 1897 Hayler, *op. cit.*

Algernon Borthwick, 'The Primrose League, *The Nineteenth Century*, July 1886, pp. 33–39.

Diana Burfield, 'Theosophy and Feminism, *Women's Religious Experience*, ed. Patricia Holden, London, 1983.

G. B. Caird, 'Paul and Women's Liberty', *The John Rylands Library*, volume 54, 1971–72.

Francis Power Cobbe, 'Life in an English Boarding School', *Victorian Women* ed. Erna O. Hellerstein *et al.*, Stanford, 1981.
Kenneth Corfield, 'Elizabeth Heyrick: Radical Quaker', in Malmgreen, *Religion in the Lives of English Women 1760–1930*, London, 1986.
T. G. Crippen, 'The Females Advocate', London, n.d. reprinted Congregational Historical Society Transaction, vol. 8, 1922.
W. M. Daniels, review M. Ostrogorski, 'Democracy and the Organization of Political Parties,' *The Nation*, vol. 76, no. 1974, April 30, 1903.
Mollie C. Davis, 'The Countess of Huntingdon: A Leader in Missions for Social and Religious Reform', *Women in New Worlds*, vol. II, ed. Rosemary Skinner Keller, Louise L. Queen and Hilah F. Thomas, Abingdon, 1982.
D. Colin Dews, 'Ann Carr and the Female Revivalists of Leeds', *Religion in the Lives of English Women, 1760–1930*, ed. Gail Malmgreen, London, 1986.
M. M. Dilke, 'Second Reply to Female Suffrage', *The Nineteenth Century*, July 1889, CXLIX.
M. E. Docwra, 'A Glimpse at Woman's Work for Temperance during the Victorian Era' papers read Bristol, October 1897, published by Women's Total Abstinence Union.
——, 'BWTA What it is, What is had done and What it had still to do'. Paper printed as tract.
Millicent Fawcett, 'Female Suffrage: A Reply', *The Nineteenth Century*, July 1889, CXLIX.
Charlotte H. Ferguson 'Woman's Work in the Temperance Reformation' in J. C. Street, F. R. Lees and D. Burns (eds), *International Temperance and Prohibition Convention*, London, 1862.
Monica C. Fryckstedt, 'The Hidden Rill: The Life and Career of Marie Jane Jewsbury', *The John Rylands University Library*, Manchester vol. 39, 1956–57.
Lady Catherine Milnes Gaskell, 'Women Today', *The Nineteenth Century*, November 1889.
Richard L. Greaves, 'The Role of Women in Early English Nonconformity', *Church History*, vol. 52, 1983, pp. 299–311.
Olwen Hufton, 'Women without Men: Widows and Spinsters in Britain and France in the Eighteenth Century', *Journal of Family History*, 1984, vol. 9, no. 4.
Margaret Hunt, 'Wife Abuse In Early Eighteenth Century London', Paper read Annual Meeting, American Historical Association, 1988.
Brian Heeney, 'The Beginnings of Church Feminism: Women and the Councils of the Church of England, 1897–1919', Malmgreen, *Religion . . . op. cit.*, pp. 260–84.
Ann R. Higginbotham, 'Respectable Sinners: Salvation Army Rescue Work with Unmarried Mothers, 1884–1914', Malmgreen, '*Religion . . .* ' *op. cit.* pp. 216–33.
Weldon T. Johnson, 'The Religious Crusade: Revival or Ritual', *American*

Journal of Sociology, March 1971, pp. 873–88.

David Jones, 'Women and Chartism', *History*, February, 1983, pp. 1–21.

Jennie Kitteringham, 'Country work girls in nineteenth-century England', *Village Life and Labour*, ed. Raphael Samuel, London, 1975.

Philippa Levine, '"So Few Prizes and So Many Blanks": Marriage and Feminism in Later Nineteenth-Century England', *Journal of British Studies*, vol. 28, no. 2, April 1989.

Lady Llangattock, 'The Primrose League Why Women Should Support It', *Lady's Realm*, June 1898, pp. 180–84.

Elizabeth Hope Luder, 'Women and Quakerism', Pendle Hill Pamphlet 196, Wallingford, 1974.

Donald Mathew, 'Women's History', *Quarterly Review*, Winter, 1981.

Harry Leon McBeth, 'The Changing Role of Women in Baptist History', *Southwestern Journal of Theology*, vol. 18, Fall 1979.

'An Appeal Against Female Suffrage, *The Nineteenth Century*, vol. 25, no. 148, June 1889, pp. 781–87.

Margaret Oliphant, 'The Condition of Women', *Blackwoods Edinburgh Magazine*, vol. 83, February 1858.

Edith Picton-Tuberville, 'The Coming Order in the Church of Christ', *Women and the Church*', ed. B. H. Streeter, 1917.

Catherine M. Prelinger, 'The Female Diaconate in the Anglican Church', Malmgreen, *Religion In the Lives . . . op. cit.*

Nina Coombs Pykare, 'The Sin of Eve and the Christian Conduct Book', *Ohio Journal of Religious Studies*, vol. 4, 1976, pp. 34–43.

Sonya Rose, 'Gender Antagonisms and Class conflict: exclusionary strategies of male trade unionists in nineteenth-century Britain', *Social History*, vol. 13, no 2, May 1988.

Lilian Lewis Shiman 'Changes Are Dangerous': Women and Temperance in Victorian England', Malmgreen, *Religion . . . , op. cit.*, pp. 193–215.

——, 'The Birstall Temperance Society,' *The Yorkshire Archaeological Journal*, vol. 46, 1974.

——, 'Temperance and Class in Bradford: 1830–60', *The Yorkshire Archaeological Journal*, January 1986.

——, 'The Church of England Temperance Society in the Nineteenth Century', *The Historical Magazine of the Protestant Episcopal Church*, vol. XLI, no. 2, June 1972.

——, '"The Blue Ribbon Army": Gospel Temperance in England', *The Historical Magazine of the Protestant Episcopal Church*, vol. 1, no. 4 (December 1981).

Derwood C. Smith, 'Paul and the Non-Eschatological Woman, *Ohio Journal of Religious Studies*, vol. 4, 1976.

Isabella Stewart, 'What do we gain by Affiliation?', BWTA Leaflet no. 6, 1887.

M. Sturge, paper published in *Women's Work in the Temperance Reform*, London, 1868, *op. cit.*

Wesley F. Swift, 'Women Itinerant Preachers of Early Methodism', Part I,

Proceedings of the Wesleyan Historical Society, XXVIII, March 1952, p. 92.
——, 'Women Itinerant Preachers of Early Methodism', Part II, *Proceedings of the Wesleyan Historical Society*, XXIX.
Dorothy Thompson, 'Women and Nineteenth Century Radical Politics', *Rights and Wrongs of Women*, ed. Juliet Mitchell and Ann Oakley, Pelican, 1976.
Myna Trustram, 'Distasteful and derogatory? Examining Victorian soldiers for venereal disease', *The Sexual Dynamics of History*, The London Feminist History Group, London, 1983, pp. 154–64.
Annmarie Turnbull, '"So extremely like parliament": the work of the women members of the London School Board, 1870–1904'. *The Sexual Dynamics of History, op. cit.*, pp. 120–33.
Louisa Twining, 'Women as Public Servants', *The Nineteenth Century*, December 1890.
Alex Tyrrell, '"Woman's Mission" and Pressure Group Politics in Britain (1825–60)', *The John Rylands University Library*, Manchester, vol. 63, no. 1.
Barbara Welter, 'The Cult of True Womanhood', *American Quarterly*, 1966, 18 (2 pt 1), pp. 151–74.
'Women and Politics', reprinted from *The Kent Times* March 12, 1887, tract.
B. Wood, 'Twenty Reasons Why All Women Should be Total Abstainers', tract, 2nd edn, revised and enlarged, Bradford (circa 1867–69).
Work We Have To Do', *The Englishwoman's Review*, October 1866.
Henry Drummond Wolfe, 'The Primrose League', *Encyclopedia Britannica*, Thirteenth Edition, 1926.

Books

A.V.L., *Ministering Women and the London Poor*, Mrs. Bayly ed., London 1870.
Richard Altick, *Victorian People and Ideas*, New York, 1973.
Herbert Asquith (The Earl of Oxford and Asquith) *Memories and Reflections 1852–1927*, Boston, 1929, vols I and II.
Margot Asquith, *An Autobiography*, New York, 1920.
Olive Banks, *Biographical Dictionary of British Feminists*, vol. i: 1800–1930, New York, 1985.
Constance Battersea, *Reminiscences*, London, 1923.
Samuel Bamford, *Passages in the Life of a Radical*, Oxford, 1984 edition.
E. Moberley Bell, *Josephine Butler, Flame of Fire*, London, 1962.
Joyce Bellamy and John Saville, ed., *Dictionary of Labour Biography*, vol. VII, London, 1972.
Annie Besant, *An Autobiography*, London, 1893.
Walter Besant, *Fifty Years Ago*, New York, 1888.

Robert Blake, *Disraeli*, New York, 1967.
Ruth Bordin, *Frances Willard: a biography*, Chapel Hill, 1986.
——, *Women and Temperance*, Philadelphia, 1981.
Nancy Boyd, *Josephine Butler, Octavia Hill, Florence Nightingale*, London, 1982.
Ian Bradley, *The Call to Seriousness. The Evangelical Impact on the Victorians*, London, 1976.
Renate Bridenthal and Claudia Koonz, *Becoming Visible*, New York, 1977.
Asa Briggs, *The Making of Modern England, 1783–1867*, New York, 1965.
Earl Kent Brown, *Women in Mr. Wesley's Methodism*, New York, 1983.
W. H. Burnett, *Sunlight in the Slums*, Manchester, 1888.
Dawson Burns, *Temperance in the Victorian Age*, London, 1897.
Jabez Burns, *A Retrospect of Forty-Five Years Christian Ministry*, London, 1875.
Joan N. Burstyn, *Victorian Education and the Ideal of Womanhood*, London, 1980.
A. S. G. Butler, *Portrait of Josephine Butler*, London, 1954.
Josephine Butler, *The Education and Employment of Women*, London, 1868.
——, *Personal Reminiscences of a Great Crusade*, London, 1898.
Edward Cadbury, M. Cecile Matheson and George Shann, *Women's Work and Wages*, London, 1906.
Karlyn K. Campbell, *Man Cannot Speak for Her*, New York, 1989, vols I and II.
Richard Carwardine, *Trans-atlantic Revivalism*, Westport, Conn., 1978.
Jennie Chapell, *Noble Workers*, London, 1910.
Arthur Compton-Rickett, *The London Life of Yesterday*, New York, 1909.
E. R. Conder, *Josiah Conder: A Memoir*, London, 1857.
Samuel Couling, *History of the Temperance Movement in Great Britain and Ireland*, London, 1862.
Robert Currie, *Methodism Divided*, London, 1968.
S. J. Curtis and M. E. A. Boultwood, *English Education Since 1800*, London, 1960.
Lenore Davidoff, *The Best Circles: Society, etiquette and the season*, London, 1986.
Rupert Davies, *Methodism*, Penguin Books, 1963.
Jacques Donzelot, *The Policing of Families*, New York, 1979.
David Doughan and Denise Sanchez, *Feminist Periodicals, 1855–1984*, Brighton, 1987.
Sarah Stickney Ellis, *The Women of England: Their Social Duties and Domestic Habits*, London, 1839.
H. J. Ellison, *The Temperance Reformation Movement in the Church of England*, London, 1878.
R. C. K Ensor, *England 1870–1914*, Oxford, 1936.
Barbara Leslie Epstein, *The Politics of Domesticity*, Middletown, 1981.
Carolly Erickson, *Our Tempestuous Day*, New York, 1986.
St. John Ervine, *God's Soldier*, New York, 1935.

Richard J. Evans, *The Feminists*, London, 1979.
David Fahey, *The Collected Writings of Jessie Forsyth 1847–1937*, New York, 1988.
Tim FitzGeorge-Parker, *Roscoe: the bright shiner*, London, 1987.
Kathleen Fitzpatrick, *Lady Henry Somerset*, Boston, 1923.
J. M. J. Fletcher, *Mrs. Wightman of Shrewsbury*, London, 1906.
Eleanor Flexner, *Century of Struggle*, New York, 1970.
Dorothy George, *England in Transition*, Pelican Edition, 1964.
Alan D. Gilbert, *Religion and Society in Industrial England*, New York, 1976.
John R. Gillis, *For Better, For Worse*, Oxford, 1985.
Anna A. Gordon, *The Beautiful Life of Frances E. Willard*, Chicago, 1898.
William Gourlay, *National Temperance A Jubilee Biograph*, London, 1906.
Doris Gulliver, *Dame Agnes Weston*, London, 1971.
Brian Harrison, *Dictionary of British Temperance Biography*, Coventry and Sheffield, 1973.
——, *Separate Spheres: The Opposition to Women's Suffrage in Britain*, London, 1978.
G. Hayler, ed., *The Prohibition Movement*, Newcastle upon Tyne, 1897.
Kathleen Heasman, *Evangelicals in Action*, London, 1962.
Brian Heeney, *The Women's Movement in the Church of England, 1850–1930*, Oxford, 1988.
Erna Olafson Hellerstein, Leslie Parker Hume and Karen Offen, editors, *Victorian Women*, Stanford, 1981.
Lady Dorothy Henley, *Rosalind Howard, Countess of Carlisle*, London, 1958.
Sheila Herstein, *A Mid-Victorian Feminist, Barbara Leigh Smith Bodichon*, New Haven, 1985.
Margaret Hewitt, *Mothers and Wives in Victorian Industry*, Rockcliffe, 1958.
J. Deane Hilton, *Marie Hilton: Her Life and Work*, London, 1897.
Eric J. Hobsbawn, *Labouring Men*, London, 1967.
Lee Holcombe, *Victorian Ladies at Work*, Newton Abbot, 1973.
Patricia Holden, ed., *Women's Religious Experience*, London, 1983.
Patricia Hollis, ed., *Pressure from Without in Early Victorian England*, New York, 1974.
——, ed., *Women in Public 1850–1900, Documents of the Victorian Women's Movement*, London, 1979.
——, *Ladies Elect: Women in English Local Government, 1865–1914*, New York, 1987.
K. S. Inglis, *Churches and the Working Classes*, London, 1963.
Elizabeth Isichei, *Victorian Quakers*, London, 1970.
Joyce L. Irwin, *Womanhood in Radical Protestantism, 1525–1675*, New York, 1979.
Dale A. Johnson, *Women in English Religion 1700–1925*, New York, 1983.
Extracts from Priscilla Johnson's Journal and Letters, privately circulated.

H. B. Kendall, *History of the Primitive Methodist Church*, London, 1919.

The Liberal Platform Historic Facts and Current Problems, London, 1895.

Jill Liddington and Jill Norris, *One Hand Tied Behind Us: The Rise of the Women's Suffrage Movement*, London, 1978.

Arnold Lloyd, *Quaker Social History 1669–1738*, London, 1950.

Colin Rhys Lovell, *English Constitutional and Legal History*, New York, 1962.

Helen M. Lynd, *England in the 1880's: Toward a Social Basis for Freedom*, New York, 1968.

Kenneth Mackenzie, *The English Parliament*, Pelican Book, 1951.

Norman Mackenzie, ed., *Letters of Sydney and Beatrice Webb*, Cambridge, 1978.

Gail Malmgreen, *Women's Suffrage in England: Origins and Alternatives 1792–1851*, Brighton, 1978.

——, editor, *Religion in the Lives of English Women, 1760–1930*, London, 1986.

G. E. Mingay, *English Landed Society in the Eighteenth Century*, London, 1963.

W. E. Moss, *Life of Mrs. Lewis*, London, 1926.

——, *Book of Memories*, Blackburn, 1951.

Kitty Muggeridge and Ruth Adam, *Beatrice Webb, A Life 1858–1943*, London, 1967.

Norman McCord, *The Anti Corn Law League 1838–1846*, London, 1958.

Eva McLaren, *The History of the Women's Suffrage Movement in the Women's Liberal Federation*, 2nd edition, 1903.

W. G. McLoughlin, *Modern Revivalism*, New York, 1959.

Wanda F. Neff, *Victorian Working Women*, New York, 1929.

Lady Dorothy Nevill, *Life and Letters of Lady Dorothy Nevill*, ed. Ralph Nevill, London, 1906.

——, *The Reminiscences of Lady Dorothy Nevill*, ed. Ralph Nevill, London, 1907.

——, *Under Five Reigns*, London, 1910.

——, *My Own Times*, London, 1912.

John Newton, *W. S. Caine, M.P.*, London, 1907,

James Obelkevich, *Religion and Rural Society*, Oxford, 1976.

Lillian O'Connor, *Pioneer Women Orators*, New York, 1954.

Elizabeth Orme, *Lady Fry of Darlington*, London, 1898.

Jessie Penn-Lewis, *The Magna Charta of Woman*, Minneapolis, 1975.

Harold Perkin, *Origins of Modern English Society*, London, 1985.

Glen Petrie, *A Single Iniquity*, New York, 1971,

J. H. Plumb, *England in the Eighteen Century 1714–1815*, Pelican, 1965.

Beatrice Potter, *My Apprenticeship*, London, 1938.

The Primrose League: Its Rise, Progress and Constitution, London, 1887.

Primrose League Manual, Statutes and Ordinances, London, 1899.

Lewis G. Pray, *The History of Sunday Schools and of Religion from the Earliest Times*, Boston, 1847.

F. K. Prochaska, *Women and Philanthropy in Nineteenth Century England*, Oxford, 1980.

Martin Pugh, *Women's Suffrage in Britain, 1867–1928*, The Historical Assn. General Series 97, London, 1980.

Marian Ramelson, *Petticoat Rebellion*, London, 1967.

Jane Rendall, *The Origins of Modern Feminism, Women in Britain, France and U.S. 1780–1860*, London, 1985.

Rosemary Reuther and Eleanor McLaughlin, *Women of the Spirit, Female Leadership in the Jewish and Christian Tradition*, New York, 1979.

Donald C. Richter, *Riotous Victorians*, Athens, Ohio, 1981.

Janet L. Robb, *The Primrose League*, New York 1968 (reprint 1942 edition).

Charles Roberts, *The Radical Countess*, Carlisle, 1962.

Elizabeth Roberts, *Woman's Work 1840–1940*, London, 1988.

Janet Roebuck, *The Making of Modern English Society from 1850*, London, 1973.

Isabel Ross, *Margaret Fell: Mother of Quakerism*, London, 1949.

Constance Rover, *Women's Suffrage and Party Politics in Britain, 1866–1914*, London, 1967.

A. Maude Royden, *The Church and Women*, London, 1924.

David Rubenstein, *Before the Suffragettes*, New York, 1986.

Lilian Lewis Shiman, *Crusade Against Drink in Victorian England*, London, 1988.

Nathan Sheppard, *Before an Audience*, London, 1886.

Esther Simon Shkolnik, *Leading Ladies: A Study of Eight Late Victorian and Edwardian Political Wives*, New York, 1987.

Frank Stenton, *Anglo Saxon England*, 3rd edition, Oxford, 1971.

Abel Stevens, *History of Methodism*, vols 1 and 2, New York, 1859.

Louisa Stewart, *Memoirs of Margaret Bright Lucas*, London, 1890.

Elizabeth Daniel Stewart, *The Crusader in Great Britain*, Springfield, 1893.

Barbara Strachey, *Remarkable Relations. The Story of the Pearsall Smith Family*, London, 1980.

Ray Strachey, *The Cause: A Short History of the Women's Movement in Great Britain*, London, 1928.

J. C. Street, F. R. Lees and D. Burns, editors, *International Temperance and Prohibition Proceedings, 1862*. London, 1862.

Elizabeth Sturge, *Reminiscences of Elizabeth Sturge*, London.

Matilda Sturge, *Memorials and letters of Ann Hunt*, London, 1898.

William Sturge, *Some Recollections of a Long Life*, Bristol, 1893.

——, *Tribute in Memory of Charlotte Sturge*, Bristol, 1894.

David E. Swift, *John Joseph Gurney, Banker, Reformer and Quaker*, Middletown, 1962.

T. W. P. Taylder, 'The History of the Rise and Progress of Teetotalism in Newcastle upon Tyne', pamphlet Newcastle upon Tyne, 1886.

Malcolm I. Thomas and Jennifer Grimmett, *Women in Protest 1800–1850*, New York, 1982.

David Thomson, *England in the Nineteenth Century*, Pelican, Baltimore,

1966.

E. M. Tomkinson, *Sarah Robinson, Agnes Weston, Mrs. Meredith: 'The World's Workers'* London, 1887.

Alex Tyrrell, *Joseph Sturge and the Moral Radical Party in Early Victorian Britain*, London, 1987.

Janet P. Treveyan, *The Life of Mrs. Humphrey Ward*, London, 1923.

F. de L. Booth Tucker, *The Life of Catherine Booth*, London,

Deborah M. Valenze, *Prophetic Sons and Daughters Female Preaching and Popular Religion in Industrial England*, Princeton, 1985.

Richard T. Vann, *The Social Development of Quakerism 1655–1753*, Cambridge, Mass. 1969.

Judith Walkowitz, *Prostitution and Victorian Society: women, class and the state*, Cambridge, 1982,

Robert Spence Watson, *National Liberal Federation*, London, 1907.

J. Steven Watson, *The Reign of George III*, Oxford, 1960.

Robert F. Wearmouth, *Methodism and the Common People of the Eighteenth Century*, London, 1945.

Julie Stewart Werner, *The Primitive Methodist Connection Its Background and Early History*, Madison, 1984.

Agnes Weston, *My Life Among the Blue-Jackets*. London, 1912.

Elizabeth Whitlegge, Maude Arnot *et al.*, editors, *The Changing Experience of Women*, Oxford, 1982.

Julia Wightman, *Haste to the Rescue*, London, 1860.

Peter Winskill, *The Temperance Movement*, vols I–IV, London, 1892.

Woman's Work in the Temperance Reformation, London, 1868.

Llewellyn Woodward, *The Age of Reform 1815–1870*, 2nd edition, Oxford, 1962.

Gayle Graham Yates, *Harriet Martineau on Women*, Brunswick, 1985.

Eileen Yeo and E. P. Thompson, *The Unknown Mayhew*, New York, 1972.

M. Young and P. Willmott, *Family and Kinship in East London*, London, 1957.

Index